PEOPLE IN CRISIS: UNDERSTANDING AND HELPING

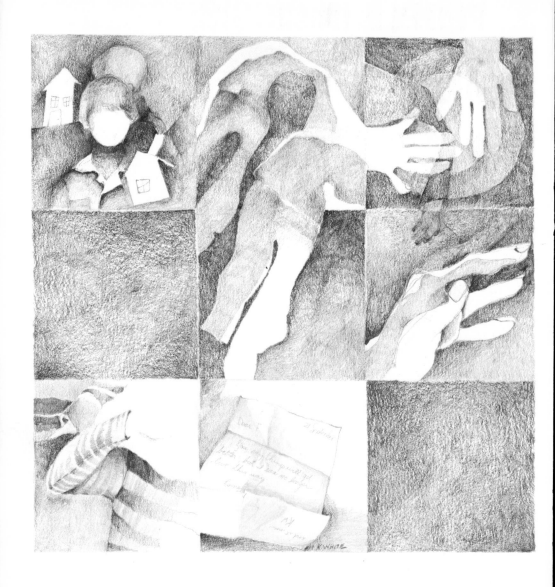

PEOPLE IN CRISIS: UNDERSTANDING AND HELPING

Lee Ann Hoff

Addison-Wesley Publishing Company

Medical/Nursing Division
Menlo Park, California • Reading, Massachusetts
London • Amsterdam • Don Mills, Ontario • Sydney

To people in crisis and those who help them
    and
To Marie and Frans

Sponsoring Editor: James Keating
Production Editor: Betsey Rhame
Cover design: Christine Butterfield
Illustrator: Karen White

Library of Congress Catalog Card No. 77-79466

ISBN 0-201-02939-1
ABCDEFGHIJ-HA-798

Addison-Wesley Publishing Company
Medical/Nursing Division
2725 Sand Hill Road
Menlo Park, California 94025

FOREWORD

It is impossible to say how many people are now doing full or part-time crisis intervention work. It seems safe to say that many are doing so who do not know it or identify it as such—and that many more should be.

During the past two and a half decades, crisis intervention has become an area of concern for mental health practitioners and those in related fields. In the late 1940's and early 1950's such giants of the profession as Erich Lindemann and Gerald Caplan established the theoretical and dynamic foundations, and crisis intervention received ready acceptance in a field which heretofore had focused only on the remediation and reconstruction of those with long-term illnesses. Crisis work brought about a number of notable changes. It brought mental health professionals out of the hospital and from behind the office desk. It took them into the community—often to the site of the event. It confronted them frequently with emergencies requiring immediate decision and direct action. It forced them to work with acute situations under conditions of high stress rather than in the reflective calm of an office. It developed the training and use of para- and non-professionals to meet the demand for services otherwise impossible to supply. It developed the use of gatekeeper groups for recognition and identification of emotional problems requiring further care.

Traditionalists in the mental health field still question whether the problems dealt with in crisis intervention are truly appropriate for the professional. Personnel in allied areas have also expressed this concern. For example, sociologists studying the emotional problems of disaster victims classify the symptoms into problems of living, mental health difficulties, and symptoms of mental illness. Mental illness and mental health have always been legitimate areas of concern for professionals—but problems of living? The difficulties brought about by an extraordinary event, such as a large-scale disaster or catastrophe, include finding clothes and substitute shelter, obtaining food, filing claims, overcoming bureaucratic red tape, mourning for lost loved ones, grieving for lost objects with their ties to the past, reconstructing a future, resettling, rebuilding, and finding a new job. Are these appropriate areas of concern for the mental health professional and for other social service workers? The answer is, of course, *yes*. In crises the stresses encountered can increase or accumulate to produce serious emotional disturbance or illness. The crisis worker's function is twofold. He or she has to be able to identify, evaluate, and handle people who are in current situations of high tension and who are demonstrating the entire range of symptoms from maladjustment to psychiatric syndrome. The crisis worker must also respond to events which he or she recognizes as potentially fraught with harmful possibilities. It is the opportunity to intervene early which is the most exciting and promising aspect of crisis work.

As Ms. Hoff emphasizes, crisis presents opportunity as well as danger. Indeed, the Chinese in their centuries-old accumulation of wisdom have devised their word for crisis from the two symbols for danger and opportunity. The opportunity arises in being forced by the crisis to react. The change may well be positive if it brings about a reorganization of defenses and attitudes, and a development of healthy adaptive responses formerly not in the individual's repertoire.

Ms. Hoff also emphasizes the need for primary prevention, a service which the mental health field as a profession is only now beginning to approach. Primary prevention is aimed at reducing, forestalling, or even preventing the crisis before it happens. It is obviously impossible to prevent all crises, but there are many which can be moderated greatly by prior activity. For example, predisaster training for social service workers would help greatly in providing trained people to work in a disaster-struck area within the shortest possible time. And time is of the essence in avoiding crises in such situations where chaos and confusion are overwhelming. The Federal Disaster Relief Act of May 1974 breaks ground by accepting the need for postdisaster intervention, but the act does not provide for predisaster training.

In suicide prevention, it is now possible to identify high-risk groups, such as the sick, the elderly, or the recently discharged mental hospital patient who is alone and lonely in the community. Ms. Hoff's suggestions for evaluation of people in crisis (Chapter 3) fit perfectly: (a) identify and reduce or eliminate the hazard—loneliness among those with the least amount of internal and external supports; (b) reduce the amount of exposure to the hazard—locate such high risk persons as quickly as possible in the community; and (c) reduce the degree of vulnerability or sensitivity—set up procedures for repeated contacts, sensitively fashioned to show continuing interest, caring, and concern.

Ms. Hoff describes not only how to help people in crisis, but also the why of crisis and crisis intervention. *People in Crisis* fills a great need in this important developing area of crisis intervention by presenting in clear, lucid, nontechnical language what crisis is, how to recognize it, and what to do about it. One does not need to be a mental health professional to be able to help people in crisis. There is room for all levels of skill and varieties of background in crisis work. Ms. Hoff does not attempt to make everyone into a mental health professional. Rather she emphasizes that all human service workers should do what they reasonably can to help people in crisis, and she notes the importance of recognizing one's limitations and not assuming too much responsibility. On the other hand, she shows convincingly how individuals in specific groups, when given more information, skills, and confidence, can become competent crisis-aware, crisis-sensitive intervenors.

NORMAN L. FARBEROW, Ph.D.
October 1977

PREFACE

This is a book about people in crisis and those who help them. None of us can escape life crises. Most of us, however, need help to weather the storm of events such as sickness, divorce, or death of a loved one. To need such help is not a sign of weakness, nor should it be a source of embarrassment. It merely means that we are human, that we are social beings who grow to our fullest capacity only when supported by others.

The crisis intervention movement addresses itself to this human need for help when in distress. Crisis intervention signals a shift in the field of mental health care from treating disturbed people to preventing emotional and mental breakdown from extreme stress.

All kinds of people help others in crisis: friends, family, physicians, nurses, clergy, social workers, crisis counselors, psychotherapists, and others. None of the professions—psychology, social work, theology, nursing, medicine, or psychiatry—can claim crisis intervention as its special domain. The work of helping people in crisis spans all of these professions and more. It is "everybody's business," not anybody's particular specialty.

Many people in crisis call suicide prevention and crisis centers. Many more go, instead, to other facilities such as hospital emergency rooms, physicians' offices, school counselors, nursing homes, or hospitals. Others are visited by clergy, police, public health, or welfare workers. Often the people in greatest need of help during a crisis are those least likely to call a crisis center. It is in these situations that the most serious crises occur, and it is in such situations that the front line crisis worker can play a vital part. Hence the need for front line crisis workers and crisis specialists—volunteers and paid-staff—to get in closer touch with one another and to pool their resources.

The examples in this book are drawn from all major racial, ethnic, and socioeconomic groups in the United States in an attempt to picture accurately the variety of people seeking help from health and human service agencies. In writing case examples I have also used my experience and study in North Dakota, Baltimore, Los Angeles, and Buffalo. The cases are real but have been disguised to protect the identity of the people concerned.

Crisis is intrinsic to life. It is a subject which I believe should not be hidden in professional jargon intelligible to only a few. In writing this book I have, therefore, avoided technical language as much as possible. Experience with health professionals and caretakers has convinced me of their willingness and ability to engage in crisis intervention when the process is not cloaked in an air of mystery.

All of us can grow in the knowledge and art of helping ourselves and others in crisis. This book is intended to assist in that learning process. *People in Crisis* was written for:

1. Front line crisis workers: nurses, physicians, police, clergy, teachers, welfare and rescue workers.

2. Specialized crisis workers, volunteer and other.

3. Health and mental health educators who train physicians, nurses, social workers, psychologists, and counselors.

4. Human service administrators and board members planning to develop crisis services according to standards recommended by the American Association of Suicidology.

5. The general reader who wants to better understand his or her own personal crises and gain from the experience.

Crisis intervention is not a panacea for all of life's problems. But at so many points in our lives it can determine whether we are enriched, or whether we stagnate, become emotionally disturbed, or die by our own hand.

It is my hope that this book will make a difference for all those who read it.

Lee Ann Hoff
East Concord, New York

ACKNOWLEDGMENTS

This book could not have been written without the generous support and encouragement of my teachers, friends and colleagues. I especially wish to thank Maureen Becker, Ron Pond, Dick Dempsey, Cathleen Getty, Lisl Goodman, Gwen Harvey, Harold Hase, Sam Heilig, Ida Horvitz, Wilton Kenney, Seymour Perlin, Al Samuelson, Ed Shneidman, Renee Spring, and Jack and Marilyn Tapp.

Thanks also go to those I have counseled, taught or supervised, who have challenged and confirmed me through the years *People in Crisis* has been in the making; the various people who kindly allowed me to interview them (they are listed in detail at the beginning of Part II and Chapter 11); Gail Sullivan for typing the manuscript in its initial stages; and David Butler, Fran Ciccia, Alan Goolden, Judy Hoff, and Florence Westheimer for their helpful suggestions about the manuscript.

I am especially grateful to Norman Farberow for writing the Foreword; Karen White for her art illustrations; Jean Higgins for bearing with me patiently—and with a wonderful sense of humor—to the end during the final stages of typing, James Keating and others at Addison-Wesley for unfailing support and direction through the publishing process; Midge Farias, Lorema Goolden, Francis Groot, Richard McGee, and my sister Marie for their most valuable critiques of the manuscript, and last but not least my friends for seeing me through the crises of writing this book.

CONTENTS

Chapter 11.
Putting It All Together:
Vignettes from the Lives of People in Crisis and Those Who
Help Them

PEOPLE IN CRISIS: UNDERSTANDING AND HELPING

PART I

THE UNDERSTANDING AND PRACTICE OF CRISIS INTERVENTION

CHAPTER 1

Understanding People in Crisis

WHAT IS CRISIS AND CRISIS INTERVENTION?

Stressful events and emergency situations are part of life. They have the potential of becoming crises. However, a crisis does not necessarily follow from a traumatic event. What is a crisis for me may not be a crisis for you. As long as we are able to handle stressful life events, we will not experience a crisis. But, if stress overwhelms us, and we are unable to find a way out of our predicament, a crisis will result.

Note that it is not the events of our life that activate crisis. Crisis occurs when our interpretation of these events leads to stress so severe that we can find no relief.

There are meaningful differences and relationships between these key words: stress, predicament, emergency, crisis. Stress is not crisis: stress is tension, strain, or pressure. Nor is predicament crisis: predicament is a condition or situation that is unpleasant, dangerous, or embarrassing. Emergency is not crisis: emergency is an unforeseen combination of circumstances which calls for immediate action. Webster defines "crisis" as ". . . a serious or decisive state of things, a turning point." Norris Hansell describes crisis as any rapid change or encounter that is foreign to a person's usual experience.[1]

Predicaments and emergencies lead to stresses which carry the potential of becoming crises. Whether such predicaments and emergencies become crises depends on our ability to handle these stresses.

Stress is a common denominator as we move from infancy through childhood to adolescence, adulthood, and old age. Your son finds himself in turmoil during adolescence; your son's friend does not. You face mid-life as a normal part of your human development; I find myself depressed; my neighbor becomes suicidal. Part of the beauty of life is the rebirth of peace following turmoil and pain. Few of us escape living through the depth and height of a crisis . . . the death of a loved one, a serious illness. Throughout life, there are numerous ups and downs, and sometimes life threatening situations.

Carl, age 50, has a heart attack and is taken to a hospital by ambulance. This is clearly a medical emergency and a source of stress for Carl and his family. However, Carl's heart attack may also precipitate an emotional crisis for him and his entire family.

Whether this crisis experience results in growth and enrichment for Carl and his loved ones, or in a lower level of functioning for one or all of them, depends largely on their previous problem solving abilities and current levels of support. These factors contribute to the subjective nature of crisis theory and make scientific inquiry into the matter very difficult.[2,3,4]

If Carl or members of his family become extremely upset as a result of his heart attack and feel unable to handle the event emotionally, they are said to be in *crisis*. It is important to remember that a crisis does not last long and is self-limiting. Through *crisis intervention,* a crisis worker—physician, counselor, nurse, minister—can help Carl and his family resolve their crisis. Crisis intervention is a short term helping process. It focuses on resolution of the immediate problem through use of personal, social, and environmental resources. This helping process and the theory supporting it is sometimes referred to as the *crisis model.*

VIEWS ABOUT PEOPLE IN CRISIS

People have been experiencing stress, predicaments, and life crises from the beginning of time. They have also found a variety of ways to resolve predicaments and live through crises. Likewise, other people have always helped in this process. Hansell cites the Biblical Noah as an example of how our ancestors handled crises.[1] Noah was warned of the serious predicament he and his family would be facing shortly. They prepared for the event and through various clever maneuvers avoided being overwhelmed by the flood.

Insights developed through the psychological and social sciences help people to understand themselves and others in crisis. The advent of a more enlightened view of people in crisis has helped put to rest some old myths about "upset people." It is not so easy anymore to write off as "crazy" and put away a person who is not his or her usual self in the face of a very upsetting event. Modern crisis theory has helped establish a new approach to people with problems. As a result of crisis theory and its unique emphasis on the helping mode, the following notions are no longer widely accepted: (a) upset people are crazy, (b) people who are upset cannot help themselves, (c) only psychiatrists or highly trained therapists can help people in crisis, and (d) people who are suicidal or upset will get over it if they are left alone.

People who can be most helpful—parents, spouses, teachers, counselors, social workers—are those who recognize that everyone has potential for vast growth. Abraham Maslow, in his study of self-actualized individuals, found them capable of virtually limitless growth and development.[5] Significantly, growth occurred in the midst of the pain and turmoil of events such as divorce and illness. Influenced by Maslow and other pioneers, there is a growing number of people—including many counselors and professional helpers—who have changed their view of people and of human problems. Those who are upset and in trouble are seen as—

- Basically normal.
- Capable of helping themselves.
- Capable of further growth with a little help from friends, family, and neighbors.

Counselors and helpers now regard the stress of human development as normal, as an opportunity to advance from one level of maturity to another. Upsetting events, such as illness or death of a loved one, are viewed as occasions for further growth, rather than for withdrawal and deterioration.

THE EVOLUTION OF CRISIS INTERVENTION

During the 1950's and 1960's ego psychologists such as Allport, Maslow, and Erikson did much to lay the philosophical base for crisis theory.[6,5,7] They stress the person's ability to learn and grow psychologically throughout life. Their views about people and human problems are based on the study of normal rather than disturbed individuals.

Decades earlier, Freud made pioneering contributions to the study of human behavior and the treatment of emotional conflict. He laid the foundation for a view of people as complex beings capable of self-discovery and change. Through extensive case studies he demonstrated the profound effect that early life experiences can have on our later development and happiness. He also found that people can resolve conflicts stemming from traumatic events of childhood and thereby live fuller, happier lives. His conclusions, however, are based largely on the study of disturbed rather than normal individuals. Psychoanalysis, the treatment method he developed from his theory, is costly, lengthy, available to few, and not applicable to the person in crisis. Certain psychoanalytic techniques, however, such as listening and "catharsis"—the expression of feelings around a traumatic event

—are useful in all psychological helping processes, including brief psychotherapy and crisis intervention.[8,9]

During World War II and the Korean War, upset members of the military were treated, whenever possible, at the front lines rather than being sent back home to psychiatric hospitals. Studies revealed that the majority of these men were able to return to combat duty rapidly as a result of receiving help on-the-spot, that is, crisis intervention individually or in a group.[1,10]

Erich Lindemann's classical study of bereavement following the Coconut Grove fire in Boston defined the grieving process people went through after sudden death of a relative.[11] His findings can be applied in working with anyone suffering a serious, sudden loss (see Chapter 7, Grief Work).

Gerald Caplan of the Harvard School of Public Health is another pioneer in the field of crisis intervention. He developed a theory of the person in crisis and emphasized a communitywide approach to crisis intervention. Public education programs and consultation with various caretakers such as teachers, police, and public health nurses are important ways to prevent destructive effects as a result of crises. All community mental health professionals should be familiar with his classical work, *Principles of Preventive Psychiatry*.[12]

James Tyhurst has helped us understand a person's response to community crises such as natural disaster.[13] During the 1940's and 1950's he studied transition states such as migration, parenthood, and retirement. His work shed light on many crisis states that occur as a result of social mobility or cultural change.

Another important historical influence on crisis intervention is the 1961 Report of the Joint Commission on Mental Illness and Health in the United States. This book, *Action for Mental Health*,[14] laid the foundation for the community mental health movement in America. It documented through five years of study the crucial fact that the masses of people were not getting the help they needed, when they needed it, and where they needed it—close to their natural social setting. The report revealed that: (a) people in crisis were tired of waiting lists; (b) professionals were tired of lengthy and expensive therapy that often did not help; (c) large numbers of people (42 percent) went initially to a physician or clergyman for *any* problem; (d) long years of training were not necessary to learn how to help distressed people; and (e) volunteers and community caretakers (e.g., police, teachers, ministers) were a large, untapped source for helping people in distress.

One of the numerous recommendations in this report was that every community should have a locally based, emergency mental health program. Federal funds were made available through legislation in 1963 and 1965 to provide comprehensive mental health services through community mental health centers. Many communities still do not have such programs. But even among those that do, emergency and other services are often far from ideal. A Ralph Nader study group recently responded to this problem with a consumers' manual entitled, *Through the Mental Health Maze.*[15]

Norris Hansell has refined many of the findings of Caplan, Tyhurst, military psychiatry, and community mental health studies into an entire system of response to the person in distress.[1] His work is especially important to crisis workers in community mental health agencies where many high risk groups of people come for help.

Lastly, there is the important historical influence of the Suicide Prevention Movement.* Richard McGee has documented in detail the work of the Los Angeles Suicide Prevention Center and other groups in launching the suicide prevention and crisis intervention movement in the United States.[16] The Los Angeles Suicide Prevention Center was born out of the efforts of Norman Farberow and Edwin Shneidman. In the late 1950's these two psychologists led the movement by studying suicide notes. From their many projects and those of numerous colleagues, suicide prevention and crisis centers were established throughout the country, numbering over 100 by 1969.[16]

It is noteworthy that the suicide prevention and crisis movement came alive during the decade when professional mental health workers had a mandate (*Action for Mental Health*) and massive federal funding to provide emergency services along with other mental health care. What makes this even more remarkable is that most crisis centers are staffed by volunteers and often were started by volunteer citizen groups such as a mental health or ministerial association. It would seem that volunteers were often willing and able to respond to an unmet community need, whereas professionals in mental health either could not or would not respond.

---

*The first suicide prevention program, the National Save-A-Life League in New York City, was founded in 1906, with no recorded offspring.

In recent years a number of these centers in the United States have shut down because of insufficient funds or inadequate leadership. Others have merged with community mental health programs.

Currently, suicide and crisis services exist in a variety of organizational frameworks. Regardless of the models, however, every community should have a comprehensive crisis program, including service for suicide emergencies. During the 1970's both volunteers and professionals have become increasingly knowledgeable about crisis intervention. One indicator of this is the launching in 1976 of a program by the American Association of Suicidology to certify suicide and crisis programs in the United States. (See Chapter 10, Standards for Crisis Services.)

DEVELOPMENTAL CRISES

Despite the lack of a well defined theoretical framework for considering human crisis states, it is useful to distinguish between developmental and situational crises. Erikson and other developmental psychologists have identified the normal states of transition in human development.[7] The major transition states are:

Prenatal to Infancy

Infancy to Childhood

Childhood to Puberty and Adolescence

Adolescence to Adulthood

Maturity to Middle Age

Middle Age to Old Age

Old Age to Death.

During each of these phases of development the person is subjected to unique stresses. He or she faces the challenge of specific developmental tasks. Failure in these tasks leads to a stunting of human growth; the personality does not mature according to one's natural potential. Growth toward maturity is an exciting process; but it is also a challenging one. People generally experience a higher level of anxiety during developmental transition states than at other times. The natural changes in roles, body image, and functions, and way of relating to self and to the world create internal turmoil and restlessness. Successful completion of developmental tasks requires energy. It also demands nurturance from others.

With appropriate support, a person normally is able to meet the challenge of growth from one stage of life to another. It is in this sense that developmental crises are considered normal. These developmental turning points are also anticipated. It is possible, therefore, to prepare for them. Developmental transition states need not be nightmares; they can be happy times. People can enjoy a sense of self-mastery and achievement from successful completion of developmental tasks.

However, these turning points can become more than a natural period of turmoil and stress. This occurs when the individual does not receive the normal social supports needed for the process of maturation. Each successive stage of development is affected by what took place in the previous phase. For some, the challenge of human growth is indeed a nightmare: life's turning points become crises with destructive effects rather than normal periods of challenge and turmoil. Some people greet adolescence, middle age, and old age with suicide attempts, depression, or withdrawal to a closed, more secure and familiar world. They approach life with a deep rejection of self and suspicion of the surrounding world.

The unique challenge in human life is to move on, not to stagnate or regress. For some, however, various situational factors make this a seemingly impossible task.

SITUATIONAL CRISES

A situational crisis is one that occurs as a result of some unanticipated traumatic event that is usually beyond one's control. Since it is unforeseen, generally there is nothing one can do to prepare for it. Some common situational crises are: loss of a parent through death or divorce, loss of job or status, urban dislocation, fire, natural disaster, diagnosis of a chronic or fatal illness. The occurrence of one of these events may or may not result in a crisis. As is true of developmental crises, much depends on the individual's personal and social resources at the time. Another factor influencing a crisis or non-crisis response to an upsetting situation is the person's stage of development when it occurs. An individual in a major transition state is already vulnerable. Add to that the stress of a traumatic event and the person is even more likely to experience a crisis.

Case Example

Carol, age 38, and Jim, age 36, decide mutually to obtain a divorce. They have been married 13 years, and have two children: Dean, age 12, and Cindy, age 9. Together they work out a custody and visiting agreement, satisfactory to both of them and taking the children's wishes into consideration. Carol and Jim had essentially untroubled childhoods and feel secure and confident as individuals. They could, therefore, avoid the common tactic of using their children as weapons against each other. The divorce was decidedly a source of additional stress to Dean and Cindy. However, neither of the children experienced it as a crisis. Both their parents were mature in their marital and parental roles. Thus Carol and Jim did not deny their children the nurturance they continued to need from their parents. The divorce also was not the occasion of a crisis for either spouse. In fact, they both saw their marriage as stagnating for their personal growth. Their decision to divorce was not a crisis; but, according to Maslow, an occasion for further "self-actualization," or growth.

In contrast let us consider Sandra and Mark, who had a less fortunate history of growth and development.

Case Example

Sandra had an unhappy childhood. She worked successfully as a bookkeeper until her marriage at age 25. However, she always felt a sense of failure as a woman before she became a wife and mother. Mark, on the other hand, feels trapped by marriage and resents the demands on him as a husband and father. Sandra definitely does not want a divorce; Mark does. Sandra wants the children but resents the role of single parent. She is also threatened by her anticipated menopause. For her, divorce is symbolic of her failure as a women. She views career and work outside the home as a necessary evil at best and has placed almost exclusive value on her role as wife and mother. Mark is glad to be free of the daily demands of marriage and fatherhood. His sense of guilt and responsibility, however, makes him lavish his children with material gifts while visiting them as infrequently as possible. Under these circumstances, divorce would almost certainly be the occasion of a crisis, especially for Sandra and probably for Mark as well. Menopause for Sandra will be more than normally stressful, unless she has the advantage of counseling to help her change her views and goals regarding self. Adolescence for their son Steve will more than likely exceed the normal level of stress during this time of his life.

These cases, in their contrasting manifestations, illustrate: (a) the highly subjective nature of the crisis experience, (b) the various factors which influence the development of a crisis state, and (c) the intrinsic relationship between developmental and situational crisis states.

The ramifications of these interlocking factors in developmental and situational crises will be examined throughout the remainder of this book.

WHY PEOPLE GO INTO CRISIS

People in crisis are, by definition, very upset emotionally; they are unable to solve life's problems in their usual way. A happy, healthy life implies an ability to solve our problems effectively. It also means that we are not lacking in basic human need fulfillment. Our basic needs include a sense of physical and psychological well being; a supportive network of friends, family, and associates; and a sense of identity and belonging to our society and cultural heritage. Caplan calls these needs "supplies."[12]

Hansell describes our essential needs as the "Seven Basic Attachments."[1] All of us have a stable arrangement of transactions between ourselves and our environment. According to Hansell, we are essentially attached to:

1. Food, oxygen, and other physical supplies necessary to life.

2. A strong sense of self identity.

3. At least one other person in a close, mutually supportive relationship.

4. At least one group which accepts us as a member.

5. One or more roles in which we feel self-respect and can perform with dignity.

6. Financial security, or a means of participating in an exchange of the goods and services we need and value.

7. A comprehensive system of meaning, or a set of values which help us to set goals and to understand ourselves and the world around us.[1]

People in crisis suffer a sudden loss of psychosocial and other supports. One or several of their basic attachments are severed or at risk of being severed.[1] For example, the shock of an unexpected death of a loved one by car accident or heart attack can leave a person feeling incomplete and at a loss about what to do, where to turn. The individual's familiar source of support and comfort disappears without warning, with no chance to adjust to the new mode of being that is required. Similar shock occurs in response to the suicide of one's friend, diagnosis of a terminal illness, or an operation, such as a mastectomy, which mutilates one's body.

Shock and a resulting crisis state can also occur at the time of normal role transitions. For example, Mary, age 19, relied very heavily on her mother for advice and support in all aspects of her life. One month after her honeymoon and the move into an apartment with her husband, she became depressed and suicidal and was unable to function at home or at work. Mary was obviously not ready for the move from adolescence into the more independent role of a young adult.

A person can also go into crisis because of a threat of loss of anything considered essential and important. A common example of this crisis-provoking occasion is the man or woman whose spouse threatens divorce.

Caplan and Tyhurst note that for some people a crisis is triggered when they meet a particularly challenging event of a psychosocial nature.[12,13] A crisis for such individuals represents a call to new action which they cannot face with their present resources.

Case Example

Edward, age 45, has been an outstanding assistant director of his company. When he is promoted to the vacated position of executive director, he becomes depressed and virtually nonfunctional. Edward, in spite of his obvious external signs of success, lacks basic self confidence; he cannot face the challenge of the new job. The thought of possible failure in his new position is unbearable. His anxiety about success is the very thing preventing him from achieving the success he desires. Edward is one of the many people who, with the help of family and friends, and perhaps a crisis counselor, can avoid possible failure and depression. He has his whole past career, including many successes, which he can draw upon profitably in his present job. With help, hopefully he will see that failure in his present position need not mean the end of a happy and productive life.

Case Example

Joan, age 19, is another example of someone who cannot meet the challenge of increasing her personal resources—that is, obtaining a college degree for teaching. She is paralyzed by her fear of the responsibilities involved in a teaching career. At examination time, she is unable to study and fails over half her courses. The challenge to increase her "supplies" in preparation for an adult teaching responsibility is more than she can face without additional resources.

HOW A CRISIS DEVELOPS

A crisis does not occur instantaneously. There are identifiable phases of development—psychosocial in character—which lead to an active crisis state. These phases were first described by Tyhurst in his study of individual responses to community disaster.[13] Victims experience three overlapping phases: (a) a period of impact, (b) a period of recoil, and (c) a post-traumatic period. (See Chapter 9, Individual Responses to Disaster, for a detailed description of these phases.)

Caplan describes four phases in the development of extreme anxiety and, finally, crisis.[12] Recognition of these phases of crisis development aids us in preventing a potential crisis event from becoming a full blown crisis.

PHASE 1:   A traumatic event causes an initial rise in one's level of anxiety. The person finds him- or herself in a predicament and responds with familiar problem solving mechanisms to reduce or eliminate the stress and discomfort stemming from excessive anxiety. For example, John, age 34, is striving toward a career as an executive in his company when he receives a diagnosis of multiple sclerosis. His wife Nancy is very supportive of him. He adjusts to this unexpected disturbing event by continuing to work as long as he can. John also has the advantage of the most advanced medical treatment available for multiple sclerosis. In addition, John's physician is skillful in applying his knowledge of the emotional impact of John's diagnosis. At this stage, John's traumatic event does not result in a crisis for him.

PHASE 2:   In this phase the person's usual problem solving ability fails. Also, the stimulus that caused the initial rise in tension continues. To continue with the illustration of John's case: The disease process is advancing despite excellent medical treatment. John's wife, Nancy, begins to cut down participation in some of her own interests so she can spend more time with her husband. The accumulating medical expenses and loss of work time strain the family's financial resources. John and Nancy receive a report from school that their son, Larry, age 14, is having behavioral problems. At this stage, since there is greater stress, the possibility of a crisis state for John increases, but a crisis is not inevitable. It depends on what happens next in John's life.

PHASE 3:   In this phase the individual's anxiety level rises even further. The increased tension moves the person to use every resource available—including unusual or new means—to solve the problem and reduce the increasingly painful state of anxiety. In John's case, he fortunately has enough inner strength, confidence, and sensitivity to recognize the strain of his illness on his wife and child. He looks for new ways to cope with his increasing stress. First, he confides in his physician, who responds by taking time to listen and offer emotional support. His physician also arranges for home health services through a public health nursing agency. This outside health assistance frees Nancy from some of her steadily increasing responsibilities. The physician also encourages John and Nancy to seek help from the school guidance counselor regarding their son, Larry. They did this.

Another way to prevent a crisis state at this phase is to redefine or change one's goals. This means of avoiding crisis is not usually possible for someone who is emotionally isolated from others and feels locked into solving a problem completely alone. With the help of his physician, John could accept his illness as something which changed his capacity to function in predefined, expected ways. However, he did not have to alter his fundamental ability to live a meaningful, rewarding life because of the illness. As John's illness progressed, it became necessary to change his role as the sole financial provider in the family. John and Nancy talked openly with each other about the total situation. Together, they decided that Nancy would take a job to ease the financial strain. They also asked the public health agency to increase the home health services, as Nancy was beginning to resent her confinement to the house and the increasing demands of being "nurse" to her husband.

PHASE 4:   This is the state of active crisis which results when:

- Internal strength and social support are lacking.
- The person's problem remains unresolved.
- Tension and anxiety rise to an unbearable degree.

An active crisis did not occur in John's case because he was able to respond constructively to his unanticipated illness. John had natural social supports and was able to use available help, so his stress did not become unbearable. The example of John illustrates how a full blown crisis (phase 4) can be avoided by various decisions and actions taken during any one of the three preceding phases.

The following example of George Sloan is in sharp contrast to that of John above. This case will be continued and discussed in subsequent chapters.

Case Example

George, age 48, works as a machinist with a construction company. Six evenings a week he works a second job as a cab driver in a large metropolitan area; his beat includes high crime sections of the city. He has just come home from the hospital after his third heart attack. The first occurred at age 44 and the second at age 47.

PHASE 1:   George has been advised by his physician to cut down on his high number of work hours. Specifically, the doctor recommended that he give up his second job and spend more time relaxing with family and friends. George's physician recognized his patient's vulnerability to heart attacks, especially as it related to his life style.[17] George rarely slowed down. He was chronically angry about things going wrong and about not being able to get ahead financially. He received his physician's advice with mixed feelings: on the one hand, he could see the relationship between his life style and his heart attacks; on the other hand, he resented what he acknowledged as a necessary change to reduce further risk of death by heart attack.

In any case, his health and financial problems definitely increased his usual level of anxiety. George talked superficially to his wife Marie about his dilemma but got very little support or understanding from her; their marital relationship was already strained. Marie is experiencing menopause and feels that she is not getting the comfort and the understanding she needs. George's discouragement and anger about not getting ahead are aggravated by Marie's complaints of never having enough money for the things she wants. George also resents what he perceives as the physician's judgment that he is not strong enough to do two jobs. At this stage, George is in a pre-crisis state, with a high degree of stress and anxiety.

PHASE 2:   George failed to obtain relief from his anxiety by talking to his wife. He does not feel comfortable in talking with his physician about his resistance to cutting down the work stress as advised. When he attempted to do so, once, he sensed that the physician was rushed. So he concluded that his doctor was only concerned about giving technical advice; not about how George would handle the advice. The prospect of quitting his second job and bringing home less money left George feeling like a failure as a bread-winner and supporter of his family. (See Chapter 8, Work Disruption.) His initial conflict and rise in tension continue. If he quits his second job, he cannot preserve his image as adequate family supporter, and he cannot reduce the risk of death by heart disease if he continues his present pace. Help outside of himself seems out of his reach.

PHASE 3:   George's increased anxiety moves him to try again talking with his wife. Ordinarily, he would have abandoned the idea based on the response he received earlier. Thus, this action constitutes an unusual effort for him, but he fails again in getting the help he needs. To make matters worse, George and Marie learn that their 16-year-old son, Arnold, has been suspended from school for a week due to suspected drug involvement. This makes George feel even more like a failure as he is seldom home during normal family hours. Also, Marie nags him about not spending enough time with the kids.

George's high level of anxiety was becoming so obvious that Marie finally suggested "Why don't you talk to the doctor about whatever's bothering you or go see our pastor?" George secretly knew that this was probably a good idea but could not bring himself to do it. He had been brought up to believe that somehow it is unmanly to get outside help to solve one's problems. His image of himself as the strong masculine supporter of the family made it impossible for him to give up the second job, although he knew the risks involved in continuing. For the same reason, he could not bear the thought of his wife's getting a job, though she herself had mentioned the idea a couple of times. Personality and social factors blocked him from redefining or changing his set goals as a means of problem resolution and prevention of crisis. Financial concerns along with the new problem of his son further increased his anxiety level. George is in a predicament he does not know how to resolve.

PHASE 4: George is at a complete loss about how to deal with all the stress in his life—the threat to his health and life if he continues his present pace, the threat to his self-image if he quits the second job, the failure in communication with his wife, and the sense of failure and guilt in his role as parent to his son. His anxiety increases to the breaking point:

- He feels hopeless.
- He does not know where to turn.
- He is in a state of active crisis.

George's case illustrates both situational and maturational factors in the development of life crises. It also highlights the subjective elements that contribute to a crisis state at different points in people's lives. George's heart disease was clearly an unanticipated, stressful event. His son Arnold's threat of suspension was unanticipated and a definite source of added stress. His wife's menopause was clearly anticipated as a normal phase of human development. So was his son's adolescence. If George's heart disease had developed at a time other than during his wife's menopause, she might have been more prone to help and support him at this time of extra stress. Also, Arnold would probably have made it through adolescence without the crisis of school suspension if there had been regular support from both parents. As it turned out, George and Marie had their first report of behavior problems with Arnold in school shortly after George's first heart attack four years earlier. They were advised at that time to seek family and/or marital counseling; they did, but stopped after a single session.

For another person, such as John in the previous case, or for George at another time of life, the same medical diagnosis and the same advice could have had an altogether different effect. This is true also for Arnold. A different response from his parents when he gave his first signals of distress, or a more constructive approach from school officials and counselors could have prevented Arnold's crisis of school suspension.

THE DURATION AND OUTCOMES OF CRISIS

People in crisis cannot stay that way forever. The state of crisis and the anxiety that accompanies it are too painful. There is a natural time limitation to the crisis experience. This is because the individual cannot survive indefinitely in such a state of psychological turmoil.

The emotional discomfort stemming from the extreme anxiety moves the person toward action to reduce the anxiety to an endurable level as soon as possible.

Experience with people in crisis has led to the observation that the acute emotional upset lasts from a few days to a few weeks.[12] The person needs to move toward some sort of resolution and expresses that need in terms such as: "I can't go on like this anymore." "Something has got to give." "Please, tell me what to do to get out of this mess—I can't stand it." "I feel like I'm losing my mind."

What, then, happens to the person in crisis? Several outcomes are possible:

1. The person can return to his or her pre-crisis state. This happens as a result of effective problem solving, made possible by one's internal strengths and social supports. Such an outcome does not necessarily imply new psychological growth as a result of the experience. Rather, the person simply returns to his or her *usual* state of being.

2. The person may not only return to the pre-crisis state but can *grow* from the crisis experience through discovery of new resources and ways of solving problems. These discoveries result from the crisis experience itself. John's case is a good example of such growth. He took advantage of resources available to him and his family such as his physician and the school guidance counselor. He found new ways of solving problems. The result for John was a process of growth: (a) His concept of himself as a worthwhile person was reinforced in spite of the loss of physical integrity from his illness. (b) He strengthened his marriage and ability to relate to his spouse regarding a serious problem. This was growth producing for both of them. (c) He developed in his role as a father by his constructive handling of the problem with his son in addition to his own personal stress.

3. The person reduces intolerable tension by lapsing into neurotic or psychotic patterns of behavior. For example, the individual may become very withdrawn, suspicious, or depressed. His or her distorted perception of events may be exaggerated to the point of blaming others inappropriately for the mis-

fortunes experienced. Others in crisis reduce their tension, at least temporarily, by excessive drinking or other drug abuse, or by impulsive disruptive behavior. Still others resort to more extreme measures by committing suicide, making suicide attempts, or by killing others.

All of these negative and destructive outcomes of the crisis experience occur when the individual lacks other more constructive ways of solving life's problems and relieving intolerable anxiety. George, for example, in the last case described, came to the conclusion in his despair that he was worth more dead than alive. Consequently, he was brought to the hospital emergency room one day after a car crash. George crashed his car deliberately, but did not die as he had planned. This was his chosen method of suicidal death; he wished to spare his family the stigma of suicide. He felt that he had already overburdened them. George's case will be continued in chapters 2 and 3 in respect to his treatment in the emergency room and his follow-up care.

Considering all of the possible outcomes of a crisis experience, it becomes obvious that we, as helpers, should have the following goals:

- To help people in crisis to at least return to their pre-crisis state.

- To do all we can to help them grow and become stronger persons as a result of the crisis and effective problem solving.

- To be alert to danger signals so we can prevent negative, destructive outcomes of a crisis experience.

This last goal we can achieve by recognizing that negative results of crisis are often not necessary but occur because of insensitivity to another's problems and a lack of appropriate resources in society's human service sector.

SUMMARY
Crisis intervention—in its practical application and the view of people on which it is based—dates informally to the beginning of time. Formally, crisis intervention began only a few decades ago. The crisis and suicide prevention movement has had an encouraging influence on the delivery of mental health services in the United States. Frequent causes of crisis are the transition from one stage of human development to another, a hazardous or unexpected situation such as

a natural disaster, death, or illness. These occurrences are often the occasion of regression, but can be opportunities for growth when proper support is offered and accepted. In order to help people in crisis, one should know why and how a crisis develops, and be aware of the positive and negative outcomes that can occur as a result of crisis.

References

1. Hansell, Norris. *The Person in Distress*. New York: Human Services Press, 1976.

2. Bartolucci, Giampiero, and C. S. Dryer. "An Overview of Crisis Intervention in the Emergency Rooms of General Hospitals," *American Journal of Psychiatry*, 130: 953–60, September 1973.

3. Dressler, David M. "The Management of Emotional Crises by Medical Practitioners," *Journal of American Medical Women's Association*, 28: 654–59, No. 12, 1973.

4. Taplin, Julian R. "Crisis Theory: Critique and Reformulation," *Community Mental Health Journal*, 7: 13–23, No. 1, 1971.

5. Maslow, Abraham. *Motivation and Personality*. Second Edition, New York: Harper and Row, 1970.

6. Allport, Gordon W. *Pattern and Growth in Personality*. New York: Holt, Rinehart and Winston, 1961.

7. Erikson, Erik. *Childhood and Society*. Second Edition. New York: W. W. Norton and Company, Inc., 1963.

8. Aquilera, Donna C., and Janice M. Messick. *Crisis Intervention*. Second Edition. St. Louis: C. V. Mosby Company, 1974.

9. Small, Leonard. *The Briefer Psychotherapies*. New York: Brunner/Mazel Publishers, 1971.

10. Glass, A. T. "Observations upon the Epidemiology of Mental Illness in Troops during Warfare," Symposium on Preventive and Social Psychiatry. Walter Reed Army Institute of Research and The National Research Council, Washington, D.C., April 15–17, 1957.

11. Lindemann, Erich. "Symptomatology and Management of Acute Grief," *American Journal of Psychiatry*, 101: 101–48, September 1944.

12. Caplan, Gerald. *Principles of Preventive Psychiatry*. New York: Basic Books, 1964.

13. Tyhurst, J. S. "The Role of Transition States—Including Disasters—in Mental Illness," Symposium on Preventive and Social Psychiatry. Walter Reed Army Institute of Research and The National Research Council, Washington, D.C., April 15–17, 1957.

14. *Action for Mental Health*. Report of the Joint Commission on Mental Illness and Health. New York: Basic Books, 1961.

15. *Through the Mental Health Maze*. Health Research Group. Washington D.C., 1975.

16. McGee, Richard K. *Crisis Intervention in the Community*. Baltimore: University Park Press, 1974.

17. Friedman, Meyer and Ray Rosenman. *Type A Behavior and Your Heart*. New York: Alfred A. Knopf, 1974.

CHAPTER 2

Identifying People in Crisis

PEOPLE AT RISK

If we can anticipate disturbing events, we can more easily prepare for them. Preparation, in turn, reduces risk of crisis and helps us avoid possible damaging outcomes of the upset. Many human experiences are predictable. Common examples are our anticipation of adolescence, adulthood, mid-life, and old age.

Many people seem unprepared to move from one phase of life to another and thus are at risk for crisis. Such unpreparedness is usually related to the individual's personality development or to social factors which inhibit him or her from normal emotional growth. For example, a youth whose parents have been overindulgent and inconsistent in their responses will find it difficult—and potentially hazardous—to move from adolescence into adulthood. Some parents are overprotective and therefore stifle a child's normal development. Consequently, the move to adulthood becomes a risk and a hazard, rather than an opportunity for further challenge and growth.

Role transitions also occur in everyone's life. Typically, a person may be first a student, then get a job, may marry and become a parent, then reach the age of retirement. Such role changes can be predicted, and precautionary measures taken to avoid a crisis. But some people do not, or cannot, prepare themselves for one or more of these events. The possibility of crisis for them is thereby increased. For example, a person need not rush into marriage, but could consider the possibility and the related role changes thoughtfully. Yet many do rush, and crises result.

Other life events are less predictable: for example, death of a loved one, serious physical illness, urban dislocation, personal and financial loss through flood, hurricane or fire, birth of a premature infant.

For the crisis worker, consideration of identifiable life events is important from the point of view of:

- Predicting crisis states in different people.

- Assessing whether a particular individual is or is not in crisis.

A person who is very upset emotionally may be judged by many observers as obviously being in a state of crisis. In fact, this is not necessarily so; accurate assessment should precede such a judgment.

However, a naive observer may quickly dismiss the need for such assessment with the conclusion that the more important task is to *help* the individual—the sooner the better. However, what is sometimes well intended as "help" turns out to have the opposite effect for the individual concerned. One way to avoid misplaced "helping" is to identify people at risk through the process of assessment.

However, assessment can be impeded by the very nature of the crisis intervention process. The positive characteristic of fast-moving helping is part of the evaluation problem. The dedication and hard work of thousands of volunteers has made crisis intervention a very human and humane function of growing popularity. Helping people in crisis is immediate, down-to-earth, and often highly rewarding. However, those human service workers who are most inclined to action and are involved in obtaining immediately observable results are often the least inclined to study and evaluate their own work.[1] Add to this factor the inherent difficulty of objectively evaluating any human helping process, and it is easy to see how crisis intervention can become a catch-all term used for all sorts of human interactions.

PREDICTING CRISIS

The assessment process need not be as vague and inaccurate as, in fact, it often is. Herbert Schulberg has developed a probability formulation which helps refine the overall assessment process.[1] According to him, we should consider several factors in assessing which persons are most crisis prone and at risk of extrusion from their natural social setting.

1. The probability that a disturbing and hazardous event will occur: For example, death of close family members is highly probable, whereas natural disasters are very improbable.

2. The probability that an individual will be exposed to the event: For example, every adolescent faces the challenge of adult responsibilities, whereas few people face the crisis of an unwanted move from their settled dwelling.

3. The vulnerability of the individual to the event: The mature adult, for example, can adapt more easily to the stress of moving than, let's say, a child in his or her first year of school.

In assessing the crisis proneness of an individual, one should consider: (a) the degree of stress stemming from a hazardous event, (b) the risk of people being exposed to that event, and (c) the person's vulnerability or ability to adapt to the stress.[1]

Application of the Probability Formulation

Case Example

Dorothy, age 38, has been in the hospital for depression three times during the past nine years. She has always been heavily dependent on her husband. Making friends is difficult for her. Dorothy's husband accepted a job transfer—his first—to a new location in another state. Dorothy dreaded the move and considered joining her husband a few months later. She thought this might allow her some time to see whether the new job was going to be permanent. However, she abandoned the idea because she couldn't tolerate the thought of being away from her husband for that length of time. One month after the move, Dorothy made a suicide attempt and was taken to a psychiatric hospital by her husband.

In this case the initial probability of the occurrence of the hazardous event, the move, was small. The probability of Dorothy's exposure to the event is high considering her marital status and her extreme dependence on her husband. Her vulnerability in view of her past history is also very high. Taken together, these factors make Dorothy a high risk for the probability of crisis. The risk of crisis for Dorothy is increased even further if she is faced with a highly probable hazardous event such as the death of her husband.

In Schulberg's formulation, probability factors which contribute to a favorable outcome of crisis include the following:[1]

1. If the person encounters and resolves a great number and variety of difficult situations, he or she is less likely to experience a crisis in future hazardous circumstances.

2. If the person has or perceives that he or she has the ability to resolve a problem, then it is more likely that the individual will successfully resolve a given problem.

3. The person who has strong social supports is very likely to resolve life crises successfully and without destructive effects.

IMPORTANCE OF CRISIS ASSESSMENT

The failure to assess prior to helping is often responsible for the misapplication or the nonapplication of the crisis model. In the human service field it is particularly unfortunate to misjudge a person in crisis by poor observation and inadequate assessment. Ultimately, these errors result in failure to help, which can have lifelong destructive effects. Paul Polak outlined this fact in his study of 104 men admitted to a psychiatric hospital in Scotland.[2] Polak found that these men or their families had typically requested psychiatric hospital admission following previous unresolved crises. These crises were everyday hazardous events such as separation, physical illness, death, and migration. Another significant fact highlighted by this study is that the psychiatric admission did indeed relieve a social crisis. However, admission also was frequently the occasion for another crisis because family patterns of interaction were disrupted, and the patient and his or her family often had disturbing and unrealistic fantasies and expectations about the purpose and meaning of hospitalization.[2]

Hansell notes how inviting a hospital environment seems to a person deprived of normal community supports.[3] Hospitalization can also be misused by families who lack personal and social resources for relating to disturbed members. Hansell suggests that crisis can just as well lead to improved friendships as to "asylum."[3]

The importance of assessment and resolution of crises as an alternative to psychiatric hospitalization is further highlighted by what happens *after* admission:

> ". . . *the admission itself tends to promote denial of the social forces in the family and community that have produced it (the admission). The patient may then emerge as the scapegoat for these family and community problems, and psychiatric assessment (vs.* crisis assessment . . . *emphasis mine) after admission tends to focus on the patient's symptomology (vs. strengths and problem solving ability) as the major cause of admission."*[2]

People in distress and some mental health workers helping them find it easier to use the temporary shelter of a hospital as a prolonged refuge than to face and seek to resolve a crisis. The upset person is diagnosed, takes on the identity of patienthood, and falls into roles expected by the institution.[4] Essentially the same thing happens to an adolescent confined to a detention home, and to an old person "put away" in a nursing home.

A more extreme example of the negative results of inadequate assessment is revealed in a study by Rosenbaum.[5] This study uncovers the destructive effects of placing disturbed people in psychiatric hospitals and labeling them with a psychiatric diagnosis such as "schizophrenia." Rosenbaum demonstrated that the professional psychiatric helpers charged with admission and diagnosis of those regarded as insane could not distinguish between pseudopatients and the truly disturbed. This was so even when the professionals were forewarned by the researcher that certain people presenting themselves for hospital admission would be pseudopatients. The study underscores Polak's observation that psychiatric hospitalization—

- Is a crisis in itself.
- Is the direct result of previously undetected and unresolved crises.
- Should be avoided whenever possible.
- Should be used only as a last resort when all other efforts to help have failed.
- Should be substituted, whenever possible, by accurate crisis assessment and intervention in the person's natural social setting.

The strong inclination of some families to place disturbed people in institutions is one of the by-products of our society's low tolerance of behavior that falls outside so-called normal limits. Unnecessary psychiatric hospitalizations also occur when mental health workers lack skill in detecting and managing life crises in a person's natural community. The person in crisis and his or her family should be advised that there are many constructive ways of resolving life's crises.[3,6] Alternatives to hospitalization will be discussed in subsequent chapters of this book.

The failure to assess adequately whether a person is in crisis has another negative result. It is ill-advised to respond with a crisis approach when there is only the *appearance* of crisis but no crisis. The ability to discriminate between a crisis and a non-crisis state requires prediction and assessment skills. Good intentions are not enough.

The development of assessment skills does not take years of intensive study and training (see Chapter 10). It does require the ability to combine what we have learned from observing and helping people in crisis with the natural tendency of human beings to help one another when in trouble. Teachers, parents, nurses, police, physicians, and clergy are in the natural front lines where life crises occur. It is here that people can do the most to help others and prevent unnecessary life casualities.

Ivan Illich claims that the bureaucratization of medicine has deprived the ordinary person of helping tools which he or she can readily use on behalf of others if allowed.[7] As many as possible of these helping tools should be available for front line people who are willing and able to help others. The assessment techniques recommended are simply elaborations or refinements of the helping responses that people have been using for centuries.

THE ASSESSMENT PROCESS

Knowledge of probability factors about crisis, then, guides us in assessing particular individuals in possible or actual crisis at any given point in time. However, the human services person—including nurses, physicians, teachers, and police—encountering someone in distress still has many questions: What do I say? What, if any, questions should I ask the individual? How do I find out what's really happening with someone who seems so confused and upset? How do I recognize a person in crisis? If the person in crisis is not "crazy," then what distinguishes him or her from someone who is mentally disturbed but not in active crisis?

There are two levels of crisis assessment that should be completed by the crisis worker. The human services person must ask himself or herself the following questions at each level:

LEVEL I: Is there an obvious or potential threat to life, either the life of the individual in crisis or the lives of others? In other words, what are the risks of suicide and/or homicide?

LEVEL II: Is there evidence that the person is unable to function in his or her usual life role? And is the person in danger of being extruded from his or her natural social setting?

Level I assessment should be done by everyone. This includes people in their natural roles of friend, neighbor, parent, and spouse, as well as people in various professional positions: physicians, teachers, nurses, police, clergy, welfare workers, prison officials. This level of assessment is critical. It has life and death dimensions and forms the basis for mobilizing emergency services on behalf of the person, family, or community in crisis.

Every person in crisis should be assessed regarding danger to self and others. Techniques for assessment of suicidal danger are presented in detail in Chapter 5. Assessment of homicidal danger includes consideration of the following:*

- History of homicidal threats
- History of assault
- Current homicidal threats and plan
- Possession of lethal weapons
- Use and/or abuse of alcohol
- Disruption of meaningful social relationships, e.g., infidelity or threat of divorce
- Threats of suicide following homicide

If assessment reveals the presence of one or several of the above, the person is a probable risk for assault or homicide. This kind of assessment should *always* include the use of consultation with an experienced professional crisis counselor and often should be done in collaboration with police (see Chapter 10).

Level II assessment involves consideration of a large number of personal and social characteristics of the person. It is usually done by a trained crisis counselor or mental health professional. A well organized worker uses tools which aid in the assessment process. If a counselor lacks direction and a sense of order, this can only add to the chaos already felt by the person in crisis. (See Appendix A for a suggested assessment tool.) Professional human service workers

*See also Appendix A.

should acquire skill in this kind of assessment if they do not already have it.

Close friends and family members are often able to make this kind of assessment as well. The chances for their success depends on: their personal level of self-confidence, general experience, and previous success in helping others with problems.

Another skill that human service workers should acquire as an aid in making assessments is the use of consultation with experienced professional crisis counselors (see Chapter 10). This is especially important in assessing persons with complex, multi-problem situations.

A basic step in crisis assessment is to identify the events which led to the person's distress. Naomi Golan differentiates between the hazardous event and the precipitating factor.[8]

HAZARDOUS EVENT: This is the initial shock or internal rise in tension that sets in order a series of reactions culminating in a crisis. The hazardous event can be anticipated: For example, a critical stage of development such as adolescence or a major transition point such as getting married. Or it may be unanticipated: For example, sudden loss of a significant person through illness or death, loss of health, or loss through natural disaster such as a flood. In order to identify the hazardous event, the helping person should ask directly "What happened?" Sometimes people are so upset or overwhelmed by a series of things that they cannot clearly identify what happened when. In these instances, it is helpful to ask the person when he or she began feeling so upset. Simple, direct questions should be asked about the time and circumstances of all the happenings perceived as upsetting. Putting all events in order, so to speak, has a calming effect on the individual. The person experiences a certain sense of self possession by the very fact of being able to make some order out of what seemed like sheer chaos. This is particularly true for the person who is afraid of "losing control" or "going crazy."

PRECIPITATING FACTOR: This is the proverbial "straw that broke the camel's back." It is the final, stressful event in a series of such events that pushes the person from a state of acute vulnerability into crisis. The precipitating event is not always easy to identify. This is particularly true when the presenting problem seems to have been present for a long time. A useful approach is to ask, "What happened *today* that made you come for help (since this apparently has troubled you for some time)?"

HOW PEOPLE IN CRISIS FEEL, THINK, AND ACT

Another important aspect of the assessment process is to recognize the usual characteristics of a person in crisis. People in distress send signals to those around them.[3] Some common signals are:

1. Difficulty in managing one's feelings.
2. Suicidal or homicidal tendencies.
3. Alcohol or other drug abuse.
4. Trouble with the law.
5. Inability to effectively use available help. (See Appendix A.)

These signals tell us that the person is threatened in regard to essential needs or the basic life attachments. (See Chapter 1.) When thus threatened, the individual alters his or her usual way of thinking, feeling, and acting.[9] Hansell calls this response the person's "crisis plumage."[3]

Feelings

People in crisis experience a high degree of anxiety and tension. They may also feel fearful, angry, guilty, or embarrassed.

ANXIETY: A certain degree of tension is a normal part of life. It serves to move us to make appropriate plans and to take productive action. For example, Terri, a student, has no anxiety about passing or failing a course. Therefore she does not exert the effort required to study and achieve a passing grade. When a person is excessively anxious, however, negative results usually occur. A state of great anxiety is one of the most painful experiences a human being can have.

Anxiety is manifested in a number of ways. Some characteristics will be peculiar to the particular person concerned. Commonly experienced signs of anxiety are:

- Sense of dread.
- Fear of losing control.
- Inability to focus on one thing.
- Physical symptoms: sweating, frequent urination, diarrhea, nausea and vomiting, tachycardia (rapid heart beat), headache, chest or abdominal pain, rash, menstrual irregularity, and sexual disinterest.

Case Example

Deborah, age 45, feels bereft after the recent death of her husband. Her friends have been supportive since his death from chronic heart disease. She chides herself and feels guilty about not being able to take the loss any better than she is. After all, she knew that her husband's condition was precarious. Nevertheless, she had depended on him as a readily available source of reassurance. Since she is basically a cheerful person, always on hand to support others in distress, she is embarrassed by what she perceives as weakness following her husband's death.

Because she cries more than usual, Deborah is afraid she may be losing control. At times she even wonders whether she is going "crazy." It should be noted that Deborah is in a major developmental transition to middle age. Also, the oldest of her three children was recently married—leaving her with a sense of loss in her usual mothering role. An additional anticipated loss was the recent news that one of her close friends will soon be leaving town. This threatened to erode further her base of support. Deborah feels angry about all these losses in her life, stating, "Why does all this have to happen to me all at once?" But she also feels guilty about her angry feelings—after all, her friend "deserves the opportunity that the move will afford her and her husband," and her daughter "has every right to get married and live her own life."

What Deborah doesn't acknowledge is that:

- She also has a right to whatever feelings she has about these disturbing events.
- She has a right and a need to express those feelings.
- Her feelings of loss and anger do not cancel the good feelings and support she can continue to have from her daughter and friend, though in an altered form.

Were it not for these various developmental and situational factors, Deborah might not have experienced her husband's death as a crisis. The stability of Deborah's life transactions was disrupted on several counts:

- Her role as wife was changed to that of widow.

- Her role as mother of her oldest daughter was altered by her daughter's marriage.

- Her affectional attachment to her husband is completely severed.

- Affectional attachment to her friend will be altered in terms of physical distance and immediacy of anticipated support.

- Her notion of a full life includes marriage, so she must adjust—at least temporarily—to a change in that concept.

Thoughts and Perceptions

Feelings—especially high anxiety—have great impact on a person's perceptions and thinking processes. In crisis, all of one's attention is focused on the acute anguish being experienced and a few items concerning the crisis event. As a consequence, the person's usual memory and way of perceiving may be altered. He or she may have difficulty sorting things out. The relationship of events may not seem clear. People in crisis seem, by their own perception, caught in a maze of happenings which they cannot fit together. They often have trouble defining who they are and what their skills are. The state of anguish and resulting confusion can alter a person's ability to make decisions and solve problems, the very skills needed during a crisis. This disturbance in perceptual processes and problem solving ability increases the individual's already heightened state of anxiety. Sometimes, the person fears that he or she is going crazy.

The distorted perceptual process observed in crisis states should not be confused with mental illness, in which a person's *usual* pattern of thinking is disturbed. In a crisis state, the disturbance arises from and is part of the crisis experience. There is a rapid return to normal perception once the crisis is resolved.

Case Example

Joan, age 34, called a mental health center stating that her husband had just left the house with a shotgun and that she didn't know where he was going. She was afraid for her life as they had had an argument the night before during which she complained about his drinking and he had threatened her. Upon further questioning, it turned out that Joan's husband had left the house at his usual time for work in a neighboring town. He had also left with the shotgun the previous evening after the argument. After three hours, he had returned during the evening and put away the gun. There was nothing in the interaction to lead an outside observer to conclude that her husband would not be home as usual after a day at work.

To be noted in this example is Joan's disturbed perceptual process. Upon questioning, she cannot recall certain details without help and cannot put all the facts into logical order. Joan is obviously very anxious about her personal safety. Complicating this feeling of anxiety is her sense of guilt about her role in precipitating the argument by mentioning her husband's drinking. Her anxiety is consistent with her *perception* of the threat to her safety. The *fact* that she is not in any immediate danger is not the determining factor. Rather, it is how she *perceives* the event.

The feelings of people in crisis are usually consistent with their perception of the situation.[10] Recognition of this fact should decrease the possibility of casting people with similar problems into a common mold. The perception of the event is one of the deciding factors that makes an event a crisis for one person but not for another.

Joan's case also illustrates how excessive anxiety interferes with effective problem solving. If Joan were not so anxious, she would probably have arrived at an obvious way to ensure her immediate safety—that is, removal of the gun or leaving the house herself and seeking help. The *use* of weapons is intrinsically connected with their availability.

Behavior

Behavior usually follows from what people think and feel. If a person feels very anxious and has a distorted perception of what is happening, he or she is likely to behave in unusual ways. A significant behavioral sign of crisis is the individual's inability to perform normal vocational functions in the usual manner. For example, a person cannot satisfactorily accomplish required household chores, concentrate on studies, or do an outside job. Another sign is a change in the individual's social behavior. The person may withdraw from usual social contacts; or he or she may make unusual efforts to avoid being alone and become "clingy" or "demanding."[3] As social connections break down, the person may also report feeling detached or distant from others. Some people in crisis act on impulse; they may drive a car recklessly, make a suicide attempt, or attack others as a desperate means of relieving tension.

Others will go out of their way to reject the assistance offered by friends. Often, this reaction rises out of the person's sense of helplessness and embarrassment at not being able to cope in the usual manner. The person fears that acceptance of help may be misinterpreted as a confirmation of one's perceived weakness. People in crisis are also observed at times to behave in ways that are inconsistent with their thoughts and feelings. For example, a young woman had witnessed a shooting accident which caused the death of her boyfriend. Initially, she was visibly upset by the event. She was brought by her family to a mental health emergency clinic. During the interview with a counselor, she laughed inappropriately when talking about the shooting and death she had witnessed. Another behavioral signal of crisis is the observation of atypical behavior such as driving while intoxicated by an individual with no previous record of such behavior.

The thoughts, feelings, and behavior of people in crisis vary from person to person. Golan describes the subjective reaction to what happened as the "vulnerable state."[8] This is the unique response of an individual to a hazardous event. No situation or disturbance affects two people alike. Also, the same person may react differently to similar events at different times in life.

As a human service worker, it is therefore important to find out how *this person* is reacting *here and now* to whatever happened. The simplest way to assess a person's vulnerability is to ask "How do you feel about what happened?" Another way to assess the person's vulnerability is to ask how he or she has already responded to the hazardous event. For example, "What have you been doing to deal with this thing that has struck you?" Mary Lee, who usually confides in her husband, has basically good coping ability. However, she feels she "shouldn't burden him" since his diagnosis of heart disease. She and her husband may need assistance in expressing their feelings and finding the support they need at this time. On the other hand, a person who copes by abusing alcohol is much more vulnerable than Mary Lee is.

Another useful technique for assessment of people in crisis is application of the paradigm developed by Aquilera and Messick.[11] This assessment model is based on the concept that people in crisis are in a state of disequilibrium (imbalance). The authors propose that if equilibrium can be maintained or regained, crisis can be avoided. Equilibrium is affected by several balancing factors:

- Realistic perception of the event.
- Adequate situational support.
- Adequate coping mechanisms.
- Resolution of the problem.

The homeostatic functioning of people implied by this view was originally proposed by Menninger[12] and Caplan.[9] This view of people in crisis has been criticized by Allport,[13] Taplin[14] and Bartolucci.[15] The problem with the homeostatic view, if applied too narrowly, is that it isolates crisis concepts from other important psychosocial concerns such as learning, perception, emotion, and communication. The view suggests that crises can be resolved by mechanistically reducing tension.[14] This implies a closed system, that is, the person as a tension holding and tension reducing organism isolated from fellow human beings and from the broader social network.

Such a view of the person in crisis is best avoided. Instead, extreme tension and anxiety associated with crisis should be regarded as feelings rising out of the person's interaction with others and affecting the person's self-concept. People learn and grow by successfully resolving crises; and crises are not simply resolved by reducing tension, which is only a part of the total crisis experience. If understood in a broader psychosocial context, the concept of disequilibrium can be helpful in ascertaining whether or not a person is in crisis. An application of the paradigm is illustrated in the following example.

Case Example

Rosemary, age 30, has been extremely upset since she learned of her husband's intention to divorce her. She perceives this event as a major blow to her desirability as a woman. She finds it difficult to imagine how she can survive happily without a husband and seriously doubts whether she can again attract and "hold" a man. Also, she is blaming herself entirely for everything that went wrong with the marriage, even though she complained earlier about her husband's seeming disregard of her. She now has frequent weeping spells.

Rosemary focused her life so exclusively on her husband that she has lost contact with all but a few of her friends. She feels ashamed to discuss her feelings with the one close friend she has. To complicate matters, she never felt close to her family; in fact, her marriage was strongly motivated by a desire to get away from her family. Even though Rosemary worked for a year as a salesclerk before her marriage, she does not want to go back to that kind of work. She hated it. She dreads the prospect of having to give up the comfortable standard of living she has grown accustomed to. Rosemary doesn't know where to turn. She considered suicide, became frightened at the thought, and decided to call the police. They recommended that she call the local crisis center.

In summary, according to the paradigm,[11] Rosemary:

• Perceives life without her husband as not worth living and sees divorce as a blow to her womanhood: *Distorted perception of the event.*

• Is ashamed to confide in her one close friend; she feels cut off emotionally from her family: *Lacks adequate situational support.*

• Responds by self-blame and consideration of suicide; she cries frequently: *Has poor coping ability.*

• Regards suicide as a scary and unacceptable solution, though she doesn't know what else to do: *Problem is unresolved.*

• Continues to feel upset, depressed, and suicidal: *Acute upset continues.*

Rosemary is in active crisis.

Regardless of the technique used, the important skill used by the helper is one's ability to identify the characteristic ways that people feel, think, and act during crisis.

THE ASSESSMENT INTERVIEW

The following interview is with George, age 48, by an emergency room nurse. George is brought to the hospital by police following an attempt to commit suicide by crashing his car. (This case illustration is continued from Chapter 1.)

Case Example: George Sloan

Signals of Distress and Crisis to be Identified	Assessment Techniques Applied to Case of Mr. George Sloan
	Nurse: Hello, Mr. Sloan. Do you mind if I call you George?
	George: No, go right ahead.
	Nurse: Will you tell me what happened, George?
	George: I had a car accident. Can't you see that without asking? (Slightly hostile and seemingly reluctant to talk)
	Nurse: Yes, I know, George. But the police said you were going the wrong way on the expressway. How did that happen?
Active Crisis State: Extreme anxiety to the breaking point	*George:* Yes, that's right——(hesitates). Well, I just couldn't take it anymore——but I guess it didn't work.
	Nurse: Sounds like you've been having a rough time, George. Can you tell me what it is you can't take anymore?
Hazardous Event: Physical illness	*George:* Well, I've got heart trouble——
Vulnerable State: Loss of external social supports or inability to use them	it's gotten to be too much for my wife——I can't expect her to do much more——
Loss of personal coping ability	we're having trouble with our 16-year-old son, Arnold——
Inability to communicate stress to significant others	I just couldn't take it anymore so figured I'd do everybody a favor and get rid of myself.

Signals of Distress and Crisis to be Identified	Assessment Techniques Applied to Case of Mr. George Sloan
High lethal suicide attempt	*Nurse:* So your car accident was really an attempt to kill yourself?
	George: That's right——that way at least my wife wouldn't lose the insurance along with everything else she's had to put up with.
	Nurse: I can see that your heart trouble and all the other troubles have left you feeling pretty worthless.
Depression	*George:* That's about it——too bad I came out alive. I really feel I'm worth more dead than alive.
	Nurse: George, I can see that you're feeling desperate about your situation. How long have you felt this way?
	George: I've had heart trouble for about four years——after my last heart attack, the doctor told me I had to slow down or it would probably kill me. Well, there's no way I can change things that I can see.
Precipitating Event: Inability to perform in expected role as father	*Nurse:* What happened this past week that made you decide to end it all?
	George: Well, our kid Arnold got suspended from school——that did it! I figured if a father can't do any better with his son than that, what's the use?
	Nurse: I gather from what you say and feel that you just couldn't see any other way out.
State of Active Crisis:	*George:* That's right——money is really getting tight; my wife was talking about getting a

Signals of Distress and Crisis to be Identified	Assessment Techniques Applied to Case of Mr. George Sloan
Vulnerability: Fixated on role expectations Inability to use outside helping resources	job to help out and that really bothers me to think that I can't support my family anymore. And if she starts working, things might get even worse with Arnold. There was no one to talk to. Suicide's the only thing left.

Nurse: With all these problems, George, have you ever thought about suicide before?

History of poor coping ability	*George:* Yes, once, after my doctor told me to really watch it after my last heart attack. I felt pretty hopeless and thought of crashing my car then. But things weren't so bad then between me and my wife, and she talked me out of it and seemed willing to stick with me.

Nurse: I see——but this time you felt there was nowhere else to turn. Anyway, George, I'm glad your suicide attempt didn't work. I'd really like to have you consider some other ways to deal with all these problems.

George: I don't know what they could be——I really feel hopeless but I guess I could see what you've got to offer.

Nurse: There are several things we can discuss ——(To be continued in Chapter 3: Helping People in Crisis)

Besides the technical aspects of asking clear, direct questions, this interview excerpt illustrates another important point. The nurse reveals an understanding of Mr. Sloan's problem and empathizes with the despair he must be feeling:

"So your car accident was really an attempt to kill yourself?"

"Sounds like you've been having a rough time, George."

"I can see that your illness and all the other troubles have left you feeling pretty worthless."

"George, I can see that you're feeling desperate about your situation."

"I'm glad your suicide attempt didn't work."

The nurse clearly comes through as a human being with feelings and concern about a fellow human being who is despairing. Concern is conveyed by a gentle voice tone and unstylized manner. Furthermore, the nurse is able to express feelings without sounding gushy and shocked and apparently is not afraid to be with a person in crisis.

As shown by this interview, effective assessment techniques are not highly complicated or veiled in mystery. The techniques require:

- Straightforward approach with simple direct questions.
- Ability to "walk in another person's moccasins."
- Ability to grasp the depth of another's despair and share the feelings that this evokes.
- Courage not to run away from frightening experiences like suicide attempts.

The interview also demonstrates that assessment for suicide risk is an integral part of thorough crisis assessment. More and more people—including parents, teachers, friends, and police—can add to their natural tendencies to help by learning these assessment techniques. Failure to use the techniques can mean the difference between life and death for someone like Mr. Sloan. It is not uncommon for people in George Sloan's condition to be treated medically and/or surgically in hospitals without anyone inquiring into underlying suicide intentions. If he receives only medical/surgical treatment and nothing else changes in his life, George Sloan will probably commit suicide within six to twelve months. He is already in a high risk category for suicide (see Chapter 5, Assessment of the Suicidal Person).

Another objective that should be accomplished during the initial interview is to provide the person in crisis with some concrete help.[16] Mr. Sloan feels the acceptance and concern of the nurse, or he would not have dropped his initial resistance to sharing his dilemma. The nurse has opened the discussion of alternatives for him to consider besides suicide.

Once an individual is identified as being in a state of crisis, the helping person proceeds to give or obtain whatever assistance is indicated. In complex situations or in circumstances involving life and death, the helper should engage the services of professional crisis workers.*

Most communities now have local crisis clinics, community mental health centers with emergency mental health services, or crisis and suicide prevention hotlines. Once the state of crisis is ascertained, the professional crisis worker will engage the person in a full scale assessment of his or her problems. Such an assessment will involve the person's family and other significant people. Assessment techniques of this nature are currently practiced in many crisis and counseling clinics and community mental health programs (see Appendix A).

SUMMARY

Some people are at greater risk of crisis than others. Identifying groups of people who are most likely to experience a crisis is helpful in recognizing individuals in crisis. People in crisis have typical patterns of thinking, feeling, and acting. There is no substitute for thorough assessment of whether a person is or is not in crisis. The assessment is the basis of the helping plan and can avoid many later problems, including unnecessary placement of people in institutions.

*Professional crisis workers may or may not be traditional mental health professionals such as psychologists, psychiatrists, and social workers. A professional who is frightened by suicide threats and who practices only traditional psychotherapy does not possess the requirements necessary for a crisis worker. (See Chapter 10.)

References

1. Schulberg, Herbert C. and Alan Sheldon. "The Probability of Crisis and Strategies for Preventive Intervention," *Archives of General Psychiatry,* 18:553–58, May 1968.

2. Polak, Paul R. "The Crisis of Admission," *Social Psychiatry,* 2:150–57, No. 4, 1967.

3. Hansell, Norris. *The Person in Distress.* New York: Human Services Press, 1976.

4. Goffman, Erving. *Asylums.* New York: Doubleday and Company, Inc., 1961.

5. Rosenbaum, D. L. "On Being Sane

in Insane Places," *Science*, 179:250–58, January 1973.

6. Polak, Paul. "A Model to Replace Psychiatric Hospitalization," *Journal of Nervous and Mental Disease*, 162:13–22, No. 1, 1976.

7. Illich, Ivan. *Tools for Conviviality*. Great Britain: Fontana/Collins, 1975.

8. Golan, Naomi. "When Is A Client in Crisis?," *Social Casework*, 50:389–94, July 1969.

9. Caplan, Gerald. *Principles of Preventive Psychiatry*. New York: Basic Books, Inc., 1964.

10. Dressler, David M. "The Management of Emotional Crises by Medical Practitioners," *Journal of American Medical Women's Association*, 28:654–59, No. 12, 1973.

11. Aquilera, Donna C., and Janice M. Messick. *Crisis Intervention*. Second Edition. St. Louis: C. V. Mosby Company, 1974.

12. Menninger, Karl; Martin Mayman; and Paul Precyser. *The Vital Balance*. New York: Viking Press, 1963.

13. Allport, Gordon W. "The Open System in Personality," *Journal of Abnormal and Social Psychology*, 61:301–10, 1960.

14. Taplin, Julian R. "Crisis Theory: Critique and Reformulation," *Community Mental Health Journal*, 7:13–23, No. 1, 1971.

15. Bartolucci, Giampiero, and Clavin, Drayer. "An Overview of Crisis Intervention in Emergency Rooms of General Hospitals," *American Journal of Psychiatry*. 130:953–60, September 1973.

16. King, Joan M. "The Initial Interview: Basis for Assessment in Crisis Intervention," *Perspectives in Psychiatric Care*, 9:247–56, No. 6, 1971.

CHAPTER 3

Helping People in Crisis

PREVENTING CRISES

Viewing crisis as both an opportunity and a danger point allows for some kind of pre-knowledge about the event. Armed with that knowledge, we can prepare for normal life events and usually prevent them from becoming crises. For many people, however, these normal events do become occasions for crisis in the sense of hazard rather than opportunity.

While we cannot predict events such as sudden death of a loved one, the birth of a premature child, or natural disaster, we can anticipate how people will react to them. In his study of survivors of the Coconut Grove fire, Erich Lindemann demonstrated the importance of recognizing crisis responses and preventing negative outcomes of crisis.[1]

In chapter 2 the following points were noted: the importance of the type of hazardous event the person is experiencing, and the person's vulnerability to the event as a base for effective crisis intervention. Once a population or individual is identified as being at risk of crisis, we can use a number of time-honored approaches to prevent crisis. Gerald Caplan speaks of primary, secondary, and tertiary prevention in the public health-mental health field.[2,3,4]

Primary Prevention

Primary prevention—in the form of education, consultation, and crisis intervention—is designed to reduce the occurrence of mental disability in a community. There are several means of doing this:

1. Eliminating or modifying the hazardous situation. Everyone is familiar with the routine practice of immunizing children against smallpox and diptheria. This practice is based on the knowledge that a failure to immunize can result in large numbers of people being exposed to the hazards of these diseases. Knowledge of social-psychological hazards should motivate us to make similar efforts to eliminate or modify the hazards. For example, alter hospital structures and practices to reduce the risk of crisis for the hospitalized child and the adult surgical patient; eliminate substandard housing for crisis prone older people and others.

2. Reducing the person's exposure to the hazardous situation. We are all familiar with public health measures which

help people avoid exposure to the risks of physical danger. For example, a flood warning allows people to escape from the disaster; a public health announcement of outbreak of infectious hepatitis at a restaurant warns people not to eat there and gives directions to persons exposed to the danger.

In the social-psychological sphere, people are advised of and screened for the risks of endeavors such as graduate school, an unusual occupation such as work in a foreign country, or a demanding occupation such as crisis counseling.

3. Reducing the person's vulnerability by helping him or her increase coping ability. In the physical health sector persons with certain diseases are directed to obtain extra rest, eat certain foods, and take prescribed medicine. All of these measures are designed to help the individual battle and recover from the disease process. In the psychosocial sphere, older people and the poor, for example, are most often exposed to the risk of urban dislocation. They can be provided with extra physical resources and social services to counter the negative emotional effects of such a hazardous event. Studies reveal that the birth of a first child constitutes a crisis situation for most parents.[5] New parents will feel less vulnerable if they are prepared for some of the hazards and experiences of rearing their first child. Marriage and retirement are other important life events which we can consider and prepare for.

The success of preventive measures in these instances depends largely on the person's openness to learning, previous problem solving success, and general social supports. Jacobson refers to anticipatory prevention as generic; that is, applicable to general target groups known to many of us.[6]

When hazardous events or a person's vulnerability to events cannot be accurately predicted, participatory techniques are used to help the person or family in crisis.[2,4,7] This approach involves a thorough psychosocial assessment and counseling of individuals or families by professional crisis workers. Participatory techniques are indicated for people who are unable to respond to generic and preventive techniques.[6] The individual and the family participate actively in resolving the crisis. (See Chapter 10 regarding development of community approaches to primary prevention.)

Secondary Prevention

The term "secondary prevention" implies that some form of mental disability has already occurred because of the absence of primary prevention activities or because of a person's inability to profit from those activities. The aim of secondary prevention is to shorten the length of time a person is mentally disabled. A major means of doing this is to provide easily accessible crisis intervention services. If such service—using a social systems model (see Chapter 4)—is offered, emotionally and mentally disturbed people can be kept out of mental hospitals. The disabling effects of institutional life are thereby avoided, as well as the destructive results of removal from one's natural community. Individuals who already respond to stress with mental or emotional disturbance are more crisis prone than others. These people need active help when in crisis more than others might.

Tertiary Prevention

The goal of this level of prevention is to reduce long-term disabling effects for those who have recovered from a mental disorder. Social and rehabilitation programs are an important means of helping these people return to old social and occupational roles or to learn new ones.[8] Crisis intervention is also important for the same reasons noted in the discussion of secondary prevention. Hopefully the recovery process includes learning new ways of coping with stress.

HOW CRISIS INTERVENTION DIFFERS FROM OTHER WAYS OF HELPING

Anticipatory prevention and participatory techniques can be viewed on a continuum of services for people with different kinds of psychosocial problems. (See Figure 3–1). The continuum suggests that people with problems have varying degrees of dependency on other people and agencies for help. Services in the continuum include the basic elements of community mental health programs:

- Consultation and education.
- Emergency mental health services, including around-the-clock crisis intervention.
- Out-care service.
- Partial hospital care.
- 24 hour in-care service.

Figure 3–1. Continuum of Mental Health Services

Lesser Dependency			Greater Dependency
Consultation and Education	Emergency Mental Health Services (including around-the-clock crisis intervention)	Out-care Service	Partial Hospital Care
			24 Hour In-care Service

These five essential services were originally mandated by the Community Mental Health Acts of 1963 and 1965. Recommendations in 1961 by the U.S. Joint Commission on Mental Illness and Health formed the basis of these mental health acts.[9] Recent federal guidelines for basic services now include rehabilitation, addiction services, services for the elderly and children, and evaluation programs. Crisis intervention is considered a part of these mental health and social services.

Certainly crisis intervention should not be regarded as a panacea for all social, emotional, and mental problems.[10] It is not synonymous with psychotherapy, even though some techniques, such as listening and catharsis, are used in both. Nor is crisis intervention a mode of helping only poor people while reserving psychotherapy for the financially secure.[11] The occurrence of crisis is not dependent on a person's socioeconomic status, and crisis intervention can be helpful regardless of that status.

It is possibly just as damaging to use a crisis intervention approach when it does *not* apply as it is to fail to use the approach when it *does* apply. To illustrate: When suicide and crisis hotlines are not effectively supervised and linked with other mental health services, there can be negative side effects. Callers seeking help from crisis centers can perceive that they must at least *act* as though they are in crisis in order to get attention and help. Thus some callers may appear to be in crisis when, in reality, they are not. For example, a person who is crying may or may not be in crisis. Judgment of crisis should be based on assessment of the caller's *total situation.*

If workers are unskilled in crisis assessment, a caller may be unwittingly encouraged to engage in crisis-like behavior when, instead, direct questions should be asked and help offered *before* a crisis occurs. The famous and sometimes tragic example is the person who "cries wolf." Listeners catch on to the individual's "act," and often ignore the person after the discovery is made that he or she is not in active crisis. In some cases, an underlying message is missed. Suicide may be the eventual outcome of the "cry wolf" syndrome if no one responds with the appropriate mode of help.

Figure 3–2 illustrates the range of services and differences among various services available to people with psychosocial problems. Crisis intervention is just one of the many services people need. Effective crisis intervention can be an important link to a mode of treatment such as psychotherapy. This is because during crisis people are more likely than at other times to consider getting help for chronic problems that made them crisis prone in the first place. Crisis intervention is also a significant means of avoiding last resort measures such as institutional care. Evaluation of a regional mental health center's clinical services revealed that short-term community oriented crisis approaches were not enough for people with serious mental and social disabilities.[13] Such individuals need long-term rehabilitation programs as well, including, for example, training for jobs, and instruction in home management.

PLANNING WITH A PERSON OR FAMILY IN CRISIS

Planning with a person for crisis resolution presumes: (a) establishment of a relationship with the person, and (b) assessment that the person is, in fact, in a crisis or precrisis state. Information obtained from careful assessment is the basis for the plan. These key questions should be answered before formulating a plan for help:[12,14]

1. To what extent has the crisis disrupted the person's normal life pattern?

2. Is she or he able to go to school or hold a job?

3. Can the person handle the responsibilities involved in the activities of daily living—for example, eating, personal hygiene?

4. Has the crisis situation disrupted the lives of others?

5. Is the person suicidal, homicidal, or both?

6. Does the person seem to be on the brink of despair?

7. Has the high level of tension distorted the person's perception of reality?

8. Is the person's usual support system present, absent, or exhausted?

9. What are the resources of the individual helper and/or agency in relation to the person's assessed needs?

The answers to these and related questions provide the worker with essential data for the intervention plan which involves: a thinking process; an ability to draw relationships between events and the way the

Figure 3–2. Differential Aspects: Crisis, Mental Health, and Social Service Models

	Psychotherapy	Medical-Institutional	Public Health-Crisis Intervention	Social-Rehabilitation
Type of People Served	Those who wish to correct neurotic personality or behavior patterns	People with serious mental or emotional breakdowns	Individuals and families in crisis or precrisis states	Those who are chronically disabled
Service Goals	Work through unconscious conflicts Reconstruct behavior and personality patterns Personal and social growth	Control-adjust Recover from acute disturbance	Growth-promoting Personal and social integration	Return to normal functioning in normal society as much as possible
Service Methods	Introspection Catharsis Interpretation Free association (Use of additional techniques depends on philosophy and training of therapist)	Medication Behavior modification Electric shock Group activities (Use of additional techniques depends on philosophy of institution)	Social and environmental manipulation Focus on feelings and problem solving May use medication to promote goals Decision counseling	Work training Resocialization Training in activities of daily living

Activity of Workers	Exploratory Non-directive Interpretive	Direct, noninvolved or Indirect	Active/Direct (depends on functional level of client)	Structured but less than in crisis intervention
Length of Service	Usually long-term	Short or long (depends on degree of disability and approach of psychiatrist) High Repeat Rate	Short—usually 6 sessions or less	Long-term—a few months to 2–3 years
Beliefs about People	Individualistic or social (depends on philosophy of therapist)	Individualistic—social aspect secondary Institution and order often more important than people	Social—people are capable of growth and self-control	People can change Mental disability or a diagnosis should not spell hopelessness
Attitudes toward Service	Emphasis on wisdom of therapist and 50 minute hour Flexibility varies with individual therapist	Scheduled Staff attitudes may become rigid and institutionalized	Flexible, any hour	Willingness to stick with it and observe only slow change Hopefulness and expectation of goal achievement

person is thinking, feeling, and acting; and an ability to formulate some problem solving mechanisms and solutions with the person and his or her family.[12]

A good intervention plan is developed in active collaboration with the person in crisis and significant other people in his or her life. Basically, the underlying philosophy is that people can help themselves with, of course, varying degrees of help from others. Doing things *to* a person in crisis without his or her active participation every step of the way almost inevitably spells failure in crisis intervention. If the goals for crisis intervention and problem solving are formulated by the helper alone, then those goals are practically worthless—no matter how appropriate they appear on the surface. Inattention to this important element of the planning process is probably responsible for more failures in crisis resolution than any other single factor. Making decisions for the person in crisis violates the growth and development concept basic to crisis intervention. The person may feel devalued. If a worker takes over, it implies that the person cannot participate in matters of vital concern to self. When a counselor makes the mistake of assuming control, other important characteristics of the plan are often overlooked, for example, attention to the person's cultural pattern.

A good plan has these additional features:[2]

1. *Problem-oriented.* The plan focuses on the immediate concrete problems which directly contribute to the crisis. For example, a teenage daughter has run away; a woman gets a diagnosis of breast cancer. The plan should avoid delving into basic personality patterns or underlying psychological or marital problems contributing to the person's crisis-proneness. These are properly the aim of psychotherapy or ongoing counseling which the individual may choose *after* resolution of the immediate crisis.

2. *Appropriate to person's functional level and dependency needs.* The helper assesses how the person is thinking, feeling, and acting. If the individual is so anxious that he or she cannot think straight and make decisions, the helper takes a more active role than might otherwise be indicated. In general, a crisis worker should never make a decision for another unless thorough assessment reveals that the person is unable to make decisions independently. Put another way, the person in crisis is allowed to borrow some ego functions of the helper on a temporary basis.

If the person is feeling pent up with emotion, the plan should include adequate time to express suppressed feelings. It is legitimate to give specific directions for action if the person's behavior and thinking are very chaotic. The key to success in this kind of action plan is an intrinsic belief in the person's basic ability to help him- or herself once the acute crisis phase is over. Such a firm confident approach, based on accurate assessment and respect for the person, inspires confidence and restores a sense of order and independence to the individual in crisis.

Success in this aspect of planning implies an understanding of human dependency needs. Obviously it is necessary for the person in crisis to depend on others for help in resolving a crisis constructively. A healthy state of *inter*dependence is considered a good balance between the person's dependence and independence needs. Some individuals have the problem of being too dependent most of the time; others have the problem of being too independent most of the time. The excessively independent person will probably have a hard time accepting his or her own need during a crisis for more dependence on others than usual. Asking for help is viewed as a blow to self-esteem. The very dependent person, on the other hand, will have the tendency to behave more dependently during a crisis than the situation warrants.

These dependency considerations underscore the need for thorough assessment of the person's strengths, resources, and usual coping abilities. A good rule of thumb is never to do something *for* a person until it is determined, with a fair degree of certainty, that the individual *cannot* do it for him- or herself. Basically, we all resent extreme dependency on others as it keeps us from growing to our full potential. Equally important is that we, as helpers, do not fail to do for a person in crisis what assessment reveals he or she cannot do for self. The Crisis Intervention Model calls for active participation by the worker. Also, the crisis counselor needs to know when to let go, so the person can once again take charge of his or her life.

3. *Consistent with person's culture and life style.* Inattention to a person's life style and cultural patterns can cause a seemingly perfect plan to fail. We must be sensitive to the person's total situation, and careful not to impose our own value system on a person whose life style and values are different.[12] Various cultural,

ethnic, and religious groups have distinct patterns of response to events such as death, physical illness, divorce, and pregnancy-out-of-wedlock. These differences merit respect by the helper.

Case Example

Sally, on the school's recommendation, talked with a public health nurse about the problems she was having in getting her six-year-old son David to go to school. During the conversation, Sally revealed that she was not married but living with a man. The nurse conveyed through her attitude (as presented to the mental health consultant) that she disapproved of Sally's living situation on moral grounds. Because Sally sensed her disapproval, the nurse's possibly constructive suggestions about David were disregarded.

4. *Inclusive of significant other(s) and social network.*   If people in crisis are viewed as social beings, then a plan that excludes their social network is lacking. Since crises occur when there is a serious disruption in normal social transactions, or in the way one perceives of the self in the social milieu, planning must attend to these important social factors. This is true even when the person's closest social contacts are very hostile and contribute significantly to the crisis.

It is tempting for a crisis worker to avoid dealing with family members who appear to want the troubled person out of their lives. Yet significant others should be brought into the planning, if for no other reason than to clarify whether they are or are not a future resource for the person. In the event that the person is no longer really wanted, for example, by a divorcing spouse, the plan will then include a means of helping the individual accept this reality and identify new social contacts.

Case Example

Jerry Bronson, a trainee in a crisis intervention group, played the role of counselor for Brenda, age 15. Brenda had run away from her mother's home where she had constant fights with her mother and her mother's second husband. She wanted to live with her father and his second wife. Brenda walked into a crisis center asking for help with the conflict she felt about her divorced parents. While she clearly wanted to live with her father, she also hoped to smooth things over with her mother.

After determining that Brenda was not suicidal and had a place to stay, Jerry's suggested approach was to exclude Brenda's mother from the helping process. The crisis trainer demonstrated the importance of *including* Brenda's mother in the intervention plan even though Brenda chose not to live with her. Not to do so would ignore an important part of Brenda's conflict and eventual resolution of her crisis.

5. Realistic, Time Limited, and Concrete. A good crisis intervention plan is realistic regarding needs and resources. For example, a person without transportation or money should not be expected to come to an office for help. The plan should also have a clear time frame. The person or family in crisis needs to know that actions A, B, and C are planned to occur at points X, Y, and Z. This kind of structure is reassuring to someone in crisis. It provides concrete evidence that:

- Something definite will happen to change the present state of discomfort.
- The seemingly endless confusion and chaos of the crisis experience can be handled in terms familiar to the person.
- The entire plan has a clearly anticipated ending point.

For the person who fears he or she is "going crazy," or who finds it difficult to depend on others, it is reassuring to anticipate that within a certain period of time events hopefully will be under control again.

An effective plan is also concrete in terms of place and circumstances. For example: Family crisis counseling sessions will be held at the crisis clinic at 7:00 p.m. twice a week; one session will be held at daughter Nancy's school and will include her guidance counselor, the school nurse, and the principal.

6. Dynamic and renegotiable. A dynamic plan is not carved in marble; it is alive, meaningful, and flexible. It is specific to *this person* with his or her unique problems and allows for ongoing changes in the person's life. It should also include a mechanism for dealing with these changes if the original plan no longer fits the person's needs, so that certain outcomes will not be perceived as "failure."

Case Example

Mary calls a crisis hotline at 11:00 p.m.—very upset over the news of her husband's threat of divorce. After 45 minutes, she and the telephone counselor agree that she will call a local counseling center the next day for an appointment. She is given the name and phone number to aid in making the contact. The plan includes an agreement that Mary will call back to the hotline for renegotiation if for any reason she is unable to complete the planned contact.

A person doubting whether anything can be done to help should be assured, "If this doesn't work, we'll examine why and try something else."

7. *Inclusive of follow-up.*   Finally, a good plan includes an agreement for follow-up contact after apparent resolution of the crisis. This feature is too often neglected by crisis and mental health workers. If it is not built into the plan initially, it will probably not be done.

There is no substitute for a good plan for crisis resolution. Crisis intervention without careful planning is like walking in the dark. A directionless helper and chaotic efforts to help can only add to the confusion already experienced by the person in crisis. Some may argue that in certain crisis situations there is no time to plan, as life and death issues are at stake. This, rather than excusing the need for planning, only underscores its urgent necessity. A good plan can be formulated in a few minutes by someone who knows the signs of crisis; is confident in his or her own ability to help; and is able to enlist additional, immediate assistance in cases of impasse or of life and death emergency.

The necessity of thinking and planning *quickly* does not eliminate the necessity of thinking and planning. Action without thought is usually fruitless.

WORKING THROUGH A CRISIS
Effective crisis management fosters growth and avoids negative, destructive effects from traumatic events. Helping a person through healthy crisis resolution means carrying out the plan that was developed after assessment. The worker's crisis intervention techniques should follow from the way the person in crisis is thinking, feeling, and acting. Caplan and others have contrasted healthy and unhealthy crisis coping in relation to each of these functional areas.[4,15] (See Figure 3-3.)

Figure 3–3. Crisis Coping

Functional manifestation of crisis	Effective crisis coping	Ineffective crisis coping
Cognitive	Realistic grasp of crisis situation	Denial of reality; distorted perception of reality
Emotional	Acceptance and expression of feelings appropriate to event	Repression or denial of feelings
		Affect inappropriate to event
Behavioral	Obtaining and using help, both personal resources and social network	Failure to seek or use help
		Resistance to problem solving
		Problem solving by drug or alcohol abuse; suicide or homicide attempts
		Lapse into neurotic or psychotic patterns of behavior
		Impulsive behavior, e.g. reckless driving

Healthy crisis coping can be achieved by using several techniques:*

1. *Listen actively and with concern.* When a person is ashamed of his or her ability to cope with a problem or feels that the problem is too minor to be so upset about, a good listener can dispel some of these feelings. Listening helps a person feel important and deserving of help no matter how trivial the problem may appear on the surface.

*The use of any psychosocial techniques of crisis intervention presumes assessment of medical emergency needs and appropriate linkage to medical resources. The most common instance of such intervention is in the event of a suicide attempt. The integration of crisis intervention with medical emergency treatment is considered in detail in Chapter 5.

2. *Encourage the open expression of feelings.*   Listening is a natural forerunner of this important crisis intervention technique. One reason why some people are crisis prone is that they habitually bottle up feelings such as anger, grief, frustration, helplessness, and hopelessness. Negative associations with feeling expression during childhood seem to put a permanent damper on such expression when traumatic events occur later in life. The crisis worker's acceptance of the person's feelings often helps him or her feel better immediately. It also can be the beginning of a healthier coping style in the future. This is one of the rewarding growth possibilities for people in crisis who are fortunate enough to get the help they need.

3. *Help the person gain an understanding of the crisis.*   The individual may ask: "Why did this awful thing have to happen to me? What did I do to deserve such treatment?" This perception of the traumatic event—threat of divorce, rape, son or daughter who has gotten into trouble—implies that the event occurred because the person in crisis was bad and deserving of punishment. The crisis worker can help the individual see the broad interplay of factors which contribute to a crisis situation, and thereby curtail self-blaming. Instead, the individual is encouraged to examine the total problem, including his or her own behavior as it may be related to the crisis. Such thoughtful reflection on oneself and one's behavior can lead to growth and change rather than self depreciation and self pity.

4. *Help the individual gradually accept reality.*   Respond to the person's tendency to blame his or her problems on others. The person in crisis may be adopting the role of "victim." The counselor can help the individual gradually accept reality and escape from the "victim" position. It is sometimes very tempting for a counselor to collude with the person in blaming others. This is particularly true when the person's story, as well as the reality, reveal especially cruel attacks, rejections, or other unfair treatment.

The tendency to blame and scapegoat is especially strong in family and marital crises. The crisis counselor should help the person understand that victim-persecutor relationships are not one-sided. This can be done effectively when the counselor has established an appropriate relationship with the person. If the counselor has genuine concern, rather than inappropriate rescue fantasies, the individual can accept the counselor's interpretation of his or her own role in the crisis event. The victim-rescuer-persecutor syndrome occurs frequently in human relationships of all kinds; it is also common in many helping relationships. People viewed as "victims" are not rescued easily. Thus crisis counselors who are bent on "rescuing" others usually are frustrated when their rescue efforts fail. Their disappointment may move them to "persecute" their "victim" for failure to respond. At this point the "victim" turns "persecutor" and punishes the counselor for the well intended but inappropriate effort to help. The reader is referred to sources such as *Born to Win* by James and Jongeward for a fuller examination of this important phenomenon.[16]

5. *Help the person explore new ways of coping with problems.* Instead of responding to crises as helpless victims, or with suicide and homicide attempts, people can learn new responses. Sometimes people have given up on problem solving devices that used to work for them.

Case Example

Jane, age 38, was able to weather a lot of storms until her best friend died. Somehow, after her friend's death, she could not find the energy necessary to establish new friendships. Exploration revealed that Jane had never worked through the grief she experienced over the death of her friend. The lack of healthy resolution of this crisis made Jane more vulnerable than she might otherwise have been when her daughter, age 18, left home and married. Jane had temporarily given up and stopped using her effective problem solving devices.

6. *Link the person to a social network.* The technique of exploring new coping devices leads naturally to this function. Just as disruption of social ties is a very important precursor of crisis, so the restoration of those ties—or, if permanently lost, the formation of new ties—is one of the most powerful means of resolving a crisis. This is such an important facet of crisis management that it will be considered in detail in the next chapter. To be noted here is the active role of the crisis counselor in re-establishing a person with his or her social network. This aspect of

crisis management is also known as social systems intervention or the ecological approach to crisis intervention (see Chapter 4).

7. *Decision counseling is another technique central to crisis management.*[17]   Decision counseling is cognitively oriented and allows the upset person to put distorted thoughts, chaotic feelings, and disturbed behavior into some kind of order. The person is encouraged to:

- Search for boundaries of the problem.
- Appraise the problem's meaning and how it can be mastered.
- Make a decision about various solutions to the problem.
- Test the chosen solutions in a clear-cut action plan.

In decision counseling the crisis counselor facilitates crisis resolution by helping the person decide:

What problem is to be solved?

How is it to be solved?

When should it be solved?

Where should it be solved?

Who should be involved in solving it?

Decision counseling also includes the setting of goals for the future and a different action plan to be used if the current plan fails or goals are not achieved.

In decision counseling the counselor must have thorough knowledge of the person's functional level and of his or her network of social attachments. Used effectively, this technique makes maximum use of the turmoil of crisis to: (a) develop new problem solving skills; (b) establish more stable emotional attachments; (c) improve the person's social skills, and (d) increase the person's competence and satisfaction with life patterns.[17]

8. *Reinforce the newly learned coping devices, and follow-up after resolution of the crisis.*   The person is given time to try out the proposed solutions to the problem. Successful problem solving mechanisms are reinforced.[12] Unsuccessful solutions are discarded and new ones sought. In either case, the person is not cut off in an abrupt manner.

A follow-up contact is carried out as agreed on in the initial plan. Some workers object that follow-up contacts maintain people in an unnecessary state of dependency. This does not occur when the follow-up plan is negotiated in collaboration with the person at the beginning of service, and when the counselor does not overprotect the person or devalue his or her abilities. Follow-up work can often be the occasion for reaching some people in precrisis states who are unable to initiate help for themselves *before* an acute crisis occurs.

These crisis management techniques can be mastered by any helping person who exerts the effort to learn them. Human service workers and community caretakers, volunteer counselors, welfare workers, nurses, physicians, police, teachers, and clergy should make it a part of their professional training to learn how to effectively help people in crisis.[18] To do so will save much time and effort spent on later problems which are secondary to earlier crises not effectively resolved. Primary prevention is much less costly both humanly and economically.

TRANQUILIZERS: WHAT PLACE IN CRISIS INTERVENTION?

We are bombarded with the idea that drugs are a solution for nearly everything. Advertisements constantly remind us: Feel upset? Can't sleep? Can't control your kids?—Take pills. Valium, a mild tranquilizer, seems to have become the all-American pill. Currently, it is prescribed more frequently than any other drug on the market. The problem with taking tranquilizers is that they relieve tension temporarily but do nothing about the problems causing the tension. At best, they are a crutch. At worst, one can become addicted and substitute them for problem solving at a psychosocial level.

For the person in crisis, tranquilizing drugs should *never* be used as a substitute for crisis counseling and problem solving. However, there are times when a tranquilizer can be used *in addition to* the crisis intervention techniques outlined above. These instances are: (a) when a person is experiencing *extreme* anxiety and is fearful of losing control, and (b) when extreme anxiety prevents sleep for a significant period of time. Sleeping pills should always be avoided. A tranquilizer is usually sufficient to correct a sleeping problem which is part of the crisis experience.

Apart from these special circumstances, tranquilizing drugs should be avoided whenever possible. By relieving anxiety on a temporary basis, tranquilizers can have the effect of reducing the person's motivation to do effective problem solving around a crisis. With such chemical tranquilization, the person loses the advantages of his or her increased energy during a crisis state. The opportunity for psychosocial growth is often lost due to the temporary tranquility of a drugged psyche.

Anything that the crisis intervention movement can do to reduce the large-scale dependence on drugs for problem solving in many Western societies will be a giant step forward.[19]

INTERVIEW EXAMPLE

Some of the recommended planning characteristics and techniques of intervention are illustrated in the following interview with George Sloan whose case is continued from chapters 1 and 2.

Case Example: George Sloan
(continued from chapters 1 and 2)

Intervention Techniques	Interview between Mr. Sloan and Emergency Room Nurse
Exploring resources	*Nurse:* You said you really can't talk to your wife about your problems. Is there anyone else you've ever thought about talking with?
	George: Well, I tried talking to my doctor once, but he didn't really have time. Then a few months ago my minister could see I was pretty down and he stopped by a couple of times, but that didn't help.
Facilitating client decision-making	*Nurse:* Is there anyone else you think you could talk to?
	George: No, not really—nobody, anyway, that would understand.
Suggestion about new resources	*Nurse:* What about seeing a regular counselor, George? We have connections here in the emergency room with the psychiatric department of our hospital where a program could be set up to help you work out some of your problems.

Intervention Techniques	Interview between Mr. Sloan and Emergency Room Nurse
	George: What do you mean? You think I'm crazy or something? (defensively) I don't need to see a shrink.
Listening, accepting client's feelings	*Nurse:* No, George, of course I don't think you're crazy. But when you're down and out enough to see no other way to turn but suicide——well, I know things look pretty bleak now, but talking to a counselor usually leads to some other ways of dealing with problems if you're willing to give it a chance.
	George: Well, I 'spose I could consider it. What would it cost? I sure can't afford any more medical bills.
Involving client in the plan Facilitating client decision making Plan is concrete and specific	*Nurse:* Here at our hospital clinic if you can't pay the regular fee you can apply for medical assistance. How would you like to arrange it? I could call someone now to come over and talk to you and set up a program, or you can call them yourself tomorrow and make the arrangements.
Involvement of significant other	*George:* Well, I feel better now, so I think I'd just as soon wait until tomorrow and call them—— besides, I guess I should really tell my wife—— I don't know how she'd feel about me seeing a counselor. But then I guess suicide really is kind of a coward's way out.
Reinforcing coping mechanism Active encouragement Expression of empathy	*Nurse:* George, you sound hesitant and I can understand what you must be feeling. Talking again with your wife sounds like a good idea. Or you and your wife might want to see the counselor together sometime. But I hope you do follow through on this, as I really believe you and your family could benefit from some help like this—after all, you've had a lot of things hit you at one time.

Intervention Techniques	Interview between Mr. Sloan and Emergency Room Nurse
	George: Well, it's hard for me to imagine what anyone could do—but maybe at least my wife and I could get along better and keep our kid out of trouble. I just wish she'd quit insisting on things I can't afford.
Conveying realistic hope that things might get better

Specific and concrete plan | *Nurse:* That's certainly a possibility, and that alone might improve things. How about this, George: I'll call you tomorrow afternoon to see how you are and whether you're having any trouble getting through to the counseling service? |
| Follow-up plan | *George:* That sounds OK. I guess I really should give it another chance. Thanks for everything.

Nurse: I'm glad we were able to talk, George. I'll be in touch tomorrow. |

THE FUNCTIONS OF THE SERVICE CONTRACT

The nature of the service contract is implied by the fact that the plan for crisis intervention is mutually arrived at by the helper and the person in crisis. If the person in crisis comes to the attention of professional crisis counselors, or mental health professionals with training in crisis intervention, the service contract should be formalized in writing. It is implicit in the contract that:

- The person is essentially in charge of his or her own life.
- The person is able to make decisions.
- The crisis counseling relationship is one between partners.
- Both parties to the contract—the person in crisis and the crisis counselor—have rights and responsibilities, as spelled out in the contract.

Institutional psychiatry and traditional mental health professions in the United States have come under serious attack in recent years for violation of people's civil rights.[20,21] Individuals have been locked up, medicated, and "treated" with electric shock against their will in mental institutions. Many human rights and consumer groups are actively advocating against such civil rights violations.[22] In an age when the protection of human rights has become such an important public issue, the idea of *contract* cannot be over-emphasized.

The importance of making crisis services available to people who need them has been stressed. Equally important, is recognition that people have the right to either use or refuse these services. The formal service contract is one of the safeguards for protecting that right. In addition to protecting a person's basic right to voluntary service and treatment, the contract establishes the following:

1. What the client can expect from the counselor.

2. What the counselor can expect from the client.

3. How the two parties will achieve their mutually agreed upon goals.

4. The target dates for achieving the goals defined in the contract.

Nothing goes into a contract that is not mutually developed by client and counselor. Both parties sign the contract, of course, and retain copies. Receiving help on a contractual basis has these effects: (a) the possibility of the helping relationship degenerating into a master-slave, or rescuer-victim stance is reduced; (b) the self-mastery and social skills of the client are enhanced; (c) growth through a crisis experience is facilitated; (d) the incidence of failure in helping a person in crisis is reduced. (See Appendix A for a service contract form which is in use in a number of crisis and counseling clinics).

SUMMARY

In the United States the tendency in health and human service programs is to react to problems rather than to prevent them. Preventive programs are much less costly in terms of money, time, and human pain. An enormous bill from only a few days in a hospital represents money that could buy many days of effective crisis counseling. Resolution of crisis should occur in a person's or family's natural setting whenever possible. Effective planning and skills in crisis management are the best way to avoid extreme measures such as hospitalization and lengthy rehabilitation programs. Active involvement of the person in his or her plan for crisis resolution is a *must* for the success of crisis intervention as a way of helping people.

References

1. Lindemann, Erich. "Symptomatology and Management of Acute Grief," In: *Crisis Intervention*. Howard J. Parad, (Ed.) New York: Family Service Association of America, 1965.

2. Caplan, Gerald, and Henry Grunebaum. "Perspectives on Primary Prevention: A Review," *Archives of General Psychiatry,* 17:331–46, September 1967.

3. Schulberg, Herbert C., and Alan Sheldon, "Probability of Crisis and Strategies for Preventive Intervention," *Archives of General Psychiatry,* 18:555–58, May 1968.

4. Caplan, Gerald. *Principles of Preventive Psychiatry.* New York: Basic Books, 1964.

5. Le Masters, E. E. "Parenthood as Crisis," In: *Crisis Intervention.* Howard J. Parad (Ed.) New York: Family Service Association of America, 1965.

6. Jacobson, Gerald F.; Martin Strickler; and Wilbur Morley. "Generic and Individual Approaches to Crisis Intervention," *American Journal of Public Health,* 58:338–43, February 1968.

7. Caplan, Gerald. *Support Systems and Community Mental Health.* New York: Behavioral Publications, 1974.

8. Berger, Mike, and Kirby Potter. "The Adjunct Consumer Group," *Community Mental Health Journal,* 12:52–60, Spring, 1976.

9. *Action for Mental Health.* Report of the Joint Commission on Mental Illness and Health. New York: Basic Books, 1961.

10. LaVietes, Ruth. "Crisis Intervention for Ghetto Children: Contraindications and Alternative Considerations," *American Journal of Orthopsychiatry,* 44:720–27, October 1974.

11. Hallowitz, David. "Counseling and Treatment of the Poor Black Family," *Social Casework,* 451–59, October 1975.

12. Aquilera, Donna C., and Janice M. Messick. *Crisis Intervention.* 2nd ed. St. Louis: C. V. Mosby Company, 1974.

13. Smith, William G. "Evaluation of the Clinical Services of a Regional Mental Health Center," Community Mental Health Journal, 11:47–57, No. 1, 1975.

14. McGee, Richard K. *Crisis Intervention in the Community.* Baltimore: University Park Press, 1974.

15. Polak, Paul R. "The Crisis of Admission," *Social Psychiatry,* 2:150–57, No. 4, 1967.

16. James, Muriel, and Dorothy Jongeward. *Born to Win.* Reading, Massachusetts: Addison-Wesley Publishing Company, 1971.

17. Hansell, Norris. "Decision Counseling Method," *Archives of General Psychiatry,* 22:462–67, May, 1970.

18. Parad, H. J., H. L. P. Resnik, and L. G. Parad (eds.) *Emergency and Disaster Management: A Mental Health Source Book.* Bowie, Maryland: Charles Press, 1976.

19. Rogers, Maurice J. "Drug Abuse: Just What the Doctor Ordered," *Psychology Today,* 5:16–24, September, 1971.

20. Szasz, Thomas S. *The Manufacture of Madness*. New York: Harper and Row, Publishers, 1970.

21. Kelly, Verne R., and Hanna B. Weston. "Civil Liberties in Mental Health Facilities," *Social Work,* 19:48–54, January, 1974.

22. *Through the Mental Health Maze*. Health Research Group, Washington, D.C.: 1975.

CHAPTER 4

Crisis Intervention and Social Systems

PSYCHOSOCIAL COMPONENTS OF HUMAN GROWTH

We are conceived and born in a social system. We grow and develop among other people. We experience crises around events in our social milieu. People near us—friends, our family, the community—help or hinder us through crises. And finally, death, even for those of us who die in isolation and abandonment, demands some response from the society left behind.

One's social network may consist of family, friends, neighbors, relatives, bartender, employer, hairdresser, teacher, welfare worker, doctor, lawyer—anyone with whom a person has regular social intercourse. It varies with different individuals. Hansell casts his entire description of persons in crisis in a social framework.[1] According to Hansell and others, successful crisis resolution is inevitably tied to the reestablishment of severed social attachments.[1,2] This view is in stark contrast to one in which emotional upsets are regarded primarily as the result of personality dynamics and the individual's internal conflicts. Advocates of this latter view do not entirely disregard social factors. Rather, it is a matter of emphasis and how one's beliefs about sources of problems influence the choice of a helping process.

Case Example

Ellen, age 16, ran away from home. Shortly after police returned her to her home, she made a suicide attempt with approximately ten aspirin and five of her mother's tranquilizers. Ellen had exhibited many signs of depression. She was seen for individual counseling at a mental health clinic for a total of twelve sessions. Ellen's parents were seen initially for one session as part of the assessment process. The counselor learned that Ellen had always been somewhat depressed and withdrawn at home, and that she was getting poor grades in school.

Counseling focused on Ellen's feelings of guilt, worthlessness, and anger centered around her relationship with her parents. She complained that her father was aloof and seldom available when there was a problem. She felt closer to her mother but said her mother was unreasonably strict about her friends, hours out, etc. At the conclusion of the individual counseling sessions, Ellen was less depressed and felt less worthless, though things were essentially the same at home and school. Two months after termination of counseling, Ellen made another suicide attempt, this time with double the amount of aspirin and tranquilizers.

This case highlights the individual versus the social systems approach to crisis intervention. The counselor's helping approach focused on Ellen as an individual. Involvement of Ellen's family and the school counselor—primary people in her social network—was not an integral part of the helping process.

By contrast, a social systems approach to Ellen's problem would also have attended to her feelings of depression and worthlessness. But these feelings would be viewed not as a natural result of her withdrawn personality and internal psychological processes, but rather as directly related to her interactions with the people closest to her. In other words, in crisis intervention people and their problems are seen in a psychosocial rather than a psychoanalytic context.

Within the psychosocial framework, Ellen's counselor would have included at a minimum her family and the school counselor in the original assessment and counseling plan. This initial move might have revealed still other persons important to Ellen and able to help. For example, when Ellen ran away, she went to her Aunt Dorothy's house. She always felt closer to Dorothy than to her parents.

One's social network is central to the process of human growth, development, and crisis intervention. Ellen is in a normal transitional stage of human development. The way she handles the natural stress of adolescence depends a lot on the people in her social network—her parents, brothers and sisters, friends, teachers, and relatives. Her relationship with these people sets the tone for the successful completion of developmental tasks. A counselor with a social view of the situation would say that necessary social supports were lacking at a point in Ellen's life when stress was already high. So, instead of normal growth, Ellen experienced stress to the point of a destructive outcome—a suicide attempt—a clear message that her social support system was weak.

Even if the person's stress reaches the point where a suicide attempt seems the only alternative, it is not too late to mobilize a shaky social network on behalf of the person in crisis. Failure to do so can result in the kind of outcome that occurred for Ellen—that is, another crisis within two months. This is not to say that individual crisis counseling was bad for Ellen. It simply was not enough.

Before considering the specifics of how a social system is engaged or developed in crisis resolution, let us examine more closely two important facets of the social network: the family and the community in crisis.*

FAMILIES IN CRISIS

Social relations are a key factor for an individual in crisis. Just as significant is the fact that a person's social network is itself often in crisis. The family unit can experience crises just as individuals can.

The probability formulation discussed in Chapter 2 can also be used to identify crisis-prone families. Reuben Hill proposes the following conceptual framework for considering families in crisis:[5]

1. Designate as A the crisis-precipitating event (also referred to as a stressor).

2. A interacts with the family's crisis-meeting resources, labelled B.

3. B then interacts with the family's definition of the event, C.

4. This produces the crisis: X.

Figure 4–1 illustrates a family in crisis.

Family researchers consider family troubles in terms of: (a) sources; (b) effect upon family structure; and (c) type of event affecting the family.[5,6]

If the source of trouble is from within the family, the event is more distressing than an external source of trouble such as a flood or racial prejudice. For example, if family members make suicide attempts or abuse alcohol, it is usually a reflection on the family's lack of basic harmony and internal adequacy—as in the case of Ellen above.

Family troubles must also be assessed according to their effect on the family configuration. Eliot[7] and Hill[5] suggest that families experience stress from dismemberment (loss of a family member), accession (addition of a member unprepared for), and demoralization (loss of morale and family unity), or a combination of all three. This classification of family stressor events recasts in a family context the numerous traumatic life events causing crises. Death and hospitalization, crisis precipitating events for individuals, are examples of

*For a deeper understanding of social systems theory the reader is referred to the works of Bertalanffy and Watzlawick.[3,4]

Figure 4–1.   ''Family in Crisis'' by Karen White

dismemberment for families. Unwanted pregnancy, a source of crisis for the girl or woman, is also an example of accession to the family and therefore a possible cause of family crisis as well. A person in crisis because of trouble with the law for delinquency or drug addiction may trigger family demoralization and crisis. Suicide, homicide, illegitimacy, divorce, imprisonment, or institutionalization for mental illness are examples of demoralization plus dismemberment or accession.

Whether or not these stressor events lead to crisis for a particular family depends on the family's resources for handling such upsets. Hill has a vivid description of the nuclear family* and its burdens as a social unit:[5]

> *Compared with other associations in society, the family is badly handicapped organizationally. Its age composition is heavily weighted with dependents, and it cannot freely reject its weak members and recruit more competent teammates. Its members receive an unearned acceptance; there is no price for belonging. Because of its unusual age composition and its uncertain sex composition, it is intrinsically a puny work group and an awkward decision making group. This group is not ideally manned to withstand stress, yet society has assigned to it the heaviest of responsibilities: the socialization and orientation of the young, and the meeting of the major emotional needs of all citizens, young and old.*

The family holds a unique position in our society. It is the most natural source of support and understanding relied on by many of us when in trouble, but it is also the arena in which we may experience our most acute distress. All families have problems, and all families have ways of dealing with their problems. Some are very successful in problem solving; others are less successful. Much depends on the resources available to them in the normal course of family life.

In addition to resources available to families in stress, a family's vulnerability to crisis is also determined by how it defines the traumatic event. For some families a divorce or a pregnancy without mar-

---

*The nuclear family (father, mother and children) is the norm in most Western societies, whereas the extended family (including relatives) is the norm in most non-Western societies.

riage are regarded as nearly catastrophic events; for others these are simply new situations to be coped with. Much depends on religious and other values. Similarly, financial loss for an upper middle class family may not be a source of crisis if there are other reserves to draw upon. On the other hand, financial loss for a family with very limited material resources can be the "last straw," as such families are more vulnerable to crises in general.[8] If the loss, however, includes a loss of status, the middle class family which values external respectability will be more vulnerable to crisis than the family with little to lose in prestige.

COMMUNITIES IN CRISIS

Just as individuals in crisis are vitally entwined with their families, so are families bound up with their community or neighborhood. An entire neighborhood may feel the impact of an individual in crisis. In one small community a man shot himself in his front yard. The entire community was obviously affected by this man's crisis, to say nothing of his wife and small children.

Communities ranging from small villages to sprawling metropolitan areas can go into crisis. In small communal or religious groups the deprivation of individual needs or rebellion against group norms can mushroom into a crisis for the entire membership. Some modern communal groups have dissolved because of such problems. Social and economic inequities among racial and ethnic groups can trigger a large-scale community crisis, for example, race riots in the United States and South Africa. The crisis-proneness of these groups is influenced by:

- Personality characteristics and personal strengths of the individuals within the group.
- Social and economic stability of individual family units within a neighborhood.
- Level at which individual and family needs are met within the group or neighborhood.
- Adequacy of neighborhood resources to meet social, economic, and recreational needs of individuals and families.

People's psychosocial needs must be met if individuals are to survive and grow. Maslow has described a hierarchy of needs we all have.[9] As a person meets basic survival needs of hunger, thirst, and protection from the elements, other needs emerge, such as the need for social interaction and pleasant surroundings. We cannot actualize our innate potential for growth if we are living from hand to mouth and using all our energy just to keep alive. To the extent that people's basic needs are unmet, they are increasingly crisis prone.

This is the case, for example, of individuals and families living in large inner city ghetto housing projects. Poverty is rampant. Slum landlords take advantage of people already disadvantaged; there is a constant threat of essential utilities being cut off for persons with inadequate resources to meet skyrocketing rates. One elderly couple in an eastern state died of exposure after a utility company cut off heat due to nonpayment of bills. Emergency medical and social services are often lacking. And where they exist, bureaucratic red tape makes them virtually inaccessible to many.

Similar deprivations exist on North American Indian reservations and among migrant farm groups. As a result of the personal, social, and economic deprivations in these communities, crime becomes widespread, adding another threat to basic survival. Another crisis prone setting is the world of the average jail or prison. Physical survival is threatened by poor health service, and there is danger of suicide. Also, prisoners fear physical attack by fellow prisoners. Social needs of prisoners are so lacking that the term "rehabilitation" becomes a mockery if applied to prisons. This situation combined with community attitudes, unemployment, and poverty, makes exoffenders highly crisis prone after release from prison.

Natural disasters such as floods, hurricanes, and severe snow storms are another source of community crisis (see Chapter 9). A community crisis can also be triggered by real or threatened acts of terrorism. This is true not only in such internationally publicized cases as Northern Ireland, but also in very small communities. In one small town, all families and individual children were threatened and virtually immobilized by an 18-year-old youth suspected but not proven to be a child molester. Another small community feared for everyone's safety when three teenagers threatened to bomb the local schools and police station in response to their individual crises of school expulsion and unemployment.

In all of these instances, communities in crisis have several common characteristics which are similar to those observed in individuals in crisis. This is true of the thoughts, feelings, and behavior of large groups in crisis. First, within the group an atmosphere of tension and fear is widespread. In riot torn U. S. cities in the 1960's, for example, such an atmosphere of suspicion prevailed. It was not uncommon for restaurant patrons to be questioned by police who were making routine rounds. Second, rumor runs rampant in a crisis ridden community. Large groups of individuals color and distort facts out of fear and lack of knowledge. Third, as with individuals in crisis, normal functioning is inhibited or at a complete standstill. Schools and businesses are often closed; health and emergency resources may be in short supply.

However, as is the case with families, certain traumatic events can also mobilize and strengthen a group or nation. Examples are instances of common external emergency, such as racial prejudice, bombing by an enemy country, Nazi persecution of the Jews in Europe.[10]

INDIVIDUAL, FAMILY, AND COMMUNITY INTERACTION
Individuals, families, and communities in crisis must be considered in relation to each other. Basic human needs and the prevention of destructive outcomes of crises form an interdependent network.

Privacy, Intimacy, Community
Human needs in regard to the self and one's social network are threefold:

    1. The need for privacy.

    2. The need for intimacy.

    3. The need for community.

To lead a reasonably happy life free of excessive strain, people should have a balanced fulfillment of needs in each of these three areas. With a suitable measure of privacy, intimate attachments, and a sense of belonging to a community, they can avoid the potentially destructive effects of the life crises they are bound to encounter. Figure 4–2 illustrates these needs concentrically.

In the center of the interactional circle is the individual with his or her unique personality; set of attributes and liabilities; view of self;

view of the world; and goals, ambitions, and set of values. The centered person who is self-accepting not only has a need for privacy but a definite capacity for it. Well adjusted people can retreat to their private world as a means of rejuvenating and coming to terms with self and with the external world.[11]

We all have differing needs and capacities for privacy. However, equally vital intimacy and community affiliation needs should not be sacrificed to an excess of privacy. The need for privacy can be violated by (a) the consistent deprivation of normal privacy; and (b) retreat to an excess of privacy, that is, isolation. Examples of privacy deprivation are the child in a family with inadequate housing, or a marriage in which one or both partners are extremely clinging.

The excessively dependent and clinging person is too insecure to ever be alone in his or her private world. Such individuals usually assume that there can be no happiness alone; their full psychosocial development has been stunted and their capacity for privacy is therefore unawakened. The person is unaware of the lack of fulfillment in an overly dependent relationship. Someone involved in this kind of relationship is a prime candidate for a suicide attempt when threatened, for example, by a crisis such as divorce. The person clung to is also deprived of essential privacy needs. He or she feels exhausted by the demand to continually relate to another person.

The problem of an excess of privacy leads to consideration of the needs for intimacy and community. In one sense, an excess of privacy is the other side of the coin of lack of intimacy and community. A person can seldom have too much privacy if his or her social needs are also met. An extreme example of social need deprivation is the isolated person who eventually commits suicide. Within the concentric circle of needs is the continuous interaction among the three components.

INNER TO OUTER CIRCLE INTERACTION: Individuals who feel in charge of themselves and capable of living in their private world are in an advantageous position to reach out and establish intimate attachments. Examples are a mature marital relationship or a small circle of intimate friends one can rely on. Need fulfillment in this sec-

Figure 4–2.   "Privacy, Intimacy, Community" by Karen White

ond circle enables the individual to establish and enjoy additional relationships in the work world and in the larger community or neighborhood. The development and flow of this interactional system can be halted in many situations. If, for example, a person feels too insecure to establish intimate or communal attachments; if a couple establishes an intimate attachment that is essentially closed and turned in on itself, thus limiting need fulfillment from the larger community;[12] or if a small communal group turns in on itself and fails to relate to society outside of its own narrow confines—the interactional system is halted.

OUTER TO INNER CIRCLE INTERACTION: The capacity of individuals to live comfortably with themselves and to move with ease in the world is influenced by families and communities. A child born into a chaotic, socially unstable family is off to a poor start in establishing him- or herself in a hostile world. Such a child is more crisis prone at developmental turning points such as entering school, puberty, and adolescence. The child's family, in turn, is affected by the kind of community surrounding it. The child and the family's crisis proneness are influenced by such factors as economic and employment opportunities, racial or ethnic prejudice, the quality of available schools, family and social services, and recreational opportunities for youth. When a sufficient number of individuals and families are adversely affected by these factors, the whole community is more crisis prone.

This concept of individuals, families, and communities in relation to one another underscores the importance of assessing and managing human crises from a social systems point of view. Certainly a person in crisis needs individual help through the ordeal. But this should always be offered in the context of the person's affectional and community needs. Seymour Halleck goes even further in urging a social approach to human problems and crises. He suggests that it may even be considered unethical, for example, for a therapist to spend professional time focusing *only* on an individual in prison who has made a suicide attempt. Besides tending to the individual in crisis, a more responsible approach would be to use one's professional skills to influence the prison system that contributes to suicidal crises.[13]

SOCIAL AND GROUP PROCESS IN CRISIS INTERVENTION

Social Systems Intervention

A social systems approach to crisis intervention never loses sight of the interactional network between individuals, families, and other social elements. Helping people resolve crises constructively involves a process of re-establishment with self, with intimate associates, and with the larger community. In practice this might mean, for example:

- Relieving the extreme isolation that led one to a suicide attempt.
- Developing a satisfying relationship to replace the loss of a close friend or spouse.
- Re-establishing ties in the work world and resolving job conflicts.
- Returning to normal school tasks after expulsion for truancy or drug abuse.
- Establishing stability and a means of family support after desertion by an alcoholic father.
- Allaying community anxiety by resolving the problems of an individual who is reacting to personal problems by child molesting.
- Relieving the fear of bomb threats in a community by helping those who are displaying their desperation by this means to resolve their problems in nondestructive ways.

In each of these instances an individual psychotherapy approach might be used. However, people with these kinds of problems need more than individual psychotherapy.

Training and practice in counseling and psychotherapy in the Western world is heavily influenced by the field of psychiatry. This influence has had its bearing on approaches to crisis intervention as well. A comprehensive plan for certain individuals in crisis may include measures available *only* through the profession of medicine and psychiatry.

A psychiatrist has a medical degree, and has certain skills and legal powers unique to his or her training and position in the field of medicine. Unlike the nonmedical counselor or psychiatric practitioner such as a psychiatric nurse or clinical psychologist, a psychiatrist can prescribe medications; admit people to hospitals; make differential diagnoses between psychological/psychiatric and neurological disturbances; diagnose and treat the symptoms of drug overdose.

However, despite the special skills and legally sanctioned treatment process needed by some troubled persons, a crisis worker strongly influenced by the medical model of treatment is at a disadvantage when working with people in their social milieu. Halleck, a psychiatrist, expresses this opinion in the *Politics of Therapy:*[13]

> *The focus of almost all psychiatric practice tends to be on the patient's internal system, that is, upon misery that the patient creates for himself. As a rule, the psychiatrist does not begin working with emotionally disturbed people until he has had considerable experience working with the physically ill. Physical illness, for the most part, implies a defect in the individual, not in society. The psychiatrist's medical training and his constant work with individuals who seem handicapped subtly encourage him to view human unhappiness as a product of individual disorder. Even if he is exceptionally aware of social forces that contribute to his patient's unhappiness, the psychiatrist's orientation as a physician tends to distract him from dealing with such forces.*
>
> *Some psychiatrists focus almost entirely upon the individual. They assume that the social institutions that regulate their patient's existence are more or less adequate. They recognize the social determinants of behaviour, but they assume that each individual who requires psychiatric assistance is somehow defective; the patient has failed to adjust to a social order that his peers find acceptable. This concept of unhappiness ignores the factors in the patient's immediate environment that make him behave peculiarly; rather it directs the physician to search for the causes of emotional suffering in the anomalies of his patient's biological and psychological past.*

The crisis intervention model—in contrast to the medical model—does not imply that the person in crisis is sick and needs treatment. Rather, the person is seen as extremely upset and needing outside help to resolve an immediate problem. The person in crisis might *also* be physically ill or mentally disturbed. If so, he or she needs medical treatment and psychiatric service *in addition to* crisis intervention.

Besides Halleck, several other psychiatrists and non-medical colleagues have markedly departed from an individually focused approach to people in distress. Among these are Langsley and Kaplan,[14] Paul Polak,[15] Virginia Satir[16,17] and Norris Hansell.[1] Despite the decades long prevalence of individual intervention techniques, social systems approaches are gaining increasing importance in many settings.

Success in the social systems method of intervention depends on the worker's belief in the role of the social system in any crisis situation. In the social systems model, the upset individual is viewed as the representative of one or more disturbed social systems. Assessment, then, of the person's total social system is paramount (see Appendix A). Polak, Hansell, and Garrison have offered many useful suggestions for developing social systems intervention techniques.[15,1,18]

Putting a social systems plan of intervention into operation involves several steps:

1. Identify the "symptom bearer" for the social system. This is the person whose upset or crisis state is most obvious. Sometimes this individual is labelled as "crazy." Mental health workers often refer to this person as the "identified client"—recognizing that the entire family or community is, in reality, the client but unaware of their role in the individual's crisis. The symptom-bearer is also commonly referred to as the "scapegoat" for a disturbed social system.

2. Identify all members of the individual's social network. This includes everyone involved with the person either before or because of the individual's crisis. These two steps will be accomplished by the comprehensive assessment suggested in Chapter 2.

3. Identify the social resources which are currently unused by

the individual but which could be an important means of successful crisis resolution.

4. Establish contact with the social resources that have been identified. Elicit the cooperation of these people in helping the person in crisis. Explain how you perceive the crisis situation and how you think someone can be of help to the person in crisis.

Case Example

"Mrs. Barrett, this is Mr. Rothman at the crisis clinic. Your daughter Alice is here and refuses to go home . . . Alice and I would like to have you join us in a planning conference."

Mrs. Barrett: "So that's where she is . . . I've done everything I know of to help that girl . . . There's nothing more I can do."

Mr. Rothman: "I know you must feel very frustrated, Mrs. Barrett, but it's important that you join us even if it's agreed that Alice doesn't go back home."

After a few more minutes, Mrs. Barrett agrees to come to the clinic with her husband. (Alice is age 34, has been in and out of mental hospitals, and cannot hold a job. She and her mother had a verbal battle about household chores. Mrs. Barrett threatened to call the police when Alice started throwing things. Alice left and went to the crisis clinic.)

5. Establish the actual linkage of the person in crisis with the social resources necessary to relieve the crisis. This is done by convening members of the social network with the person in crisis for a Screening-Linking-Planning (SLP) Conference.[1,18] The SLP conference should be held wherever it is most conducive to achieving the conference objectives. A conference might be held in the home, office, or hospital emergency room.

6. Conduct the SLP conference with the person in crisis and members of his or her social network. During this time, the problem is explored as it pertains to everyone involved. The complaints of all parties are aired, and possible solutions are proposed and considered in relation to available resources.

Case Example

Conference leader to Alice: "Alice, will you review for everyone here how you see your problem?"

To Mr. Higgins, counselor from Emergency Hostel: "Will you explain your emergency housing service, eligibility requirements, and other arrangements to Alice and her parents?"

To Alice: "How does this housing arrangement sound to you, Alice?"

To Alice's parents: "What do you think about this proposal?"

7. Conclude the conference with a definite plan of action for resolution of the crisis. For example, the person in crisis is actively linked to a social resource such as welfare, emergency housing, emergency hospitalization, or job training. The specifics of the action plan are clearly defined: *who* is going to do *what* and within *what time frame*.

8. Establish a follow-up plan. That is, determine the time, place, circumstances, membership, and purpose of the next meeting.

Social systems intervention is one of the most practical and effective techniques available to crisis workers. Its success in resolving highly complex crisis situations is unparalleled in mental health practice. The reason for the technique's effectiveness is that it is based on recognition and acceptance of the person's basic social nature.

An effective crisis worker has faith in the social network and in the technique. A worker's lack of conviction translates itself into a negative self-fulfilling prophecy; that is, the response of the social network is highly dependent upon the worker's *expectations* of response. A counselor skilled in social network techniques approaches people with a positive attitude and conveys an expectation that the person will respond positively, that he or she has something valuable or essential to offer the individual in crisis. Such an attitude eliminates the need to be excessively demanding, an approach that could alienate the prospective social resource. Workers confident in themselves and the use of social network techniques can successfully use an assertive approach that yields voluntary participation by those whose help is needed.

Crisis Groups

The idea of helping people in groups developed during and after World War II. Because of the large number of people needing help, it was impossible to serve all of them individually with a limited number of helping personnel. From the experience of working with people in groups, the group mode of helping was often found to be the method of choice rather than of expediency. The use or non-use of group modes in crisis intervention is heavily influenced by the worker's training and experience with group methods. Use of groups has been strongly influenced by the psychiatric/psychoanalytic or medical model of practice which emphasizes individual rather than social factors.

Traditional emphasis on individual rather than group approaches has contributed to the relative lack of study of group methods in crisis intervention.[19,20,21,22] As is true of social network techniques, the successful use of crisis groups depends on the worker's conviction of the group's usefulness and on appropriate application in the crisis intervention process.

Group work in crisis intervention is indicated in several instances:

1. As a means of assessing a person's coping mechanisms which are revealed through interaction with a group. Direct observation of a person in a group setting can uncover behaviors that may have contributed to the crisis situation. Examination of how a crisis developed is part of the process of crisis resolution. The individual is helped to grasp the reality and impact of his or her behavior in relation to others.[21] Such understanding of the crisis situation gained in the group assessment process forms the base for discovering more constructive coping mechanisms in interaction with others. The group is an ideal medium for such a process.

2. As a means of crisis resolution through the helping process inherent in a well defined and appropriately led group. For the group members in crisis the number of helpers is extended from one counselor to the total number in the group. The process of helping others resolve crises restores a person's confidence in self. It can also relieve a member's fear of going crazy or losing control.

3. As a means of relieving the extreme isolation of some individuals in crisis. For persons almost completely lacking in social resources or the ability to relate to others, the crisis group can be a first step in reestablishing a vital social network.

4. As a means of immediate screening and assessment in settings where large numbers of people come for help and the number of counselors is limited. This is the case in some metropolitan areas where the population is more crisis prone due to housing, financial, employment, and physical health problems.

Crisis Assessment in Groups

A crisis assessment group should be used only when counseling resources are so limited that the people asking for help would otherwise not be seen at all or would be placed on a waiting list. The chief value of a crisis assessment group is as a triage mechanism. That is, people in most serious need of help are screened out and assisted before those in less critical need. The usual place where this kind of screening is necessary is in busy emergency mental health clinics. All the people who come to such clinics are not in crisis; others most surely are. The crisis assessment group is a means of identifying, as soon as possible, those persons in need of immediate help. This method of assessment should not be used as a substitute for a comprehensive social network evaluation.

Suggested Procedure for Group Crisis Assessment

Ideally, crisis assessment group work proceeds as follows:

1. Several people appear for service in an emergency mental health clinic within one hour: Joe, age 28; Jenny, age 36; Charles, age 39; Louise, age 19. There are only two counselors available for assessment, one of whom is involved in an assessment interview.

2. Each person is asked whether he or she is willing to be seen for initial assessment with a group of people who have similar problems. During this initial presentation the person is also told that: (a) the reason for the group assessment is to give some immediate assistance and prevent a long period of waiting due to staff shortages; (b) the group assessment is not a substitute for individual assessment and counseling that are revealed in the group. If the person refuses, obviously he or she is not forced, but rather is reassured of being seen individually as soon as a counselor is available.

3. The crisis counselor explores with each group member the crisis nature of his or her problem. Each is asked to share the reason for coming to the emergency mental health service. Members are specifically asked why they came *today*. This line of questioning will usually reveal the precipitating event as well as the person's current coping ability. Some responses might be:

Joe: "I had another argument with my wife last night and I felt like killing her——I couldn't control myself and got scared——Today I couldn't face going to work, so I thought I'd come in."

Jenny: "I've been feeling so depressed lately——The only reason I happened to come today is that I was talking with my best friend and she convinced me I should get some help."

Charles: "I've been so nervous at work——I just can't concentrate. Today I finally walked off and didn't tell anyone——I'm afraid to face my wife when I get home because we really need the money, so I decided to come here instead."

Louise: "I took an overdose of pills last night and they told me at the hospital emergency room to come in here today for some counseling."

4. Coping ability and resources are explored in detail. The counselor ascertains in each case the degree of danger to self or others. Members are asked how they have resolved problems in the past. Group members are invited to share and compare problem areas and ways of solving them:

Joe: "Usually I go out drinking or something just to keep away from my wife——Maybe if I'd have done that last night, too, I wouldn't have felt like killing her——No, I've never hit her, but I came pretty close to it last night."

Jenny: "Usually it helps a lot to talk to my girlfriend——We both think I should get a job so I can get out of the house, but my husband doesn't want me to——No, I've never tried to kill myself, but I've thought about it lately——No, I've never planned anything in particular to kill myself."

Charles: "I find, too, that it helps to talk to someone——

My wife has been really great since I've had this trouble on the job——She convinced me to talk with the company doctor ——Maybe I could do that tomorrow and get medical leave or something for a while.''

Louise: ''My mother said I had to come in here——They think I'm crazy for taking those pills last night——I feel like you, Joe, I can't stand going back home but I don't know where else to go——Maybe if someone else could just talk to my folks.''

5. Action plans are proposed to the members. Again, members are invited to share ideas:

Joe's Plan: An individual assessment is scheduled for later in the afternoon. A phone call to Joe's wife asking her to participate in the assessment is also planned. Joe is extremely tense and uses alcohol to calm his nerves. This, in turn, upsets his wife, so tranquilizing medication will be considered after the full assessment.

Jenny's Plan: An individual assessment interview is planned for Jenny three days later as Jenny is not in crisis or in any immediate danger of harming herself. She is also given the agency's emergency number should an upset occur between now and her scheduled appointment. (See Chapter 5: Assessment of the Suicidal Person.)

Charles' Plan: He agrees to talk with the company doctor tomorrow and request medical leave. He will call in the results and return for a detailed assessment and exploration of his problem the next day.

Louise's Plan: A phone call is planned to Louise's parents to solicit their participation in working with the counselor on behalf of Louise. If they refuse to come in, a home visit will be planned within 24 hours.

This example illustrates the function of the crisis assessment group as a useful way to focus helping resources intensely on people whose problems are most critical—without neglecting others. The crisis assessment group rapidly reveals the degree of stress that people are feeling and their ability to cope with problems. It is apparent, for example, that Jenny has a problem with which she needs help, though she is not in crisis.

Mental health agencies with limited counseling resources need to develop techniques to assure that those in crisis or in life and death emergencies receive immediate attention. The assessment worker attuned to social network techniques also facilitates the use of resources outside the agency and the individual. Charles, for example, is supported in his self-preservation plans of seeing the company doctor for medical leave, with the intent of resolving his basic problem through counseling.

As is true with crisis groups generally, crisis assessment groups develop rapid cohesion. Members receive immediate help in a busy agency. Sharing their problems voluntarily with others and assisting fellow group members with similar or more difficult problems gives people a sense of self mastery. It also strengthens their sense of community with others. An appropriately conducted crisis assessment group can lay the foundation for: (a) network techniques in each individual's particular social system; (b) later participation in a crisis counseling group that may be recommended as part of the total plan for crisis resolution; (c) participation in self-help groups such as AA (Alcoholics Anonymous), widows' clubs,* Parents-in-Crisis, and others.[1]

Crisis Counseling in Groups

An important facet of group work in crisis intervention is determining when it is indicated. Counselors need to guard against an attitude of unnecessary protection of people in crisis from groups. This attitude is often revealed in worker's statements such as: "I'll see her individually just for a few sessions;" or "She's not ready for a group yet." These statements can be interpreted in several ways:

1. A person actually needs individual crisis counseling.

2. A person is so terrified of the prospect of a group experience that he or she is, in fact, not ready.

3. The counselor basically believes that counseling people

---

*An example of one such club is The Solos of Western New York, founded in 1972 by Adele Meyer. In this self-help group, widows help one another with understanding, companionship, and guidance to cope with problems during their grief.

individually is always better and that a group approach is indicated *only* when there is not enough time for individual work.

Consider the following responses to these interpretations:

1. The need for individual crisis counseling does not cancel out the need for group crisis counseling. If both are indicated, both should be offered to the person simultaneously.

2. If a person is indeed terrified of a group experience, this may be an even greater indication of his or her need for the experience. In the individual sessions preparatory to the group experience, the counselor should convey the expectation that the group work will be a helpful process. A counselor's overprotective attitude will confirm the person's fear that groups are basically destructive and should be avoided. The person's learning of coping skills will thus be limited to one-to-one encounters.

3. If the counselor believes in group work only as an expediency measure, rather than the intervention of choice according to assessed needs, he or she will not use this very effective method of crisis counseling in many instances when it is indicated.

Group Structure

Another facet of crisis counseling in groups is the structure, content, and conduct of the group itself. Some crisis workers recommend structuring the group to a strict limit of six sessions.[19] A more flexible approach takes into consideration the different coping abilities and external resources available to individuals in crisis. Therefore, while group members should be asked to attend a minimum of six sessions (average session length 1½ to 2 hours) once or twice a week, they might be permitted a maximum of ten sessions if a particular crisis situation warrants it. Group "crisis counseling" beyond ten sessions indicates that: (a) the counselor does not recognize the difference between crisis counseling and long term therapy; (b) the person in crisis also has an underlying mental health problem of a chronic nature which should be dealt with in a traditional group therapy setting; (c) the person in crisis may be substituting the group for other, more regular social contacts, and the counselor is inadvertently fostering such restricted social engagement by failure to limit the number of group sessions.

The content and conduct of the crisis counseling group are determined by its purpose: resolution of crisis by means of a group process. Therefore, the group sessions focus on the crises identified by the group members. Individual historical information and feelings not associated with the crisis are restricted in group discussion. There is a continued focus on resolution of the crisis that brought the person to the group. This includes use of all the techniques employed in crisis management for individuals—encouraging expression of feelings appropriate to the traumatic event, gaining an understanding of the crisis situation, and exploring resources and possible solutions to the problem. A major difference between group and individual work is that in group work the counselor facilitates the process of all group members helping one another in the resolution of crises. Another difference is that individuals in crisis inevitably feel less isolated socially as a result of the bonds created in the group problem solving process.

We also need to consider the question of whether a crisis group should be open or closed. This depends to some extent on the size of the agency and the potential number of individuals for whom a crisis counseling group is indicated. In an agency where several or dozens of individuals in crisis are seen each day or two, closed groups are indicated. That is, six or eight people are assigned to a crisis counseling group with the understanding of the six to ten session contract, and no new members are admitted to the group once it is formed.

In an agency with fewer clients where it is difficult to form an initial group of even five people, the group might be structured in an "open" fashion. This means that new members can be admitted up to a maximum group number of eight or ten. To avoid constantly dealing with the initiation of new members, admissions are best limited to every third session. Even though the group is "open" to new members, each individual is expected to abide by the six to ten session contract around his or her particular crisis situation. The nature and structure of the group are explained to prospective members in pregroup orientation sessions conducted by the group crisis counselor.

Admission to and termination of the group can serve as a medium for discussion about the events that are often an integral part of life crises: admission of a new family member by birth of a baby, a divorce, an unwanted pregnancy, a rape, death or absence of a family member through illness. As individuals come and go to and from the group, members are provided an opportunity to work through possible feelings associated with familiar personal losses.

Group counseling is a valuable means of facilitating individual and social growth from a crisis experience. Hopefully more and more counselors will avail themselves of this method of helping people in crisis.

Counseling Families in Crisis

Social network techniques apply in general to the family. A significant feature among families in crisis is the phenomenon of scapegoating. Assessment of the "scapegoat" or identified symptom bearer in crisis, along with his or her social network, will reveal the purpose of this person's symptoms in maintaining family balance. For example, Julie, age 15, is identified by the school as a "behavior problem." She violates all of the family rules at home. John, age 17, by contrast is seen as a "good boy." Through this convenient labeling process, the mother and father can overlook the chronic discord in their marital relationship and child rearing practices. The fights that Julie's mother and father have always seem to be about disciplining Julie. It is, therefore, easy for them to conclude that they would not be fighting if it weren't for Julie's behavior problems. Julie becomes very withdrawn and finally runs away from home to her friend's house. A naive counselor could simply focus on Julie as the chief source of difficulty in the family. If, however, the counselor is attuned to the principle of human growth, development, and life crises within a social system, the analysis would be different. Julie would be viewed as the symptom bearer for a disturbed family system. The entire family would be identified as the client.

Crisis intervention for a family such as Julie's (or Ellen's cited earlier) includes the following elements:

1. Julie's mother brings her to the crisis clinic as recommended by the school guidance counselor.

2. Julie and her mother are seen in individual assessment interviews.

3. A brief joint-interview is held in which the counselor points out the importance and necessity of a family approach if Julie is to get any real help with her problem. The mother is directed to talk with her husband and son about this recommendation with the understanding that the counselor will assist in this process as necessary.

4. Individual assessment interviews are arranged with the husband and son.

5. The entire family is seen together and a six to eight session family counseling contract is arranged.

6. Crisis counseling sessions are conducted. As in group crisis counseling, the counselor facilitates the participation of all family members in resolution of the crisis. The family group process will inevitably reveal that Julie indeed has a problem, but that the entire family has contributed to and is an integral part of her problem. For example, mother and father give Julie conflicting messages regarding their expectations of her. Brother John is an ''ideal boy,'' and Julie ''never does anything right.'' Julie feels her father basically ignores her. The guidance counselor had asked Julie's parents to come to the school for a conference, but they ''never had time.''

The sessions will focus on helping Julie and her parents reach compromise solutions regarding discipline and expected task performance. Parents are helped to recognize and change their inconsistent patterns of discipline. All members are helped to discover ways to give and receive affection in needed doses. Parents and John are helped to see how John's favored position in the family has isolated Julie and contributed to her withdrawal and running away.

7. A conference is held after the second or third session with the entire family, school guidance counselor, and Julie's friend. This conference will assure proper linkage to and involvement of the important people in Julie's social network.

8. During the course of the family sessions, the basic marital

discord between Julie's mother and father becomes apparent. They are recommended to receive ongoing marital counseling from a family service agency.

9. Family sessions are terminated with satisfactory resolution of the crisis as manifested by the family symptom bearer, Julie.

10. A follow-up contact is agreed on by the family and the counselor.

In some families the underlying disturbance in the social system is so deep that the symptom bearer is forced to remain in his or her scapegoat position. For example, if Julie's mother and father refused to seek help for their marital problems, Julie would virtually have no choice but to continue "acting out" on behalf of the basic family disturbance. Unfortunately, in these situations things often "get worse before they get better." For example, if Julie in her desperation becomes pregnant or makes a suicide attempt, the family may be jolted into doing something about the underlying problems leading to such extreme behavior.

For children and adolescents in crisis, family crisis counseling is recommended as the preferred helping mode in nearly all instances. To bypass this intervention method for young people is to do them a grave disservice. It also ignores the basic concepts of human growth and development and the key role of family in this process. Langsley and Kaplan have demonstrated the effectiveness of family crisis intervention in many other instances as well.[14]

SUMMARY

Individuals, families, and communities interact with one another in inseparable ways. Crises arise out of this interaction network and are resolved by restoring people to their normal place in the world. Attention to social systems principles can be the key to success in crisis intervention; inattention to these systems is often a source of destructive resolution of crises. In spite of the heavy influence of individualistic philosophies in all helping professions, a social systems approach is being used effectively by increasing numbers of human service workers.

References

1. Hansell, Norris. *The Person in Distress*. New York: Human Sciences Press, 1976.

2. Miller, Warren B. "Special Issues in Consultation: The Psychosocial Interface," In: *Psychiatric Treatment: Crisis, Clinic, Consultation.* C. Peter Rosenbaum and John E. Beebe III., eds. New York: McGraw-Hill Book Company, 1975.

3. Bertalanffy, Ludwig von. *General Systems Theory.* New York: George Braziller, 1968.

4. Watzlawick, Paul; Janet Beavin; and Don Jackson. *Pragmatics of Human Communication*. New York: W. W. Norton and Company, Inc., 1967.

5. Hill, Reuben. "Generic Features of Families Under Stress," In: *Crisis Intervention.* Howard J. Parad, ed. New York: Family Service Association of America, 1965.

6. Parad, Howard, and Gerald Caplan. "A Framework for Studying Families in Crisis," In: *Crisis Intervention.* Howard J. Parad, ed. New York: Family Service Association of America, 1965.

7. Eliot, Thomas D. "Handling Family Strains and Shocks," In: *Family, Marriage and Parenthood.* Howard Becker and Reuben Hill, eds. Boston: Heath and Company, 1955.

8. Hollingshead, A. B. and F. D. Redlich. *Social Class and Mental Illness.* New York: John Wiley and Sons, Inc., 1958.

9. Maslow, Abraham. *Motivation and Personality.* 2nd ed. New York: Harper and Row, 1970.

10. "The Holocaust." Yad Vashem, Jerusalem, Israel: Martyrs' and Heroes' Remembrance Authority, 1975.

11. Moustakas, Clark. *Individuality and Encounter.* Cambridge, Massachusetts: Howard A. Doyle Publishing Company, 1968.

12. O'Neill, Nena, and George O'Neill. *Open Marriage.* New York: M. Evans and Company, Inc., 1972.

13. Halleck, Seymour, L. *The Politics of Therapy.* New York: Science House, Inc., 1971.

14. Langsley, D., and D. Kaplan. *The Treatment of Families in Crisis.* New York: Grune and Stratton, 1968.

15. Polak, Paul R. "Social Systems Intervention," *Archives of General Psychiatry,* 25:110–17, August 1971.

16. Satir, Virginia. *Peoplemaking.* Palo Alto, California: Science and Behavior Books, Inc., 1972.

17. Satir, Virginia; James Stackowiak; and Harvey A. Taschman. *Helping Families to Change.* New York: Jason Aronson, Inc., 1975.

18. Garrison, John. "Network Techniques: Case Studies in the Screening-Linking-Planning Conference Method," *Family Process,* 13:337, 53, September 1974.

19. Aquilera, Donna C., and Janice M. Messick. *Crisis Intervention.* 2nd ed. St. Louis: C. V. Mosby Company, 1974.

20. Allgeyer, Jean. "The Crisis Group:

Its Unique Usefulness to the Disadvantaged," *International Journal of Group Psychotherapy,* 20:235–40, April 1970.

21. Walsh, Joseph A., and Thomas W. Phelau. "People in Crisis: An Experimental Group," *Community*

Mental Health Journal, 10:3–8, No. 1, 1974.

22. Strickler, M., and J. Allgeyer. "The Crisis Group: A New Application of Crisis Theory," *Social Work,* 12:28–32, July 1967.

CHAPTER 5

Response to Crisis by Suicide and Other Self-destructive Behavior

BACKGROUND INFORMATION, ATTITUDES, ETHICAL ISSUES

Suicide: A Serious and Growing Problem[1,2]

Some people respond to life crises with suicide or other self-destructive acts. George Sloan, whose case was noted in previous chapters, tried to kill himself in a car crash when he saw no other way out of his crisis.

Suicide is viewed as a major public health problem in many countries. In the United States it is the tenth leading cause of death among adults. Among adolescents it is the second leading cause of death. There are 25,000 reported deaths from suicide annually in the United States. The rate of suicide in the U. S. varies between nine and eleven per 100,000 population per year. This rate has remained relatively constant for several decades, and there is little difference between urban and rural regions. Some countries reporting much higher rates are Finland, Denmark, Sweden, Hungary, West Germany, and Austria. Lower rates are reported by England, Japan, Italy, Norway, and Spain. For every suicide there are eight to ten suicide attempts in the United States.

Because reporting systems differ widely, there are probably more suicides than are reported. Cultural taboos, insurance policies, and other factors strongly influence the reporting of suicide. Some coroners, for example, will not certify a death as suicide unless there is a suicide note. However, everyone who commits suicide does not leave a suicide note. Because of all these factors, we lack accurate and comprehensive statistics about suicide.

Suicide as a response to crisis is used by all classes and kinds of people—including our relatives or neighbors—people with social, mental, emotional, and physical problems. In short, people of every age, sex, religion, race, and social or economic class commit suicide. And perhaps most important of all, suicide is the first and leading cause of unnecessary and stigmatizing death.

Common Beliefs and Feelings About Self-destructive People

Nearly everyone has had contact with self-destructive people. Some of us have relatives and friends who have committed suicide or made suicide attempts. We know others who slowly destroy themselves by excessive drinking or abuse of other drugs.

Among the readers of this book, a certain percentage will have
responded to a life crisis by some kind of self-destructive act. For
example, the suicide rate among physicians is one of the highest of
any occupational group. Also, narcotic addiction, as a way of coping
with stress, is prevalent among physicians and nurses. It is one of the
tragedies of life that those whose main work is service to others,
often find it difficult to ask for help for themselves when in crisis.
Perhaps more than any other group, physicians and nurses, particularly in hospital emergency rooms, come in direct contact with
self-destructive people—individuals who have cut their wrists,
attempted to kill themselves in a car crash, overdosed on pills, or
attempted to drown their troubles in alcohol. These are only a few of
the many consequences of self-destructive incidents that emergency
room personnel have to deal with.

Volunteers and other workers in suicide and crisis centers are
another group that has frequent contact with self-destructive people.
About 30 percent of callers to these centers are in suicidal crisis.
Counselors and psychotherapists also work with self-destructive
persons.

All of these workers and people in general have varying degrees
of knowledge about suicide and self-destructive people. Myths and
false beliefs about suicidal people are also widespread. Some of the
most common myths are:[3]

Only "crazy" or insane people commit suicide.

"Good circumstances"—a comfortable home, good job, etc.
—prevent suicide.

People who talk about suicide won't commit suicide.

People who make suicide attempts that are medically nonserious are not a risk for suicide.

The reader will probably recognize some of these myths as being
held by self, among family, friends, and associates. Even among professional mental health workers, these myths are more common than
one would expect.

Professional suicidologists (those trained in the study of suicide
and suicide prevention) believe that "suicide prevention is everybody's business." This is a tall order, however, considering how
many false beliefs about suicide still persist. It is not uncommon for
nurses and physicians to resist dealing with self-destructive persons

with the mental note, "That's somebody else's job." Yet, people can hardly deal with something they know little about. We face a number of difficulties in trying to learn more about self-destructive people:

- Cultural taboo against suicide.
- Strong feelings that people have about suicide and other self-destructive acts.
- Limitations of doing research on human beings.
- Intrinsic difficulty of examining the self-destructive process in those who commit suicide; such study is limited to determining the probable causes of suicide from survivors closely associated with the person.

However, in spite of these limitations, research and direct work with self-destructive persons have had promising results. "Suicidology" (the study of suicide and suicide prevention) is by no means an exact science. Yet the scientific knowledge and practices developed over the past fifteen years are a considerable advancement over responses to suicidal people based on myths and taboos.

Knowledge about something is no guarantee of use of the knowledge. Many false beliefs about self-destructive people and responses to them persist because of intense feelings about suicide, death, and dying. Suicide and self-destructive behavior have been part of the human condition from the beginning of time.

Views about suicide, its honorability or shamefulness, have varied throughout antiquity to the present time.[4] In the Judeo-Christian tradition, neither the Hebrew Bible nor the New Testament prohibits suicide. Jews (defenders of Masada) and Christians (martyrs) alike justified suicide in the face of military defeat or personal attack by pagans. However, over the centuries suicide took on the character of a sinful act. In modern times the taboo persists among most peoples more as a socially disgraceful act than as a moral offense. Thus, feelings and views about suicide have deep historical roots.

Failure to acknowledge and deal with one's feelings about suicide and death can prevent one from being helpful to self-destructive people. What are some of the most common feelings people have about a self-destructive person? And why are these feelings particularly intense in the helper-client interaction?

As we try to help self-destructive people, we may feel sadness, pity, helplessness, desire to rescue, anger, or frustration. Some of these feelings are mirrored in the following comments:

Curious Bystander: "Oh, the poor thing."

Friendly Neighbor: "What can I possibly do?"

Family: "Why did she have to disgrace us this way?"

Nurse: "I can't stand wasting time on these people who are just looking for attention."

Physicians, nurses, and other helpers have a particular frustration in working with self-destructive people. Suicidal persons defeat the medical role of fostering and maintaining life. A suicide attempt appears as a deliberate flaunting of the natural instinct to live. George Vlasak notes that the person attempting suicide requests directly or indirectly a departure from the usual defined roles of patient and helper.[5]

This fact places a heavy burden on emergency room and rescue personnel. Faced with these feelings, helping people need an opportunity to express and work through their feelings about self-destructive behavior (see Chapter 10: p. 393). This is a basic step in a worker's acquiring the knowledge and skills necessary to help people in suicidal crisis.

Responsibility and the Right to Die by Suicide[6,7]

Closely related to this first step in coping with self-destructive behavior is the issue of responsibility for the lives of others. Some workers may confuse suicide prevention efforts with a distorted sense of obligation to prevent any and all suicides whenever physically possible. Such confusion is based on the assumption that no one has the right to end his or her own life. This misguided belief often exists along with lack of scientific knowledge about self-destructive behavior and inability to assess suicidal risk. What can result is a set of practices which promote rather than prevent suicide:

1. Placing a hospitalized, suicidal person in isolation. This is done, presumably, for closer observation; but merely increases the person's sense of abandonment.

2. Involuntary commitment of a suicidal person to a mental hospital. This can be a basic attack on the person's sense of dignity and self-worth, yet mental health laws in many states encourage the practice among those working in public agencies or mental health professions.

3. Use of the largest tube to remove stomach contents of the person who has taken an overdose of pills. Such a punitive practice is based on the belief that physical discomfort will discourage future suicide attempts. In fact, the self-destructive person feels attacked and more worthless than ever.

The hidden function of these practices among workers is probably the expression of anger against the self-destructive person for violating the suicide taboo and for frustrating their helper roles. The suicidal person has little or no ability to deal with such negative value messages. He or she already has an overdose of self-hatred. Rejection by helpers as they carry out their service responsibilities can only increase a person's self-destructiveness.

Ethical and other opinions differ regarding the issue of responsibility to save others and the right of people to determine their own death. The prevailing opinion in the ethical and suicidology fields is that people have a basic right to choose death by suicide. However, we should consider the right to commit suicide in relation to our responsibility to help people find alternatives to suicide.

Case Example
Dorothy, age 69, lived with her daughter and son-in-law and was dying of cancer. The public health nurse learned that she was suicidal. In fact, Dorothy spoke openly of her "right" to kill herself. After the nurse worked with the daughter's feelings regarding her dying mother, the relationship between the two of them improved. Dorothy was no longer suicidal and decided not to exercise her "right" to kill herself.

This case illustrates the importance of a worker's not using the right to suicide concept as an excuse to "cop out." In the above example the nurse does what she realistically can for a despairing person.

On the other hand, failure to acknowledge this right can lead to extreme and unrealistic measures to "save" people from suicide.

Case Example

John, age 48, was locked up in a state mental hospital against his will when he became highly suicidal after his wife divorced him. John also had a serious drinking problem. The main reason for hospitalizing John was to prevent him from committing suicide. John had two very close friends and a small business of his own. John found the hospital worse than anything he had experienced. He had no contact with his friends while in the hospital. After two weeks, John begged to be discharged. He was no longer highly suicidal but was still depressed. John was discharged with antidepressant medicine and instructed to return for a follow-up appointment in one week. He killed himself with sleeping pills (obtained from a private physician) and alcohol two days after discharge.

It is possible that this suicide could have been prevented with a different treatment approach, including, especially, helping John to reestablish himself socially (see Chapter 4). It could also be argued that committment of John to the hospital was the proper exercise of professional responsibility on John's behalf. That is, John has friends, and by objective standards "something to live for," even though he could not see that at the time he decided to kill himself. Therefore, his decision for suicide could be regarded as not in his own best interests, thereby justifying the extreme "saving" action of the helpers.

For some people, suicide is chosen even after considering other alternatives. This is not to say, however, that suicide is inevitable once a person considers it.

Case Example

Joe, age 64, had chronic heart disease. He was depressed after his wife died three months earlier. When he was laid off from his job, he became suicidal and talked with his doctor. Joe's doctor referred him to a community mental health center for therapy. He received individual and group psychotherapy and antidepressant drugs. After three months, Joe's depression lifted somewhat, but he was still unconvinced that there was anything left to live for. He had been very dependent on his wife and seemed unable to develop other satisfying relationships. Joe killed himself by carbon monoxide poisoning after terminating therapy at the mental health center.

Explicit acknowledgment of a person's right to suicide can have a curious suicide prevention effect.

Case Example
Diane, a medical student, age 21, resisted all alternatives to suicide as proposed by a crisis counselor. She learned she was pregnant, was rejected by her lover, and could not share her distress with her parents or friends. Abortion was not an acceptable alternative to her. She feared that continuing the pregnancy would mean failure in medical school. The counselor agreed with Diane regarding her basic right to suicide, but expressed regret if she followed through on that decision during the peak of her crisis. This acknowledgement seemed to give Diane a sense of dignity and control over her life and a new will to live even though her only perceived resource at the moment was the counselor.

The following is offered as a practical guideline to helpers in respect to the "rights and responsibility" issue regarding suicide: Everyone has the final responsibility for his or her own life. This includes the way one chooses to live it or end it. We have a communal responsibility to do what we reasonably can to help others live as happy a life as possible. This includes the prevention of suicide when it appears to be against the person's own best interests. Such responsibility, however, does not mean that one must prevent a suicide at all costs. Workers in human service professions such as nursing, medicine, mental health, and law enforcement have an additional responsibility: They should learn as much as they can about self-destructive people and how to help them find alternatives to suicide.

CHARACTERISTICS OF SELF-DESTRUCTIVE PEOPLE
To be understood is basic to the feeling that someone cares, that life is worth living. When someone responds to stress with a deliberate suicide attempt, those around the person are usually dismayed and ask "Why?" The wide range of self-destructive acts that people engage in adds to the observer's confusion. There are many overlapping features of self-destructive behavior. For example, Mary, age 50, has been chronically destroying herself through alcohol abuse for 15 years, but she also takes an overdose of sleeping pills.

The development of precise definitions of self-destructive acts is therefore a complex task. Opinions differ as to the meaning and causes of suicidal behavior. However, in spite of academic differences, one should recognize that a person engaging in self-destructive behavior is in some kind of turmoil.

Self-destructiveness: What Does It Include?

Self-destructive behavior includes any action by which a person damages or ends his or her life emotionally, socially, and physically. Broadly, the spectrum of self-destructiveness includes nail biting, hair pulling, scratching, wrist or other cutting, swallowing toxic substances or harmful objects, cigarette smoking, head banging, alcohol and other drug abuse, reckless driving, neglect of life-preserving measures such as taking insulin, direct suicide attempts, and outright suicide.[8]

At one end of the spectrum of self-destructiveness is Jane, who smokes but is in essentially good emotional and physical health. She knows the long-range effects of smoking and chooses to live her life in such a way that it may in fact be shortened. However, Jane would hardly be regarded as suicidal on a lethality assessment scale. Smoking by Arthur, however, who has severe emphysema (a lung disease) is another matter. His behavior could be considered a slow form of deliberate self-destruction. At the other end of the spectrum is James who plans to hang himself. Unless saved accidentally, James will most certainly die by his own hand.

There are four broad groups of self-destructive people:

1. *Those who complete suicide:* Suicide is defined as a fatal act which is self-inflicted and consciously intended. It is difficult to determine, however, whether the act is suicidal or accidental if full information about the victim's intentions is not available.[9]

2. *Those who threaten suicide:* This group includes those who talk about suicide and whose plans for suicide may be either very vague or highly specific and well thought out. Some in this group have made suicide attempts in the past, others have not. To be noted here is that only *suicidal* people threaten suicide.

3. *Those who make suicide attempts:* Stengel defines *suicide attempt* as any nonfatal act of self-inflicted damage with self-destructive intention, however vague and ambiguous. Sometimes the individual's intention must be inferred from the person's behavior.[9]

Some suicidal persons are in a state of acute crisis—in contrast to some who are chronically self-destructive—and therefore experience a high degree of emotional turmoil. As noted in Chapter 1, one characteristic of people in crisis is a temporary upset in cognitive functioning. This upset can make it difficult for a person to clarify his or her intentions. The resulting ambiguity arising out of the crisis state should not be confused with a psychotic process which may or may not be present. Nor should one go along with the prevalent myth that "only a crazy person could seriously consider, attempt, or commit suicide." Loss of impulse control influences some suicide attempts and completed suicides. In the large majority of instances, however, self-destructive behavior is something which people consciously and deliberately plan and execute.

4. *Those who are chronically self-destructive:* Persons in this group may habitually abuse alcohol and/or other drugs. Others may destroy themselves by the deliberate refusal to follow life-sustaining medical programs such as for heart disease or diabetes. Still others engage in high risk life styles or activities which bring them more or less constantly into the face of potential death. Such individuals seem to need the stimulation of their risky life style to make life seem worth living.[10] These behaviors are not, of course, explicitly suicidal. However, individuals who engage in them may, like others, become overtly suicidal. This, of course, complicates whatever problems already exist.

The Path to Suicide

Suicidal behavior can be viewed on a continuum. The continuum might be described as a "highway leading to suicide." The highway begins with the first suicide threat or attempt and ends in suicide. As in the case of any trip destined for a certain endpoint, one can always change one's mind, take a different road to another destination, or turn around and come back. A destiny of suicide is not inevitable. Whether one continues down the highway to suicide depends on a variety of circumstances. People traveling down the suicide highway give clues to their distress. The suicide continuum, therefore, can be interrupted at any point: after a first attempt, fifth attempt, or as soon as clues are recognized. Much depends on the help available and the ability of the suicidal person to accept and use help.

Lacking such resources, suicidal persons usually attempt to relieve their pain by repeating suicide attempts. Their gamble with death becomes more dangerous. As they move along the suicide highway repeating their "cries for help," they are often labeled and written off as "manipulators" or "attention seekers." This usually means that professional helpers and others regard them as devious and insincere in their "demands" for attention. Some conclude that if the person were really "serious" about suicide he or she would try something that "really did the job." Such a judgment implies a gross misunderstanding of the meaning of a suicidal person's behavior. Unfortunately, his or her real needs are therefore ignored.

Individuals who are thus labeled and ignored will probably make more suicide attempts of an increasingly serious nature. They may also engage in the "no lose game" as they plan the next suicide attempt. The "no lose game" goes something like this (the method chosen is usually fatal, but with the possibility of rescue, such as swallowing pills):

> "If they (e.g., spouse, friend, family) find me, they care enough and therefore life *is* worth living . . ." (I win by living.)

> "If they don't find me, life *isn't* worth living." (I win by dying.)

Such reasoning is ineffective in instances when one could not reasonably expect rescue (e.g., a family member checking on the person at 2:00 a.m.). It is nevertheless an indication of the person's extreme distress and follows from the logic of the "no lose game."

What Are Self-Destructive People Telling Us?

Interrupting the suicide continuum depends very much on the response a person receives to messages of distress. Practically everyone who has worked with suicidal people agrees that they are trying to tell us something by their behavior. Most individuals get what they need or want by simply asking for it. Or friends and family are sensitive and caring enough to pick up the clues to distress before the person becomes desperate.

Some people, however, spend a lifetime trying without success to obtain what they need for basic survival and happiness. This may be because they cannot directly express their needs; because their needs are insatiable and, therefore, unobtainable; or because others don't listen and try to meet their needs. Finally, they give up and make a suicide attempt as a "last ditch" effort to let someone know that they are hurting and probably desperate.

The general message of the person threatening or attempting suicide is a "cry for help":[11] "Please save me from myself . . . Help me find something to live for." The helper must also determine the meaning of the suicidal behavior for the particular person concerned. Specific messages of self-destructive behavior might include:

"I'm angry at my mother . . . She'll really be sorry when I'm dead."

"I can't take any more problems (e.g. financial, alcoholic husband, housing) without some relief."

"I can't live without my boyfriend . . ." i.e., "I don't really want to die, I just want him back or somebody in his place."

"I can't take the pain (e.g. from the cancer) anymore."

"There's nothing else left since my wife left me . . . I really want to die."

And there are many more.

These examples illustrate that self-destructive behavior is intended by some to result in death. Others use it in desperate attempts to make some change in a life situation.

Self-destructive behavior is, in fact, a very powerful means of communicating. After a person's first suicide attempt, family and other significant people in the individual's life are usually shocked. They are more disturbed by a suicide attempt than by anything else the person might have done. Typically, a parent, spouse, or friend will say: "I knew she was upset and not exactly happy, but I didn't know she was *that* unhappy." In other words, the first suicide attempt is the most powerful of a series of behavioral messages or clues given over a period of time.[12]

We should all be familiar with suicidal clues or cries for help such as: "You won't be seeing me around much anymore." "I've about had it with this job." "I can't take it anymore."

Behavioral clues may include making out a will, taking out a large life insurance policy, giving away precious belongings, despondency after a financial setback, distress from a critical life event, engaging in behavior unusual for the individual, or various forms of "acting out."[12]

Ambivalence: Weighing Life and Death

Suicidal people usually struggle with two irreconcilable wishes: the desire to live and, at the same time, the desire to die. Simultaneously, they consider the advantages of life and death. This state of mind is known as *ambivalence*.

As long as the person has ambivalent feelings about life and death, it is possible to help the individual consider choices on the side of life. Suicide is not inevitable. People can always change their minds if they find some realistic alternatives to suicide. Those who are no longer ambivalent do not usually come to emergency rooms or call police and suicide hotlines.

Case Example

Sally, age 16, made a suicide attempt by swallowing six sleeping pills, which is a medically non-serious attempt. Though she contemplated death, she also wanted to live. That is, she hoped that the suicide attempt would bring about some change in her miserable family life so that she could *avoid* the last resort of suicide itself. Before her suicide attempt, Sally was having trouble in school, she ran away from home once, experimented with drugs, and in general engaged in behavior that brought disapproval from her parents.

All these behaviors are Sally's way of saying "Listen to me," "Can't you see that I'm miserable . . . that I can't control myself . . . that I can't go on like this anymore?" Sally had been upset for several years by her parents' constant fighting and favoritism among the children. Her father drank heavily and frequently was away from home. When Sally's school counselor had recommended family counseling, they refused out of shame. Her acting out was really a cry for help. After her suicide attempt, Sally's behavior improved generally, and she made no further suicide attempts.

If Sally had not obtained the help she needed, it is highly probable that she would have made more suicide attempts, continuing down the highway to suicide. The usual pattern in such a case is that the attempts become more serious in the medical sense; the person becomes more desperate and finally commits suicide.

Helping the ambivalent person move in the direction of life is done by understanding and responding to the meaning of his or her behavior. It is not uncommon for people to exclaim after a suicide: "But he had everything going for him . . . there was no reason for the suicide." The truth is, there may have been no *apparent* reason. What is revealed by this conclusion is that survivors were not aware of the clues and messages given by the person. Studies reveal that 20 to 65 percent of persons who commit suicide have made previous suicide attempts. And in the absence of attempts, 80 percent have given other significant clues of their suicidal intent.[13,14]

Unfortunately, many people lack the knowledge or resources to respond helpfully to a suicidal person. The self-destructive person is often surrounded by others who potentially *could* help him or her, but whose own troubles prevent them from providing what the self-destructive person needs from them. Some families are so needy that the most they can do is obtain medical treatment for the suicidal person. This sad situation is not helped by the fact that crisis services may be absent or inadequate in some communities.

How, then, can we discover what a person is trying to tell us through self-destructive behavior? One obvious and simple means is to ask him or her. "What did you hope would happen when you took the pills?" "Did you intend to die?" There is no substitute for simple, direct communication by a person who cares. Besides providing the information we need in order to help, it is directly helpful to the suicidal person. It tells the person that we are interested and concerned about what the contemplated suicide means to him or her. More often than not, self-destructive people have lacked the advantage of such direct communication all their lives.

Would-be helpers fail to use this useful tool in the false belief that "talking to the person about possible suicide intentions may trigger the person into the idea, if he or she doesn't already have it." The process of deciding to commit suicide is much more complicated than that. A person who is not suicidal will not become so by a direct question from someone intending to help. In fact, experience reveals that suicidal people are relieved when someone is sensitive enough to guess their despair and thus help protect them from themselves.

ASSESSMENT OF THE SUICIDAL PERSON

Communication leads to understanding which is the foundation for decision and action. Helping suicidal people without understanding the meaning of their behavior and the degree of suicide risk is like groping in the dark. *Lethality assessment* is the process of determining the likelihood of suicide for a particular person. The assessment tries to answer the question: What is the risk of lethality or death for this individual?

Some workers use lethality assessment scales to predict suicidal risk. Most of these scales are not very effective.[14] The problem with most scales is that they do not exclude the non-suicidal population. For example, let's consider depression as a predictive sign. A large number of people who commit suicide (approximately 70 percent) have been diagnosed as depressed; however, the majority of depressed people do not commit suicide. Standard psychological tests such as the Minnesota Multiphasic Personality Inventory (MMPI) are also not very helpful in suicide prediction.

Importance of Assessing Suicide Risk

The importance of lethality assessment can be compared to the importance of diagnosing a person's cough before beginning treatment. Effective assessment of lethality should accomplish the following:

- Cut down on a guesswork approach in working with self-destructive people.
- Reduce the confusion and disagreement that often occur among those trying to help suicidal people.
- Provide a scientific base for service plans for self-destructive people.
- Increase the appropriate use of hospitalization for suicidal persons.
- Decrease a worker's level of anxiety in working with suicidal persons.

Failure to assess the degree of suicide risk results in unnecessary problems while helping self-destructive people. For example, Linda, age 23, who lives alone and feels alienated from her family is treated medically for her cut wrists and discharged without follow-up counseling. The emergency room staff assumed that she was "just seeking attention." Since the "message" and long-range risk of Linda's suicide attempt were missed, we can predict that she will very probably make another suicide attempt in the future.

Another problem arising out of inaccurate lethality assessment is unnecessary hospitalization. It is inappropriate to hospitalize a suicidal person when the degree of suicidal risk is very low and other sources of protection are available. Thus a person who hopes, by a suicide attempt, to relieve his or her isolation from family may feel even more isolated in a psychiatric hospital. This is especially true when community and family intervention are indicated instead.

Sometimes community and hospital workers hospitalize suicidal people out of their own anxiety about suicide. Unresolved feelings of guilt and responsibility issues surrounding suicide usually precipitate such action. On the other hand, as we assess highly suicidal persons we should recognize the hospital as a possible resource to relieve isolation and prevent suicide when social supports in the community are lacking.

Lethality assessment techniques are based on knowledge obtained from the study of completed suicides. Suicide research is one of the most difficult among human scientific studies. Nevertheless, the study of completed suicides has shed some light on the problem of predicting suicide. Brown and Sheran,[14] Warren Breed,[15] Beck, Resnik, and Lettieri,[16] and others have identified signs which help us predict the degree of risk for suicide. The most reliable predictors help us distinguish persons who commit suicide from the population at large and also from those who make only suicide attempts. These signs, however, have their limitations. For instance, there is not enough research on suicide to warrant general conclusions about suicide for different population groups.[15,17,18] One should be careful not to be overly certain in applying signs to a suicidal person. It is impossible, at present, to predict suicide in any absolute sense. However, attention to the predictors we know about is a considerable improvement over an approach based on myth, taboo, and unresearched guesswork.

Signs That Help Predict Suicide

The following material regarding signs which help us predict suicide is summarized from the works of Brown and Sheran,[14] Breed,[15] Beck, Resnik, and Lettieri,[16] Farberow,[17] Bush,[18] Jacobs,[19] Neuringer,[20] Dublin,[21] Hendin,[22] Maris,[23] Durkheim,[24] Shneidman,[25] and Alvarez.[26]

1. SUICIDE PLAN: Studies reveal that the majority of persons who die by suicide have planned deliberately to do so. This is in contrast to the myth still held by many that people who commit suicide "do not know what they are doing," or are "crazy." In respect to plan, persons suspected of being suicidal should be asked several direct questions concerning the following subjects:

Suicidal Ideas: "Are you so upset that you're thinking of suicide?" or "Are you thinking about hurting yourself?"

Lethality of Method: The interviewer should ask: "What are you thinking of doing?"

High Lethal Methods
Gun
Jumping
Hanging
Drowning
Carbon monoxide poisoning
Barbiturates and prescribed
sleeping pills
Aspirin (high dose)
Car crash
Exposure to extreme cold

Low Lethal Methods
Wrist cutting
House gas
Non-prescription drugs
(excluding aspirin and Tylenol)
Tranquilizers

The helper should also determine the person's knowledge about the lethality of the chosen method. For example, a person who takes ten tranquilizers with the mistaken belief that the dose is fatal is alive more accidentally than by intent.

Availability of the Means: "Do you have a gun? Do you know how to use it? Do you have ammunition?" "Do you have pills?" Lives have often been saved by removal of very lethal methods such as guns and sleeping pills. A highly suicidal person who calls a crisis center is often making a final effort to get some help, even though he or she may be sitting next to a loaded gun or bottle of pills. Such an individual will welcome a direct, protective gesture from a telephone counselor such as: "Why don't you put the gun away (e.g. dresser drawer) . . . or throw the pills out . . . and then let's talk about what's troubling you." When friends and family are involved, they, too, should be directed to get rid of the suicide means.

Specificity of Plan: "Do you have a plan worked out for killing yourself? How do you plan to get the pills . . . the gun?" A person who has a well-thought-out plan—including time, place, and circumstances—with an available high lethal method is an immediate high risk for suicide. We should also determine whether any rescue possibilities are included in the plan: "What time of day (or night) do you plan to do this?" "Is there anyone else around at that time?" We should also find out about the person's intent. Some people really intend to die; others intend by a suicide attempt to bring about some change which, in fact, will help them avoid death and make life more liveable.

It is important to remember that we can seldom discover a person's suicide plan except through direct questioning. An individual who believes in the myth that "talking about suicide may put the idea in the person's head," will hesitate to ask direct questions.

The person's suicide plan is a less important predictive sign in the case of people with a history of impulsive behavior. This is true for some adults and for adolescents in general, who are inclined to be impulsive as a characteristic of their stage of development.

2. HISTORY OF SUICIDE ATTEMPTS: In the U. S. adult population, suicide attempts occur eight to ten times more often than actual suicide. Among adolescents there are about 50 attempts to every completed suicide. It is encouraging to know that most people who make suicide attempts do not go on to commit suicide. Usually some change has occurred in their psychosocial world that makes life more desirable than death. A history of suicide attempts (20 to 65 percent of completed suicides) is especially prominent among suicidal people who find that self-destructive behavior is the most powerful means they have of communicating their distress to others. Those who have made previous high lethal attempts are at greater risk for suicide than those who made low lethal attempts.

Another historical indicator is a change in method of suicide attempt. A person who makes a high lethal attempt after several less lethal attempts which elicited increasingly indifferent responses from significant others is a higher risk for suicide than a person with a consistent pattern of low lethal attempts. This is particularly true in the case of suicidal adolescents.

We should also determine the outcome of previous suicide attempts. For example: "What happened after your last attempt?" "Did you plan any possibility of rescue? or were you rescued accidentally?"

A person living alone who overdoses with sleeping pills, has unexpected company and is rescued, is alive more by accident than by intent. He or she falls into a high risk category for future suicide if there are other high risk indicators as well. Suicide risk is also increased if the person has a negative perception of a psychiatric hospital or counseling experience. This finding underscores the importance of extreme caution in employing mental health laws to hospitalize suicidal people against their will for "self protection."

3. RESOURCES AND COMMUNICATION WITH SIGNIFICANT OTHERS: Internal resources consist of a person's strengths, problem solving ability, and personality factors that help or hinder one in coping with stress. External resources include a network of persons on whom one can rely routinely and during a crisis. Communication as a suicide sign includes: (a) The statement to others of intent to commit suicide; (b) The quality of the bond that exists between the suicidal person and significant others. A large number of people who finally commit suicide feel ignored or cut off from significant people around them, some to the point of feeling there are no significant persons in their lives. This is extremely important in the case of adolescents, especially regarding their attempt to communicate with their parents. Peck and Litman found that most adolescents who kill themselves are at odds with their families and feel very misunderstood.[18]

Institutionalized racism and the unequal distribution of material resources in the United States appear to contribute to the rapidly increasing rate of suicide among minority groups. This is especially true among the young (under 30) who realize early in life that many doors are closed to them. Their rage and frustration eventually lead to despair, suicide, and other violent behavior. An example of violence which is closely linked to suicide is *victim-precipitated homicide*. In this form of homicide, the person killed is, in fact, suicidal, but instead of committing suicide, the victim incites someone else to kill, thus precipitating the homicide.

Others may have observable resources such as a supportive caring spouse, but the conviction of their worthlessness prevents them from accepting and using such support. This is especially true for suicidal people who are also extremely depressed. Adequate personality resources include the ability to be flexible and accept mistakes and imperfections in oneself. Some people who kill themselves apparently have happy families, good jobs, and good health. Observers therefore assume that these people have "no reasons to kill themselves." Research by Warren Breed reveals that this kind of person perceives him- or herself in very rigid roles imposed by culture, sex identity, or socioeconomic status.[15] A typical example is the middle-aged male executive who rigidly commits himself to success by climbing up the career ladder in his company. A threatened or actual failure in this self-imposed rigid role performance can precipitate suicide for such a person.

Such failure is usually sex specific: work failure for men and family or mate failure for women. Investigation of completed suicides reveals that this kind of person commits suicide *after* receiving, for example, a long anticipated promotion. Such rigidity in personality type is also revealed in the person's approach to problem solving. The individual sees narrowly—perceiving only one course of action or one solution to a problem: suicide. We should recognize this characteristic as a possible barrier in our efforts to help suicidal people consider alternatives. Thus a person of this type whose personal and social resources are exhausted and whose only remaining communication link is to a counselor or helping agency is a high risk for suicide.

Researchers note that workers should look not only at the predictive signs, but also at the complex patterning of signs.[14,17] Let us apply this analysis to the patterning of the signs considered above. If the person (a) has a history of high lethal attempts; (b) has a specific, high lethal plan for suicide with available means; (c) lacks both personality and social resources, his or her immediate and long range risk for probable suicide is very high regardless of other factors. The risk increases, however, if other factors are also present. These are discussed next.

4. AGE, SEX, AND RACE: The ratio of suicide among American men and women is approximately 3 (male): 1 (female). Among children between the ages of 10 and 14, the suicide rate is 0.3 to 0.6 per 100,000. Among children below the age of 10, suicide is almost non-existent, less than one annually in the United States. Suicide risk increases with age only for white males. Among blacks, Chicanos, and Native Americans, the suicide rate reaches its peak below the age of 30.

The overall suicide rate among white persons is three times that among black persons. However, among young urban black persons between 20 and 35 years of age, the rate is twice that of white people the same age. In Native American communities the suicide rate varies from group to group. In general, the rates are increasing in these populations:

- Adolescents: rate doubled in Los Angeles County between 1967–1971.

- Black women: rate increased 80 percent in the past twenty years.

- Black men: rate increased 33 percent in the past twenty years.[18]

- White women: rate increased 49 percent in the past twenty years.

If a person is separated, widowed, or divorced, the risk of suicide increases. Those who are married or who have never been married are at less risk. This seems related to the loss factor among suicidal people, but does not seem to apply to two specific groups: older married white men who are simply "tired of living," and married black people who have lost a love relationship.

5. RECENT LOSS: Personal loss or threat of loss of a spouse, parent, status, money, or job increases a person's suicide risk. This is a very significant suicide indicator among adolescents.

6. PHYSICAL ILLNESS: Studies reveal that many people who kill themselves are physically ill. Also, three out of four suicide victims have been under medical care or have visited their physician within

four to six months of their death. The visit to a physician does not necessarily imply that the person is physically ill. But it highlights the fact that a large number of people with *any* problem seek out either physicians or the clergy. In the case of suicidal people, the visit may be their last attempt to find relief from distress.

These facts suggest the influential role physicians can have in preventing suicide if they are attentive to clues. The physician's failure to ascertain the suicide plan or to examine the depression disguised by a complaint with no physical basis, often leads to the common practice of prescribing a mild tranquilizer without listening to the person and making a referral for counseling. Such a response by a physician can be interpreted by the individual as an invitation to suicide.

The possibility of suicide is even greater if a person receives a diagnosis which affects his or her image of self or demands a major switch in life style; for example: heart disease, breast cancer, amputation of limb, cancer of sex organs.

7. DRINKING AND DRUG ABUSE: Drinking increases impulsive behavior and loss of control and therefore increases suicide risk, especially if the person has a high lethal means available. Alcohol also reduces the number of sleeping pills needed for a lethal overdose. Alcohol is involved in many deaths by suicide. Peck and Litman found that nearly half of the adolescents who died by suicide were involved in drug or alcohol abuse before their death.[18]

8. ISOLATION: If a person is isolated both emotionally and physically, risk of suicide is greater than if he or she lives with close significant others. According to Durkheim, "egoistic" suicide occurs when people feel they do not belong to society; "anomic" suicide occurs among people who cannot adjust to change and social demands.[24] One of the basic human needs is approval by others of our performance in expected roles. The lack of such approval leads to social isolation.

Negative or rejecting reactions from significant people are incorporated into the sense of self. If significant others are rejecting, this can lead to a conviction of worthlessness. When this happens, the person believes that others also see him or her as worthless. People who suffer from discrimination are a risk group for "egoistic" suicide. However, once minority groups and women achieve equality and better conditions, studies indicate that their risk for "anomic" suicide will increase. If white society or male dominance can no longer be blamed, the person may internalize failure. This process can lead to suicide. As Christopher Holmes put it: "being on the ground floor left no room to jump."[18] Thus, upward mobility increases suicide risk.

A person who is physically alone and socially isolated is often a candidate for hospitalization or other extraordinary means to relieve isolation. In such cases this can be a life-saving measure.

9. UNEXPLAINED CHANGE IN BEHAVIOR: Changes in behavior such as reckless driving and drinking by a previously careful, sober driver can be an indicator of suicide risk.

10. DEPRESSION: Depressed people may experience sleeplessness, early wakening, slowed down functioning, weight loss, menstrual irregularity, loss of appetite, inability to work normally, disinterest in sex, crying, restlessness, and feelings of hopelessness. Depressed adolescents are often overactive, may fail in school, or withdraw from usual social contacts. Not all people who kill themselves show signs of depression. However, a sufficient number of suicide victims are depressed to make this an important indicator for suicide. This is particularly true for the depressed person who is convinced of his or her worthlessness and is unable to reach out to others for help.

11. SOCIAL FACTORS: Social problems such as family disorganization, a broken home, and a record of delinquency and truancy increase a person's risk of suicide. Peck and Litman found that 42 percent of adolescents who killed themselves had prior physical fights with their families.[18] A person with a chaotic social background is also likely to *repeat* suicide attempts and eventually commit suicide if there is increasing indifference to suicide attempts by significant others. Suicide risk also increases for people who are unemployed or are forced to retire or move, especially when these upsets occur during a developmental transition stage.

12. MENTAL ILLNESS: Some people believe, falsely, that only a mentally ill person could commit suicide. If an individual hears voices directing him or her to commit suicide, the risk of suicide is obviously

increased. However, the number of individuals who fall into this category is extremely small. Others who are diagnosed as mentally ill should be assessed for suicide risk according to the criteria outlined.

Immediate and Long-range Risk for Suicide

People tend to classify self-destructive behavior as more or less serious according to whether there is immediate danger of death. A person might engage in several kinds of self-destructive behavior at the same time. For example, an individual who chronically abuses alcohol may threaten, attempt, or commit suicide—all in one day. We should view these behaviors on the continuum noted earlier; *all* are serious and important in terms of life and death. The difference is that for some the danger of death is *immediate,* whereas for others it is long-range. Still others are at risk because of a high risk life style, chronic alcohol or drug abuse, and neglect of medical care.

In this book, suicidal behavior is classified according to three types. This schema assists in assessing suicide risk and in planning appropriate responses.

TYPE I SUICIDAL BEHAVIOR: This includes verbal threats of suicide with no specific plan or means of carrying out a plan. Also defined as Type I behavior is an attempt which, with knowledge of the effects of the method, involves no physical danger to life or clearly provides for rescue. Ambivalence in Type I behavior tends more in the direction of life than death.
Suicide Risk Rating: The immediate risk of suicide is low whereas the risk for an attempt, a *repeat* attempt, and eventual suicide is high—depending on what happens after the threat or attempt. The risk is increased if the person abuses the use of alcohol and other drugs.

Case Examples of Type I Behavior

Jean, age 36, thinks of suicide as a long sleep, as a way of just not having to wake up to the day's problems, though she does not really wish to die. Jean has no history of suicide attempts nor does she abuse drugs or alcohol. She is troubled by her boredom and mild depression; she lacks outlets beyond her homemaking duties. She is not threatened by any immediate loss.

Immediate Risk of Suicide: Low
Risk of Suicide Attempt: Low to moderate depending on what she

does about her problem and the occurrence of a critical event in her life.

Case Example

Sarah, age 42, took five sleeping pills at 5:00 p.m. with full knowledge that the drug would not kill her, and obtained the temporary relief she wanted in sleep. When her husband found her sleeping at 6:00 p.m., he had at least some message of her distress. Sarah is troubled by her marriage. She really wants a divorce but is afraid she can't make it on her own. Sarah also takes an average of six to eight Valium per day. She has not made any other suicide attempts.

Immediate Risk of Suicide: Low
Risk of Repeat Suicide Attempt: Moderate to high depending on what she is able to do about her problem.

TYPE II SUICIDAL BEHAVIOR: This includes verbal threats with a plan and available means more specific and potentially more lethal than those involved in Type I behavior. Also included are attempts in which the rescue possibility is more precarious. The chosen method, though it may result in temporary physical disability, is not fatal regardless of whether there is rescue or not. Ambivalence is strong: life and death are seen more and more in an equally favorable light.

Suicide Risk Rating: The immediate risk for suicide is moderate. The risk for a repeat suicide attempt and eventual suicide is higher than for Type I behavior if no important life changes occur after the attempt or revelation of the suicide plan. The risk is significantly increased in the presence of chronic alcohol and drug abuse.

Case Example of Type II Behavior

Susan, age 21, came by herself in a taxi to a local hospital emergency room. She had taken ten 5 mg tablets of Valium a half hour earlier. Susan and her four-year-old child, Debbie, live with her parents. She has never gotten along well with her parents, especially her mother. Before the birth of her child, Susan had a couple of short-lived jobs as a waitress. She dropped out of high school at age 16 and has experimented off and on with soft drugs. Beginning at age 17, Susan had made four suicide attempts prior to the present one. She took overdoses of non-prescription drugs three times and cut her wrists once. These attempts were assessed as being of low lethality.

At the emergency room, Susan had her stomach pumped and was kept for observation for one hour. She was discharged without a referral for follow-up counseling. While in the emergency room, Susan could sense the impatience and disgust of the staff. A man with a heart attack had come in around the same time. Susan felt that no one had the time or interest to talk to her. She and the nurses knew each other from emergency room visits after her other suicide attempts. Twice before Susan had refused referrals for counseling, so the nurses assumed that she was hopeless and didn't want any help.

Suicide Risk: Susan is not in immediate danger of suicide. She does not have a high lethal plan and has no history of high lethal attempts. Her personal coping ability is poor, for example, drug use and school failure, but she is not cut off from her family, though her relationship with them is disturbed. She has not suffered a serious personal loss. However, because there is no follow-up counseling or evidence of any changes in her disturbed social situation, she is at risk of making more suicide attempts in the future. If such attempts increase in their medical seriousness, Susan's risk of eventual suicide also increases significantly.

TYPE III SUICIDAL BEHAVIOR: This includes a threat or attempt with an anticipated fatal outcome unless accidental rescue occurs. Such behavior also includes instances when the method fails to end in death for an unplanned reason, such as in a suicide attempt by car crash. Another example is a threat which will be carried out unless a potential rescuer (such as friend, family member, crisis worker, or other) can convince the person that there are good reasons to go on living. Ambivalence in Type III behavior tends more in the direction of death than life.

Suicide Risk Rating: The present and long-range risk of suicide is very high unless immediate help is available and accepted. Chronic, self-destructive behavior increases the risk even further.

Case Example of Type III Behavior

Edward, age 41, had just learned that his wife Jane had decided to get a divorce. He threatened to kill himself with a gun or carbon monoxide on the day she files for the divorce. Jane's divorce lawyer proposed that their country home and the twenty adjoining acres be turned over completely to Jane.

Edward told his wife, neighbors, and a crisis counselor that his family and home were all he had to live for. He and Jane have four children. Edward also has several concerned friends but doesn't feel he can turn to them. Jane's decision to divorce Edward has left him feeling like a complete failure. He has several guns and is a skilled hunter. A major factor in Jane's decision to divorce Edward was his chronic drinking problem. He had threatened to shoot himself eight months earlier after a violent argument with Jane when he was drinking.

Several strong predictive signs of suicide can be identified in Edward's case:

1. He has a specific plan with an available high lethal means, the gun.

2. He threatened suicide with a high lethal method eight months previously and is currently communicating his suicidal plan.

3. He is threatened with a serious interpersonal loss and feels cut off from what he regards as his most important social resources—his family and home.

4. Edward has a rigid expectation of himself in his role as husband and provider for his family. He sees himself as a failure in that role and has a deep sense of shame about his perceived failure.

5. His coping ability is apparently poor as he resorts to the abuse of alcohol and is reluctant to use his friends for support during a crisis.

6. Edward is also a high risk in terms of his age, sex, race, marital status, and history of alcohol abuse.

Suicide Risk: Edward is in immediate danger of committing suicide. Even if he makes it through his present crisis, he is also a long-range risk for suicide because of his chronic self-destructive behavior— abuse of alcohol and threats of suicide by available high lethal means.

The immediate and long-range risks of these suicidal behaviors are summarized in Figure 5–1. (Case examples of various suicide types will be continued in Chapter 6).

A final point about assessment of suicide risk is that it is an ongoing process. A person's risk for suicide should be reassessed continually. If important social and attitudinal changes occur as a

Figure 5–1. Suicide Risk Differentiation

Suicidal behavior	Immediate risk	Long range risk
Type I	Low	High depending on immediate response, treatment, and
Type II	Moderate	High follow-up
Type III	Very High	High

result of a suicide attempt, the person who is suicidal today may not be suicidal tomorrow or ever again. The opposite is also true: a critical life event or other circumstances can drastically affect a person's view of life and death. Someone who has never been suicidal may become so. These factors should be actively considered by health workers, counselors, friends, and family involved with a troubled person.

SUMMARY
Suicide and self-destructive behavior are extreme ways in which some people respond to crisis. The pain and turmoil felt by a self-destructive person can be compared to the confusion and mixed feelings of those trying to help. People destroy themselves for complex reasons. Understanding what a self-destructive person is trying to communicate is basic to helping the individual find alternatives to suicide. Assessment of suicide risk is a difficult task. It is made possible by recognition of signs that predict the likelihood of suicide for particular individuals. Assessment of suicide risk is an important basis for appropriate response to self-destructive people.

References

1. Linden, Leonard L. and Warren Breed. "The Demographic Epidemiology of Suicide." In: *Suicidology: Contemporary Developments*. Edwin S. Shneidman (ed.). New York: Grune and Stratton, Inc., 1976.

2. Monk, Mary. "Epidemiology." In: *A Handbook for the Study of Suicide*. Seymour Perlin, ed. New York: Oxford University Press, 1975.

3. Pokorny, Alex D. "Myths about

Suicide." In: *Suicidal Behaviors: Diagnosis and Management.* H. L. P. Resnick, ed. Boston: Little, Brown and Company, 1968.

4. Rosen, George. "History." In: *A Handbook for the Study of Suicide.* Seymour Perlin, ed. New York: Oxford University Press, 1975.

5. Vlasak, George J. "Medical Sociology." In: *A Handbook for the Study of Suicide.* Seymour Perlin, ed. New York: Oxford University Press, 1975.

6. McGuire, Daniel C. "Death by Chance, Death by Choice," *The Atlantic.* 233:56–65, January, 1974.

7. Brandt, R. B. "The Morality and Rationality of Suicide." In: *A Handbook for the Study of Suicide.* Seymour Perlin, ed. New York: Oxford University Press, 1975.

8. Menninger, Karl. *Man Against Himself.* New York: Harcourt, Brace and Company, 1938.

9. Stengel, Ervin. "Attempted Suicides," In: *Suicidal Behaviors: Diagnosis and Management,* H. L. P. Resnick, ed. Boston: Little, Brown and Company, 1968.

10. Weisman, Avery. "Death and Self Destructive Behaviors," In: *Suicide Prevention in the 1970's.* Washington, D.C.: U. S. Government Printing Office, Pub. No. (HSM), 72–9054, 1973.

11. Farberow, Norman L., and Edwin S. Shneidman, eds. *The Cry for Help.* New York: McGraw-Hill Book Company, 1961.

12. Shneidman, Edwin S., and Norman L. Farberow, eds. *Clues to Suicide.* New York: McGraw-Hill Book Company, 1957.

13. Dorpat, Theodore, and Herbert S. Ripley. "The Relationship Between Attempted Suicide and Committee Suicide," *Comprehensive Psychiatry,* 8:74–79, No. 2, 1967.

14. Brown, Timothy R., and Tamera J. Sheran. "Suicide Prediction: A Review," *Life-Threatening Behavior,* 2:67–97, Summer, 1972.

15. Breed, Warren. "Five Components of a Basic Suicide Syndrome," *Life-Threatening Behavior,* 2:3–18, Spring, 1972.

16. Beck, Aaron T.; Harvey L. P. Resnik; and D. J. Lettier, eds. *The Prediction of Suicide.* Bowie, Maryland: The Charles Press Publishers, Inc., 1974.

17. Farberow, Norman L., ed. *Suicide in Different Cultures.* Baltimore: University Park Press, 1975.

18. Bush, James A., ed. "Suicide and Blacks." *Proceedings of Black Suicide Workshop.* Charles R. Drew Postgraduate Medical School, Department of Psychiatry and Human Behavior, Los Angeles, California, 1973.

19. Jacobs, Gerald. *Adolescent Suicide.* New York: Wiley and Sons, Inc., 1971.

20. Freeman, Douglas J.; Karl E. Wilson; Joe D. Thigpen; and Richard K. McGee. "Assessing Intention to Die in Self-Injury Behavior." In: *Psychological Assessment of Suicidal Risk* by Charles Neuringer, ed. Springfield, Illinois: Charles C. Thomas Publishing Company, 1974.

21. Dublin, Louis I. *Suicide: A Sociological and Statistical Study.* New York: Ronald Press, 1963.

22. Hendin, H. *Black Suicide*. New York: Basic Books, 1969.

23. Maris, Ronald. "Sociology." In: *A Handbook for the Study of Suicide*. Seymour Perlin, ed. New York: Oxford University Press, 1975.

24. Durkheim, E. *Suicide*. 2nd ed. Translated by J. A. Spaulding and G. Simpson. Glencoe, Illinois: Free Press, 1951.

25. Shneidman, Edwin, ed. *Suicidology: Contemporary Developments*. New York: Grune and Stratton, Inc., 1976.

26. Alvarez, A. *The Savage God*. London: Weidenfeld and Nicolson, 1971.

CHAPTER 6

Helping Self-destructive People and Survivors of Suicide

COMPREHENSIVE SERVICE FOR SELF-DESTRUCTIVE PERSONS

Everyone who threatens or attempts suicide should have access to all the services the crisis calls for. Three kinds of service should be available for suicidal and self-destructive people:

1. Emergency medical treatment
2. Crisis intervention
3. Follow-up counseling or therapy

Emergency Medical Treatment

This is indicated for anyone who has already made a suicide attempt. Unfortunately, this is still *all* that is received by a large number of people who attempt suicide. Everyone—friend, neighbor, family member, passer-by—is obligated by simple humanity to help a suicidal person obtain medical treatment. The first-aid aspects of such treatment can be performed by police, volunteer fireworkers, rescue squads, or anyone familiar with first-aid procedures.

In any situation when there is immediate danger of death, the police should be called, for police and attached rescue squads have the greatest possibility of assuring rapid transportation to a hospital. If there is any question about the medical seriousness of the suicide attempt, a physician should be called. The best way to obtain a medical opinion in such cases is to call a local hospital emergency room. In large communities, there is always a physician there; in small ones, a physician is on call.

Most communities also have poison control centers, usually attached to a hospital. In cases of drug overdose when the lethality level of the drug is not certain, a poison control center should be called. The amount of drug necessary to cause death depends on the kind of drug, the size of the person, and the person's tolerance for the drug in cases of addiction. Sleeping pills are the most dangerous.

In general, *a lethal dose is ten times the normal dose.* In combination with alcohol, only *half* the amount is necessary to cause death. Aspirin is also much more dangerous than is commonly believed. One hundred five grain tablets can cause death; less is needed if other drugs are also taken. Tylenol, an Aspirin substitute, is even more dangerous, as it cannot be removed from body tissue by dialysis. Tranquilizers are less dangerous as suicide weapons.

Some suicidal persons have gone through hospital emergency rooms, intensive care, and surgical units, and on to discharge, with no explicit attention paid to the primary problem, which caused the suicide attempt. The urgency of medical treatment for a suicidal person can be so engrossing that other aspects of crisis intervention are omitted. For example, if a person is in a coma from an overdose, or is being treated for injuries from a car crash, a careful lethality assessment may be forgotten after the person is out of physical danger. Great care should be taken to assure that this does not happen.

If a person whose suicide attempt is medically serious does not receive follow-up counseling, the risk of suicide within a few months is very high. Medical treatment, of course, is of primary importance when there is danger of death; but we should always remember that the person's physical injuries are a *result* of the suicide attempt. Dealing with those injuries is only a first step. The attitude of hospital emergency room staff can be the forerunner of more serious suicide attempts or the foundation for crisis intervention and acceptance of a referral for follow-up counseling.

Crisis Intervention

People who threaten or attempt suicide as a way of coping with a crisis usually lack more constructive ways of handling stress. The crisis intervention principles outlined in chapters 3 and 4 should be used on behalf of self-destructive persons. Several techniques are particularly important for a person in suicidal crisis:

1. *Relieve isolation*. If the suicidal person is living alone, such physical isolation must be relieved. If there is no friend or supportive relative with whom the person can stay temporarily, and if the person is highly suicidal, he or she should probably be hospitalized until the active crisis is over.

2. *Remove lethal weapons*. Lethal weapons and pills should be removed either by the counselor, a relative, or friend.

3. *Encourage alternate expression of anger*. If the person is planning suicide as a way of expressing anger at someone, we should actively explore with the individual other ways of expressing anger short of the price of his or her life.

4. *Avoid final decision of suicide during crisis*. The suicidal person should be actively assured that the suicidal crisis, that is,

seeing suicide as the only option, is a temporary state. Also, we should try to persuade the person to avoid a decision about suicide until he or she has considered all other alternatives during a non-crisis state of mind.

5. *Reestablish social ties.* Every effort should be made to help the suicidal person reestablish social bonds if they are broken. Family crisis counseling sessions, or finding satisfying substitutes for lost relationships should be planned. Active links to such self-help groups as Widow-to-Widow or Parents Without Partners clubs can be a life-saving act.

6. *Relieve extreme anxiety and sleep loss—medication.* If a suicidal person is extremely anxious and also has been unable to sleep for several days, he or she may become even more suicidal as a result. To a suicidal person, the world looks more bleak, and death seems more desirable at 4:00 a.m. after endless nights of sleeplessness. A good night's sleep can temporarily reduce suicide risk and put the person in a better frame of mind to consider other ways of solving life's problems.

In such cases, it is appropriate to consider medication on an emergency basis. This should *never* be done for a highly suicidal person apart from daily crisis counseling sessions. Without effective counseling, the extremely suicidal person may interpret such an approach as an invitation to suicide. A tranquilizer will usually take care of both the anxiety and the sleeping problem, since anxiety is the major cause of sleeplessness. If medication seems needed, the person should be given a *one to three day supply at most,* and *never* without a specific return appointment for crisis counseling.

Sometimes non-medical crisis counselors need to seek medical consultation and emergency medicine for a suicidal person. In such cases the counselor must clearly advise the consulting physician of the person's suicidal state and of the recommended limited dose of drugs. This is particularly important when dealing with physicians who lack training in suicide prevention or who seem hurried and disinterested. It should never be forgotten that the majority of suicide deaths in the United States are by *prescribed* drugs.

There is probably no instance when crisis assessment is as important as it is in working with a self-destructive person. It determines our immediate and long-range response to the individual. A person who is threatening or has attempted suicide is either in active crisis, or is already beyond the crisis, and at a loss to resolve the crisis in any other way.

Everyone who engages in self-destructive acts is not in a life and death emergency situation. However, anyone distressed enough to be self-destructive at *any* level should be listened to and helped; but if the suicide attempt is medically nonserious, the counselor's response should not convey a sense of life and death urgency. This does not mean that the person's action is "written off" as nonserious. Rather, the underlying social message of the behavior should receive the *greatest part* of our attention. To do otherwise may inadvertently lead to further suicide attempts. A helper thereby reinforces self-destructive behavior by a dramatic and misplaced life and death medical response, while ignoring the problems signaled by the self-destructive act.

Thus persons at all levels of risk should be responded to. The helper must differentiate between the *types* of response. Emergency measures are used when there is immediate danger of death from a failed suicide attempt which is medically serious. For the person whose suicide risk is long-range, the approach should also be precisely that: long-range. If the attempt is medically nonserious, one should avoid a medical-treatment-only approach on the one hand, and a life-and-death approach on the other. Rather, the person should be helped to bring about needed psychosocial changes by means other than self-destructive acts.

Follow-up of Suicidal People

COUNSELING AND PSYCHOTHERAPY: Beyond crisis counseling, all self-destructive persons should have the opportunity to receive counseling or psychotherapy as an aid in solving the problems that led them to self-destructive behavior. Such therapy is the proper work of specially trained people. Usually these are clinical psychologists, psychiatric nurses, psychiatrists, and psychiatric social workers. Others who do such counseling may be clergy, lay volunteers, and counselors in community mental health settings. The main concern is that the counselor or psychotherapist be properly trained and supervised.

Counseling should focus on the resolution of situational problems and the appropriate expression of feelings. The person is helped to change various behaviors that are causing discomfort and which he or she is usually consciously aware of. Psychotherapy involves the uncovering of feelings that have been denied expression for a long time. It may also involve changing certain aspects of one's personality and deep rooted patterns of behavior. People usually engage in psychotherapy because they are troubled or unhappy about certain features of their personality or behavior.

In most instances counseling or psychotherapy should be made available to the suidical person. It is particularly recommended for crisis-prone people who solve everyday problems by drug and alcohol abuse and other self-destructive behavior. This kind of person has such difficulty expressing feelings verbally that self-destructive acts become an easier way to communicate. People who are extremely dependent, or who have rigid expectations for themselves combined with inflexible behavior patterns are also good candidates for psychotherapy. A severely depressed, suicidal person should always have follow-up counseling or psychotherapy.

Counseling and psychotherapy can take place on an individual or group basis. A group experience is valuable for nearly everyone, but it is particularly recommended for the suicidal person who has underlying problems with social interaction and communication of feelings. For adolescents who have made suicide attempts, family therapy should frequently follow family crisis counseling. Marital counseling should be offered whenever a disturbed marriage has contributed to the person's suicidal crisis. These therapies can be used in various combinations—depending on the needs of the individual and family.

Whether in a group or individually, counseling and psychotherapy goals should be directed toward:

- Correcting psychological and social disturbances in the person's life.
- Improving the person's self-image.
- Finding satisfactory social resources.
- Developing approaches to problems other than self-destructive behavior.
- Discovering a satisfying life plan.

Crisis counselors should always keep in mind that a satisfying and constructive resolution of a crisis is an excellent foundation for persuading people to seek follow-up counseling or psychotherapy around the problems that made them crisis-prone in the first place.

DRUG TREATMENT FOR DEPRESSION: Antidepressants are not emergency drugs. However, these drugs may be used successfully for some suicidal persons who are also severely depressed. Two of the most commonly used antidepressants are Elavil and Tofranil—tricyclic drugs. Another group of antidepressant drugs, the mono-amine-oxidase (MAO) inhibitors, (Parnate is a common example), are also very effective but have the disadvantage of more serious side effects.[1] These drugs should not be used for a person who is going through normal grief and mourning. Nor should they be used when the person is suffering from a reactive depression.[2,3] A reactive depression occurs when a person in crisis surrounding a loss does not express normal feelings of sadness and anger *during* the crisis, and later reacts with depression. Sometimes this is referred to as a "delayed grief reaction." Psychotherapy—not an antidepressant drug—is indicated for such persons. Antidepressant drugs do seem to help a large number of people (about 30 percent) who have what is called endogenous or clinical depression.[2] Classical symptoms include weight loss, early morning wakening, loss of appetite, slowed down body functions, sexual and menstrual abnormality, and extreme feelings of worthlessness. The symptoms usually cannot be related to a conscious loss or specific life event.

Antidepressant drugs are dangerous and should be prescribed for suicidal persons with extreme caution. When taken with alcohol, death can easily result from an overdose. Also, a person using these drugs can experience side effects such as feelings of confusion, restlessness, or loss of control.[1] Persons with a past history of psychosis or with symptoms of "borderline psychosis" can have serious side effects from antidepressants.[3]

Another problem with antidepressant drugs is that it takes 10 to 14 days before there is any noticeable lifting of the depression, even though the person sleeps better as a result of a sedative side effect. This delayed drug action should be explained very carefully, because most people expect to feel better immediately after taking a drug.

During the pre-therapeutic phase, a suicide could occur as a result of side effects of confusion and agitation.

Case Example
Marilyn, age 42, was suffering from a delayed grief reaction a year after the death of her husband. She was also distressed about handling her adolescent daughter, Roseann, age 13. Marilyn had no history of suicide attempts. She had a close relationship with a brother and sister who lived nearby, and in general had a stable undisturbed life until the loss of her husband. Marilyn had seen a physician, was given a prescription for Tofranil, and referred to a counseling center. After four days of taking the antidepressant drug, Marilyn killed herself by extensive and bizarre body mutilation, even though she had seen a counselor twice during the past four days. (The counselor was highly trained and experienced and had done a careful lethality assessment.) Evaluation of this case led to the conclusion that Marilyn probably had a side reaction to the antidepressant drug, which should not have been prescribed in the first place since she was suffering from a reactive depression.

Another danger of suicide occurs after the depression lifts during drug treatment. This is especially true for the person who is so depressed and physically slowed down that he or she did not, previously, have the energy to carry out a suicide plan.[1, 3] Because of all these factors, it is preferable to use antidepressant drugs in combination with psychiatric hospitalization for a depressed person who is highly suicidal, especially if he or she is also socially and physically isolated.

Case Example
Jack, age 69, had seen his physician for bowel problems. He was also quite depressed. Even after complete examination and extensive tests, he was obsessed with the idea of cancer and was afraid that he would die. Jack also had high blood pressure and emphysema. Months earlier he had had prostate surgery. His family described him as a chronic complainer. Jack's doctor gave him a prescription for an antidepressant drug and referred him to a local mental health clinic for counseling. Jack admitted to the crisis counselor that he had ideas of suicide, but he had no specific plan or history of attempts. After two counseling sessions, Jack killed himself by carbon monoxide poisoning. This suicide might have been prevented if Jack had been hospitalized, and if the delayed reaction of the drug had been properly explained. He lived alone and probably expected to feel better

immediately after taking the *antidepressant*. Another alternative might have been prescribing a drug to relieve his acute anxiety in combination with a plan to live with relatives for a couple of weeks.

Crisis counselors should not lose sight of the fact that antidepressants are not emergency drugs. These drugs should usually not be prescribed for a highly suicidal person during the acute crisis state—unless the individual is hospitalized. The crisis counselor should routinely ask a person in crisis what drugs he or she is taking or has in his or her possession. Also, the prescription of *any* drug as a substitute for effective crisis counseling is irresponsible. Not only can drug use precipitate a suicide, but the unwarranted prescription of drugs can also lead to serious drug abuse problems.[4]

EXAMPLES OF SERVICE PLANS
The following cases are continued from Chapter 5.

Case Example: Sarah
Sarah exhibited Type I Suicidal Behavior (low risk)

Emergency Medical: Medical treatment for Sarah is not indicated because pills are absorbed from the stomach into the blood stream within a half hour. The dose of five sleepings pills is not lethal or extremely toxic. Therefore, other medical measures such as dialysis are not indicated.

Crisis Intervention: Crisis counseling should focus on the immediate situation related to Sarah's suicide attempt and decision making about her marriage.

Follow-up: In follow-up counseling Sarah hopefully will examine her extreme dependency on her marriage, her personal insecurity, and her dependency on Valium as a means of problem solving.

Case Example: Susan
Susan exhibited Type II Suicidal Behavior (moderate risk).

Emergency Medical: Treatment for the overdose is stomach lavage (washing out the stomach contents).

Crisis Intervention: Crisis counseling for Susan should include contacts with her parents and should focus on the various situational problems she faces: unemployment, upsets with her parents, and dependence on her parents.

Follow-up: Since Susan has had a chaotic life for a number of years, she could benefit from ongoing individual counseling or psychotherapy, if she so chooses. Family therapy may be indicated if she decides to remain in her parents' household. Group therapy is strongly recommended for Susan.

Case Example: Edward

Edward exhibited Type III Suicidal Behavior (high risk).

Emergency Medical: Not indicated—no suicide attempt has been made.

Crisis Intervention: Remove guns (and alcohol, if possible) or have wife or friend remove them. Arrange to have Edward stay with a friend on the day his wife files for divorce. Try to get Edward to a self-help group, Alcoholics Anonymous, and rely on an individual AA member for support during his crisis. Arrange daily crisis counseling sessions for Edward.

Follow-up: Edward should have ongoing therapy—both individually and in a group—focusing on his alcohol dependency problem, his rigid expectations of himself, and ways of finding other satisfying relationships after the loss of his wife by divorce.

HELPING SURVIVORS OF SUICIDE

When a suicide occurs, it is almost always the occasion of a crisis for survivors: children, spouse, parents, other relatives, friends, crisis counselor, therapist, anyone closely associated with the person. The usual feelings associated with any serious loss are felt by most survivors of a suicide: sadness that the person ended life so tragically, and anger that the person is no longer a part of one's life.

In addition, however, survivors often feel enormous guilt. This arises usually from two main sources:

1. The sense of responsibility that somehow one should have prevented the suicide. This is especially true when the survivors were very close to the person.

2. The sense of relief that some survivors feel after a suicide. This happens when relationships were very strained or when the person attempted suicide many times and either could not or would not use available help.

A common tendency among survivors of suicide is to blame or "scapegoat" someone for the suicide. This reaction often arises from a survivor's sense of helplessness and guilt about not preventing the suicide.

Some survivors deny that the suicide ever took place. This seems to be the only way they can handle the crisis. Often, this takes the form of insisting that the death was an accident.

Case Example
One couple instructed their nine-year-old daughter, who was a patient in the pediatric ward, to tell the hospital supervisor that her older brother died of an accident. (The supervisor knew the family through the hospital psychiatric unit.) The parents had insisted that he be discharged from psychiatric care, even though he was highly suicidal and the physician advised against it. A few days later, the boy shot himself at home with a hunting rifle. These parents were apparently very guilt ridden and went to great lengths to deny the suicide.

Albert Cain and others have documented the many problems that can occur throughout survivors' lives if they do not have help at the time of the crisis of suicide.[5] Problems for survivors include depression, serious personality disturbances, and obsession with suicide as the predestined fate for oneself, especially on the anniversary of the suicide or when the person reaches the same age. A mother of 35 became very depressed and suicidal on the second anniversary of her 15-year-old son's death by suicide. Counseling at a community mental health clinic helped this woman eventually accept and live with the reality of her son's suicide.

The tragic effect of a suicide is particularly striking in the case of children following a parent's suicide. In studies of child survivors, some of the symptoms found were learning disabilities, sleepwalking, delinquency, fire setting, and many others.[6] Crisis counseling should therefore be available for all survivors of suicide. Shneidman calls this "postvention," an effort to reduce some of the possible harmful effects of suicide on the survivors.[7]

Some people commit suicide while receiving therapy or counseling through a crisis center, mental health agency, or private practitioner, or while receiving hospital or medical care. In these cases, the counselor, nurse and/or physician is in a natural, strategic position to help survivors. Unfortunately, what often happens is that workers pass up golden opportunities for postvention because they may be struggling with the same mixture of feelings that beset the family. It is obviously much better to prevent this kind of impasse than to deal with it after it happens.

The most useful preventive measure is for helpers to learn as much as they can about suicide and constructive ways of handling the many feelings one can have in working with self-destructive people. There will always be strong feelings following a suicide. However, a worker with a realistic concept of the limits of responsibility for another's suicide can help other survivors work through their feelings and reduce the scapegoating that often occurs.

In counseling and health care settings, a counselor or nurse should immediately seek consultation from a supervisor after a suicide occurs. Team meetings are another important step (see Chapter 10, Team Relationships). They provide staff an opportunity to air feelings, evaluate the total situation, and determine who is best able to make postvention contact with the family. If the counselor who has worked most closely with the victim is too upset to deal with the family, a supervisory person should handle the matter, at least initially. In hospitals or mental health agencies where no one has had training in basic suicide prevention and crisis counseling, outside consultation with suicidologists or crisis counselors should be obtained whenever possible.

Most suicides do not occur among people receiving help from a health or counseling agency. This is one reason why many survivors of suicide get so little help. In some communities there are special bereavement counseling programs or self-help groups such as widow-to-widow clubs which help survivors of suicides. Ideally, every community should have an active reach-out program for suicide survivors as a basic part of comprehensive crisis services. Survivors are free to refuse these offers of support, but such offers should at least be available.

In the absence of these formal avenues of help, survivors of suicides can still be reached by police, clergy, and funeral directors, if such caretakers are sensitive to survivors' needs. These key people should be very careful not to increase a survivor's possible sense of guilt and denial, recognizing how strong the suicide taboo and scapegoating tendency are in most of us. The least any of us can do is to offer an understanding word and suggest where the person might find an agency or person who can help one through the crisis.

Techniques in helping a survivor of suicide are essentially the same as those used in dealing with other crises. A survivor should be helped to:

- Express feelings appropriate to the event.
- Grasp the reality of the suicide.
- Obtain and use the help necessary to work through the crisis (including sometimes his or her own suicide crisis).

If a survivor depended on the suicide victim for financial support, he or she may also need help in managing money and housing, for example. A surviving spouse with young children also needs special help in explaining to the children the death by suicide of their parent. The almost universal tendency is to hide the facts from children in the mistaken belief that they will thus be spared unnecessary pain. What adults often fail to realize is that children know a great deal more than they are usually given credit for. Even if children do not know the full facts, they do know that something much more terrible than an accident has occurred. If the suicide is not discussed, the child is left to fill in the facts alone in the very rich fantasy life every child has; and usually a child's fantasies are much more scary than the actual facts. For example, a child may fear that the surviving parent killed the dead parent, or that the child's own misbehavior may have caused the parent's death. The child may have unrealistic expectations that the dead parent will return—"Maybe if I'm extra good, Daddy will come back."

What children do not create in their fantasy life will often be filled in by information from neighborhood and school companions. Some child survivors also suffer from jeers and teasing by other children about the parent's suicide.

Survivors should explain the death by suicide clearly, simply, and in a manner consistent with the child's level of development and understanding. The child should have an opportunity to ask questions and express feelings. He or she needs to know that the surviving parent is also willing to answer questions in the future, as the child's understanding of death and suicide grows. A child should never be left with the impression that it is a closed issue, never to be discussed again.

EXAMPLES OF DISCUSSIONS WITH CHILDREN:

"Yes, Daddy shot himself . . . No, it wasn't an accident . . . He did it because he wanted to."

"Mommy will not be coming back anymore . . . No, Mommy didn't do it because you misbehaved last night . . ."

"No one knows exactly why Daddy did it . . . Yes, he had a lot of things that bothered him . . ."

Surviving parents who cannot deal directly with their children about the other parent's suicide have usually not worked through their own feelings of guilt and responsibility regarding the suicide. In these cases, parents need the support and help of a counselor for themselves as well as for their children. Most often parents simply do not understand the serious results that can occur by hiding the true facts from children. Counseling should include a full explanation of the advantages of talking openly with children about the suicide.

In some cases, a child is completely aware that the parent committed suicide, especially if there were many open threats or attempts of suicide. Sometimes a child finds the dead parent or has been given directions by the other parent to "call if anything happens to Mommy."[5] If the suicidal person was very disturbed or abusive prior to committing suicide, the child may feel relief. In all of these cases, surviving children are strapped with an enormous load of guilt and misplaced responsibility for the death of his or her parent.[5]

Parents will usually need the assistance of a crisis worker or a child guidance counselor to help a child through this crisis. Robert Jarmusz reported the successful use of a natural play group for four young boys who had found a man hanging.[8] All four boys became restless and fearful and refused to sleep in their own beds. Crisis intervention programs for such children are far too uncommon.

Help for survivors of suicides has always been one of the goals of the suicide prevention movement. This is obviously an important but very difficult work to carry out. Many people, including some coroners' offices, are still inclined to cover up the reality of a suicide. The suicide taboo in modern times continues, despite a growing acceptance of the morality of suicide in certain instances.[9]

One means of reaching a large number of survivors is through coroners' offices. It is there that every death is eventually reported and recorded. In Los Angeles County all suicide deaths as well as equivocal deaths (those in which suicide is suspected but not certain) are followed up by staff from the Los Angeles Suicide Prevention Center. Suicidologists do a "Psychological Autopsy."[10] This is an intensive examination to determine whether in fact the death was by suicide, and if it was, to define the probable causes of the suicide. Information for the psychological autopsy is obtained from survivors and from medical and psychiatric records.

The psychological autopsy is an excellent means of contacting the large number of survivors who are not in contact with a crisis center, physician, or mental health agency. Survivors are, of course, free to refuse participation in such post mortem examinations. Experience reveals, however, that the majority of survivors do not refuse to be interviewed, and welcome the opportunity to talk about the suicide. This is especially true if they are contacted within a few days of the suicide when they are most troubled with their feelings. Many survivors use this occasion to obtain some help in answering their own questions and dealing with suicidal inclinations following a suicide. The "official" interview situation is somehow a more acceptable circumstance for some people to open up about an otherwise taboo subject. This is an ideal opportunity for the interviewer to suggest follow-up counseling resources to the survivor. If weeks or months pass, survivors may resent the post mortem interview. By that time they have had to settle their feelings and questions on their own and in their own way, which may include denial and resentment. A delayed interview may seem like unnecessary opening of an old wound.

McGee has documented the excellent postvention work done by the Death Investigation Team in Gainesville, Florida.[11] The Suicide Prevention Center in Detroit, Michigan also conducts an extensive survivor counseling program. Most communities do not have similar formal programs available to survivors of suicides. Obviously a great deal.of work remains to be done in this important area.

SUMMARY

People who get help after a suicide attempt or other self-destructive behavior may never commit suicide. Much depends on what happens in the form of emergency, crisis, and follow-up intervention. However, when suicide does occur, survivors of suicides usually are in crisis and are often neglected because of taboos and the lack of aggressive reach-out programs for them. Children, spouses, and parents pay an especially high price in after-effects of a suicide when they do not receive support during this crisis. This is an area of great challenge for crisis centers.

References

1. Kline, Nathan S., and John M. Davis. "Psychotropic Drugs," *American Journal of Nursing,* 73:54–62, January 1973.

2. Klerman, Gerald L.; A. Dimascio; M. Weissman; B. Prusoff; and E. Paykel. "Treatment of Depression by Drugs and Psychotherapy,"

American Journal of Psychiatry,
131:186–91, February 1974.

3. "Elavil-Product Summary Information." West Point, Pennsylvania:
Merck, Sharp and Dome, September
1972.

4. Rogers, Maurice J. "Drug Abuse:
Just What the Doctor Ordered."
Psychology Today, 5:16–24, Septem-
ber 1971.

5. Cain, Albert C., ed. *Survivors of
Suicide.* Springfield, Illinois: Charles
C Thomas, Publisher, 1972.

6. Cain, Albert C., and Irene Fast.
"Children's Disturbed Reactions to
Parent Suicide: Distortions of Guilt,
Communication and Identification."
In: *Survivors of Suicide.* Albert C.
Cain, ed. Springfield, Illinois:
Charles C Thomas, Publisher, 1972.

7. Shneidman, Edwin S. "Foreword."

In: *Survivors of Suicide.* Albert C.
Cain, ed. Springfield, Illinois:
Charles C Thomas, Publisher, 1972.

8. Jarmusz, Robert T. "Crisis Intervention with Four Boys, Members
of a Natural Play Group," *Vita,*
Official Newsletter: The International Association for Suicide Prevention, February 1976.

9. Hall, Elizabeth with Paul Cameron.
"Our Failing Reverence for Life."
Psychology Today, 9:104–13, April
1976.

10. Litman, Robert E.; E. S.
Shneidman; N. L. Farberow; and
N. D. Tabachnick. "Investigation of
Equivocal Suicides." *Journal of the
American Medical Association,*
184:924–29, June 1963.

11. McGee, Richard K. *Crisis Intervention in the Community.* Baltimore: University Park Press, 1974.

PART II

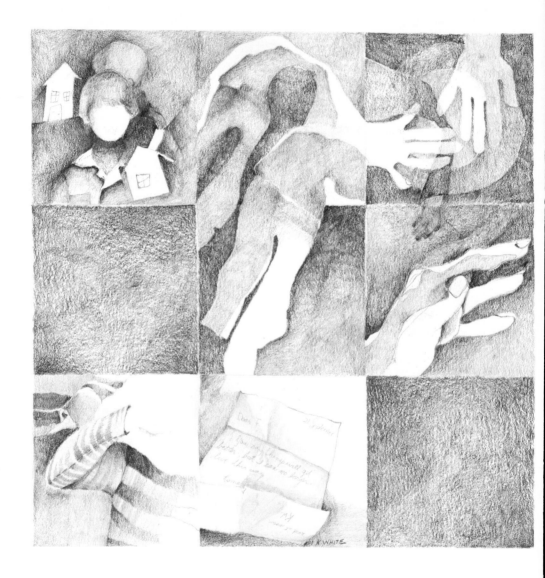

INTERVENTION IN SPECIFIC CRISES[*]

*Material for this section of the book is drawn from the author's experience and from interviews with the following people: Martha Bilski, Fran Ciccia, Eleonora Dykstra, David Hallowitz, Arden Hefren, Margaret Ireland, Earl and Ella Kemmerer, Sharon Kern, Melvin Kuechle, Nursing Staffs of Erie County Department of Health Division of Nursing and the Millard Fillmore Suburban Hospital in Buffalo, New York, Jean and Joe Oddo, Elsa Pacheco, Father Benedict Pfaller, and Florence Weinberg.

CHAPTER 7

Crises Threatening Health and Self-Image

INTRODUCTION

The unique hazard of some life events is that our health, image of self, or life itself is threatened. To avoid a crisis state, all of us need to have:

- Sense of physical well being.
- Some control in everyday life functions.
- Ability to be creative and productive in a way that is meaningful to us and accepted by others.
- Membership in a supportive community.

These aspects of life are acutely threatened by illness, accidents, birth of a handicapped child, criminal attacks, and uncontrolled use of alcohol and other drugs. Several of our basic needs are in jeopardy when hazardous events like these occur. A full-blown crisis experience can be avoided only if the threatened person is supported by family, friends, community caretakers, or health workers. Self-defeating outcomes such as suicide, homicide, mental illness, and depression can also be avoided if immediate help is available when these unanticipated situations occur.

Some of these events, such as child abuse and rape, can often be traced to ineffective crisis resolution at a critical earlier point in the life of the attacker. The mother who eventually abuses a child may not have wanted a baby, or was probably a victim of abuse herself as a child and felt helpless. As an abused child, she may have felt hopelessly dependent on her parents and afraid of further abuse if she reported their behavior. At each of these points, the destructive effects of a crisis situation might have been avoided by the intervention of an observant, caring person: by a pastor who detected unsound approaches to child rearing; by a maternity nurse or physician when a mother-in-crisis delivered her child; by a public health nurse who is sensitive to the early signs of child neglect and abuse.

A rape victim is often the next person encountered by a man who has fought with his lover or mother, has argued with his parole officer, or feels unable to cope with his disturbed sex life. Society's attitude toward the rape victim and the treatment she may receive from police officers and hospital workers can compound her crisis.

The person who abuses alcohol or other drugs often knows of no other way to make it through the day. Friends, family, hairdressers, and bartenders are the frequent listeners for this type of person. He or she is already beyond a crisis and is coping in a chronic self-destructive manner. The poor problem solving ability and disturbed life style of a person abusing drugs and alochol makes him or her even more prone to crises concerning housing, money, family, and the legal system.

Physical illness or an accident are often the beginning of a series of problems for the individual as well as for his or her family. If struck by a potentially fatal illness such as cancer, the person experiences the same sense of dread and loss that death itself implies. A person's self-image is also threatened by physical deformity resulting from a mastectomy, amputation of an arm or leg, or scars from an accident or extensive burns.

In addition to facing the illness or accident itself, the sick person in a hospital faces another crisis: hospitalization. Crisis intervention should be viewed as a routine part of comprehensive health care. When nurses and physicians do not communicate openly, they can become part of the person's problems rather than a source of help.

People in these kinds of crisis situations rarely come to the attention of mental health or crisis specialists at the high point of their crises. It is not uncommon, however, for mental health workers to see many of these people *after* the crisis, when they become dependent on alcohol or drugs, have lapsed into depression, or experienced other emotional disturbance. This fact highlights the enormously important role of front line workers: people at the scene of an accident; in police departments; in doctors' offices; in lawyers' offices; in emergency, intensive care, and other general hospital units; in welfare departments; in public health offices; and in residential settings for those who need supervision of daily living activities.

Workers in these community settings are not expected to function as counselors or psychotherapists. The failure to distinguish between psychotherapy and crisis intervention may account, in part, for the reluctance of some workers to engage in crisis intervention. Many front line people are already doing crisis intervention but may lack self-confidence because they have had no formal training. They often need reinforcement and confirmation from crisis specialists of the work they are doing for people in distress.

In the following pages the principles and techniques of crisis intervention are applied on behalf of people in crisis on the battleground of life. Case examples illustrate how health, welfare, and rescue workers can collaborate with mental health and crisis specialists to avoid destructive outcomes of hazardous events.

ILLNESS AND HOSPITALIZATION[1,2,3]

Case Example—History

Mr. Michael French, age 55, had suffered from cancer of the prostate gland for several years. During the past year he was forced to retire from his supervisory job in a factory. The cancer had spread to his bladder and colon, causing continuous pain as well as urinary control problems. Michael became very depressed and highly dependent on his wife, Maria, age 51. Michael and Maria grew further apart in their marriage as stress for both of them increased. Michael began to suspect Maria of infidelity.

Maria went to the hospital for a hysterectomy for fibroids of the uterus. Five days after hospital admission, she received a message from a friend that her husband was threatening to kill her when she came home. He had also dismissed their tenants without notice and had changed the locks on all the doors. The friend, who was afraid of Michael in this state, also called a local public health nurse who, in turn, called a nearby crisis clinic. The nurse had been making biweekly visits to supervise Michael's medication.

When Maria finally entered the hospital for surgery, she did so after repeated cancellations. Her husband always protested her leaving and, at the last minute, she would cancel. Finally her doctor pressed her to go through with the operation. Since she was not visibly sick, according to Michael's observations, he felt Maria was abandoning him unnecessarily. Along with the ordinary fears of anyone facing a major operation, Maria was very worried about her husband's condition when she went to the hospital. However, she was too embarrassed by Michael's accusations of infidelity to discuss her fears with the nurses or with her doctor.

Crisis Management

1. The crisis counselor called Maria in the hospital to talk about her concerns and to determine whether Michael had any history of violence, whether guns were available, etc. Michael's accusations of infidelity—which, according to Maria, were unfounded—may have been related to concern about his forced dependency on his wife and feelings of inadequacy as a man with cancer of the sex gland.

2. The crisis counselor called Michael, and let Michael know
that he (the counselor), Maria, and the neighbor were all concerned about him. Michael accepted an appointment for a home
visit by the counselor within the next few hours. He expressed
his fears that people were trying to take advantage of him during
his wife's absence. This was his stated reason for dismissing the
tenants and changing the locks. Further exploration revealed that
he felt inadequate to handle household matters and the everyday
requests of the tenants which his wife usually managed.

3. Michael agreed to the counselor's recommendation for a
medical-psychiatric-neurological check-up to determine whether
metastasis (spreading of the cancer) to the brain had occurred.
The counselor explained that brain tumors can contribute to acute
emotional upsets such as Michael was experiencing.

4. Since Michael had no means of visiting Maria in the hospital, the counselor arranged for such a visit. The counselor also
scheduled a joint counseling session between Michael and Maria
after they had had a chance to visit. This session revealed that
Michael and Maria each had serious concerns about the welfare
of the other. In their two telephone conversations during Maria's
stay in the hospital, Michael and Maria were unable to express
their fears and concern. As it turned out, the joint counseling session was the highlight in successful resolution of their crisis.
Michael's threats to kill Maria were a once-in-a-lifetime occurrence triggered by his unexpressed anger at Maria for leaving
him, and the troubles he experienced during her absence.

5. When Maria returned from the hospital, a joint session was
held at the French's home between the two of them, the public
health nurse, and the friend who made the original calls. This
conference had several positive results: (a) It calmed the neighbor's fears of Michael. (b) It broadened everyone's understanding of the reactions people can have to the stress of illness and
hospitalization. (c) The public health nurse agreed to enlist further home health services for the Frenches to relieve Maria's
increasing role of "nurse" to her husband. (d) Michael and Maria
agreed to several additional counseling sessions to explore ways
in which Michael's excessive dependency on his wife could be
reduced. Also, Michael and Maria had never before discussed

openly the feelings they both had about Michael's progressive cancer. Future sessions were to deal with ways that the Frenches could resume social contacts with their children and friends whom they had cut off almost completely.

Preventive Aspects

This case history reveals at least three earlier points at which crisis intervention should have been available to the Frenches:

1. At the time Michael received his diagnosis of cancer.

2. When Michael was forced to retire.

3. At the point of Maria's actual hospitalization, plus each time she had previously delayed her operation.

In each of these instances, nurses and physicians were in key positions to help the Frenches through the hazardous events of Michael's illness and Maria's operation. Sessions with the crisis counselor confirmed the fact that the Frenches, like many other people facing illness, received little or no attention regarding the fears and social ramifications of their illness and hospitalization.

When Maria expressed to the public health nurse her original concern about Michael's early retirement, the nurse might have extended her ten-minute visits to a half hour, thus allowing time for communication of concerns. *Example:* "Maria, you seem really concerned about your husband being home all the time . . . Can we talk about what's bothering you?" Or the nurse might have made a mental health referral after observing Michael's increasing depression.

The gynecologist attending to Maria's health problems might have explored the reasons for her repeated cancellations of the scheduled surgery. *Example:* "Mrs. French, you've cancelled the surgery appointment three times now . . . There must be some serious reason for this, as you know that the operation is necessary . . . Let's talk about what's at the bottom of this." Such a conversation might have led to a social service referral.

The nurse attending Maria prior to her operation—as well as the public health nurse visiting the home—might have picked up her concerns about the effect of her absence on Michael. Such a response requires listening skills and awareness of the psychological cues always given by people in stress.

Case Example

Hospital nurse: Mrs. French, you've been terribly quiet, and you seem tense. You said before that you're not particularly worried about the operation, but I wonder if something else is bothering you . . ."

Maria: "Well, I wish my husband were here, but I know he can't be."

Nurse: "Can you tell me more about that?"

Maria: "He's got cancer and isn't supposed to drive . . . I hated leaving him by himself."

Nurse: "How about talking with him by phone?"

Maria: "I've done that, but all we talk about is the weather and things that don't matter . . . I'm afraid if I tell him how worried I am about him, he'll think I'm putting him down."

Nurse: "Mrs. French, I understand what you're saying. A lot of people feel that way . . . But you know there's really no substitute for telling people honestly how we feel, especially those close to us."

Maria: "Maybe you're right . . . I s'pose I could try but I'd want to be really careful about what I say . . . There's been a lot of tension between us lately."

Nurse: "Why don't you start by letting him know that you wish he could be here with you and that you hope things are OK with him at home . . . (Pause) . . . You said there's been a lot of tension . . . Do you have anyone you can talk to routinely about the things that are bothering you?"

Maria: "No, not really."

The nurse might then explain the hospital resources such as social services or pastoral care—ways of helping Maria explore the problem further if she wishes.

In this brief interaction around a hazardous event such as surgery, the nurse has: (a) helped Maria express her fears openly; (b) conveyed her own understanding of Maria's fears; (c) helped Maria put her fears (of not communicating with her husband) in a more realistic perspective; (d) offered direct assistance in putting Maria in touch with the person most important to her at this time;

and (e) made available the resources for obtaining counseling service if Maria so desires.

This type of intervention should be made available to everyone with a serious illness or who experiences the traumatic effects of an operation, burns, or an accident. The person whose physical integrity, self-image, and social freedom are threatened or actually damaged by these hazards to health shows many of the usual signs of a crisis state.

FEELINGS: An amputation or diagnosis such as heart disease, diabetes, or cancer leaves people feeling

- Shock and anger: "Why me?"

- Helplessness and hopelessness in regard to future normal functioning: "What's left for me now?"

- Shame of the obvious scar, handicap, or reduced physical ability and dependence on others: "What will my husband/ lover think?"

- Anxiety about the welfare of spouse or children who depend on them: "How will they manage at home without me?"

- Deep sense of loss of body integrity and loss of goals the person hoped to achieve before the illness or accident: "I don't think I'll ever feel right again."

- Doubt of acceptance by others: "No one will want to be around me this way."

- Fear of death which may have been narrowly escaped in an accident or which now must be faced in the case of cancer: "It was almost the end"; or "This is the end."

THOUGHTS AND PERCEPTIONS: The fears raised by a serious illness, accident, or operation usually color the person's perception of the event itself—the understanding of the event, and how it will affect his or her future life. For example, a young woman with diabetes assumed that her cocktail party circuit, which she felt was necessary in her high executive position, would be completely cut off. She obviously lacked knowledge about what social limitations might be imposed by diabetes.

A person with heart disease may assume a future as an invalid; the reality is that he or she must change the manner and range of performance. The woman with a mastectomy may perceive that all men will reject her because of the deformity; in reality only some men would do so. A woman who does not have a secure relationship with a man before a mastectomy may experience rejection. We can help such a woman consider the value to her of a relationship with a man who can accept her only for her body. In fact, women with stable relationships are seldom rejected by their husbands or lovers following a mastectomy.

BEHAVIOR: The behavior of people who are ill or suffering from the physical effects of an accident or surgery is altered by several factors. Hospitalization forces on people a routine of dependency which is often necessary because of their physical condition. However, the enforced dependency role of the "patient" also serves to keep the hospital running according to established rules of hierarchy among physicians, nurses, and others. This hierarchy has little or nothing to do with patient welfare. In fact, rigidity in the hierarchy often defeats the very purpose for which hospitals claim they exist—that is, quality care of patients.

The environment of an intensive care unit—the tubes, lights, and electrical gadgets—is a constant reminder to the conscious patient of his or her proximity to death itself.[4] Furthermore, a patient's fears, anger, and lack of knowledge about illness, hospital routines, and expectations, can elicit the worst possible behavior from a person who is otherwise cooperative and likable.

Nurses, physicians, chaplains, and others familiar with these common behavior signs of patients in crisis can do much to relieve unnecessary stress and harmful outcomes of the hospital experience. The patient in crisis needs an opportunity to:

- Express the feelings related to his or her condition.

- Gain an understanding of the illness, what limitations it imposes, and in general what to expect in the future.

- Have his or her behavior understood by the staff, how it relates to the person's feelings and perception of the illness, and how the behavior is related to the attitudes and behavior of the entire staff and of the hospital itself.

SELF-HELP GROUPS: Putting people in touch with self-help
groups is another important means of reducing the hazards of illness
and hospitalization. These groups exist for nearly every kind of illness
or operation a person can have: heart disease, leukemia, diabetes,
mastectomy, amputation, and others. Many hospitals hold teaching
and discussion groups among patients while still in the hospital. This
is an excellent forum for people to air their feelings with others who
have similar problems, gain a better understanding of the illness or
operation and how it will affect their lives, and establish contacts with
people who may provide lasting social support in the future.

Crisis Intervention in Mental Institutions and Hostels

As noted in Chapter 2, admission to a mental hospital is a cardinal
sign that crises have not been constructively resolved at various
points along the way. Whenever possible, crisis hostels and other
alternatives to psychiatric hospitals should be used if a person cannot
be helped in the home environment.[5] Although mental hospitals are
intended to relieve acute breakdowns or stress situations, they—like
general hospitals—create another kind of crisis.

Case Example

Angela, age 18, highly suicidal, upset, and dependent on her family, was
brought to a private mental hospital by her mother on the advice of a psychiatrist whom the mother had called a few hours earlier. Angela and her
mother arrived at the hospital at 3:00 p.m. The admitting nurse stayed with
them until 3:30 p.m. when she was scheduled to go off duty. Angela was just
beginning to calm down but became very upset again when the nurse left.
The nurses were attempting to obtain an order from the psychiatrist for tranquilizing medication, but could not reach the doctor. Meanwhile, visiting
hours ended at 4:00 p.m., and Angela's mother was asked to leave. At this
point, Angela became even more upset. The nurse on the evening shift was
unable to quiet or console her. By 6:00 p.m. there was still no medical order
for tranquilizing medication. Angela's behavior now became uncontrollable,
and she was placed in a high security room as she became more suicidal.

In this case the rules and regulations of the hospital and the absence
of a call system to obtain doctor's orders for emergency medication
clearly contributed to Angela's crisis state which reached the point of
panic.

In general, the same principles of crisis management discussed in earlier chapters apply in mental hospitals and residential settings: (a) help people to express their feelings; (b) help them understand their situation and develop new ways of problem solving; and (c) help them to re-establish themselves with family and community resources. The staff in residential facilities should examine the programs and routines to determine whether people become *more* upset than they were originally as a result of the rules, thus defeating the purpose of a residential program.

ALCOHOL AND DRUG ABUSE

Alcoholism and drug abuse are not crises in themselves. The person who abuses drugs or alcohol is engaging in a chronic form of self-destructive behavior. It can usually be assumed that such people were in crisis at earlier points in their lives and lacked the social support and personal strength to resolve the crises in a more constructive manner. People abusing drugs and alcohol commonly avoid getting help for their problem until another crisis occurs as a result of the addiction itself. Frequently, a crisis takes the form of a family fight, eviction from an apartment, loss of a job, or trouble with the law. Depending on the attitude and skill of helpers at such times, these later crises can be the occasion of a turning point for the person dependent on drugs and/or alcohol.

Chronic Self-Destructive Behavior and Crisis Intervention

The opportunity to change a self-destructive life style is often missed. This is due, in part, to the lack of appropriate long-term treatment facilities, and in part to the attitude of hospital and clinic staffs whose hopelessness often matches that of the drug dependent people themselves. Careful application of crisis intervention techniques can greatly reduce the sense of defeat experienced by client and staff alike.

Crisis principles to be highlighted in regard to the drug or alcohol dependent person are:

1. Crisis represents a turning point, hopefully in this case away from drugs as a means of coping with stress.

2. In crisis intervention we avoid doing things *for* rather than *with* people. Proposed solutions to problems are mutually

agreed on by client and staff person. The drug dependent person will often act helpless and try to get staff to do things *for* him or her unnecessarily, thus increasing dependency even more. While expressing concern, staff should avoid falling into this rescue or "savior" trap.

3. Basic social attachments which have been disrupted must be reinstated or a substitute found to help avoid further crises and more self-destructive behavior. Usually, people who abuse drugs and alcohol are more isolated than most.

Failure to observe these points can only lead to greater dependency of the client and increasing frustration of the staff.

These crisis management techniques should be practiced in hospitals, in doctors' offices, and by police and rescue services—wherever the drug or alcohol dependent person is in crisis. Substituting these approaches for the current widespread attitudes of rejection would not miraculously cure one of the country's most serious health and mental health problems. However, the use of these techniques would be a first step for many persons toward a life free of these harmful chemical substances.

Case Example

Mrs. Emma Jefferson, age 42, had been drinking heavily for about 15 years. At age 35 her husband divorced her after repeated pleading that she do something about her drinking problem. He also obtained custody of their two children. Emma was sufficiently shocked by this turn of events that she gave up drinking, joined AA (Alcoholics Anonymous), remarried at age 37, and had another child at age 38. She had hurried into her second marriage, the chief motive being that she wanted another child.

A year later Emma began drinking again and was threatened with divorce by her second husband. Emma made superficial attempts to stop drinking again and began substituting Valium when she had episodes of anxiety and depression. Her second husband divorced her six months later. This time Emma retained custody of her child, though it was a close fight. Emma took a job, was fired, went on welfare assistance, and began spending a lot of time in bars. On the urging of a friend, Emma finally decided to seek help for her alcohol and Valium dependency problem. She gave up drinking but continued a heavy use of Valium, sometimes taking as many as six 5 mg tablets a day. Emma was inconsistent in carrying out plans to reorganize her life to include less dependence on drugs and more constructive social outlets.

One day a neighbor reported to the Child Protection Agency that she believed Emma was neglecting her child and should be investigated. The Child Welfare worker learned that Emma indeed had few social contacts outside the bars and occasionally left her two-year-old child unattended. Emma was allowed to maintain temporary custody of her child with regular home visitations by a welfare worker to supervise her parenting activity. The threat of loss of her third child was apparently a sufficient crisis to act as a turning point for Emma. The welfare worker urged Emma to seek continued help with her life problems from her counselor. Emma finally gave up her dependency on Valium, developed a more satisfying social life, and returned to work. She also made plans for another marriage, this time being more selective of a mate and less desperately dependent on a man for security.

A crisis resulting from Emma's chronic dependence on alcohol and drugs was the occasion for her finally giving up her self-destructive life style. Two divorces as a result of her drug dependence were *not* crisis occasions impelling her to make a change. In fact, Emma did not seek available counseling on either of these occasions. She stated that she was ashamed to ask for help, and in any case did not think she could afford it. (See Chapter 10, Community Education.)

Other people abusing drugs and alcohol seek help and make changes after serious financial or job failure, threat or actual experience of imprisonment, or a brush with death such as DT's (delirium tremens, a sign of advanced alcoholism), bleeding ulcers, liver damage, or a near-fatal suicide attempt. Hopefully, the increasing availability of crisis services and follow-up treatment programs will result in earlier choices toward growth rather than self destruction for drug dependent people.

Influence of Societal Attitudes

The attitudes of a given society naturally affect the use of drugs in that society. In the U.S., many attitudes toward drug use need changing. For example a drug such as marijuana is often regarded as "dangerous," while the excessive use of alcohol is considered by many as acceptable. A stable, law-abiding citizen can be censored or convicted for the use of marijuana, yet if the same person chose to use alcohol instead there would be no legal restrictions.

If consumed privately with no damage to others, there are no sanctions against even the excessive use of alcohol. Yet those who use alcohol chronically often suffer eventual liver and/or brain damage.[6] A crisis can occur for the user of alcohol only if he or she indulges in excess publicly and then damages others or others' property, as in the case of reckless driving.

The user of other drugs, however, can experience a crisis simply by the purchase or possession of a substance like marijuana. In the U.S., a few states have changed the laws in this regard, but the use of drugs other than alcohol is still predominantly a political issue. Unfortunately, at present little effort is made in the public arena to distinguish between the *user* of drugs and the *abuser* of drugs.[8] Many crises, such as arrest and imprisonment of people using illegal drugs, appear to occur by design of the social system. These crises are perpetuated by other practices such as racism and political pay-offs in exchange for information about drugs. In fact, the most serious drug abuse problems receive the least attention. The most widespread and dangerous abuse problems today are alcoholism and the overuse or misuse of prescribed drugs: both legal.[7]

RAPE

Because of society's attitude toward the crime of rape, the crisis of rape victims has not received appropriate attention until very recent years. Efforts of feminists and others who have become sensitized to the horrors of this crime against women are slowly bringing about necessary changes in the legal system. This system results in a double victimization of the woman or girl who has been attacked. We still have a long way to go in reforming that system. Some rape victims are still greeted with attitudes of contempt, blame, or disbelief. Also, rape, as one of the common crimes of war, still goes unpunished. Yet there is no question (society's attitudes aside) that girls and women who have been raped are people in crisis.[9] They feel angry, fearful for their lives, and physically violated. Sometimes, they feel shame because of misplaced blame of themselves. These feelings all lead to a temporary halting of their usual problem solving ability. This often results in a delay in reporting the crime. Rape is sometimes accompanied by robbery and abandonment at the scene of the crime where the victim was taken by the rapist. Such a series of events further reduces the person's normal problem solving ability.

Crisis Response to the Rape Victim

The rape victim is sometimes hesitant to ask for the help she needs from family and friends. Active reaching out in the form of crisis intervention is indicated in every case of rape. This should begin with the police officer who investigates the case. Emergency room personnel who treat rape victims medically should not only listen to and support the victim emotionally, but should actively link her with follow-up crisis counseling services. Some hospital emergency rooms are staffed with such counselors. If this is not the case, nearly all large cities have rape crisis services either in connection with crisis hotlines or women's centers. Where such specialized services do not exist, rape victims should be offered the services of local community mental health agencies which exist in nearly every community.

Ann Burgess and Lynda Holmstrom in *Rape: Victims of Crisis* have described the crisis and treatment of rape victims.[9] Susan Brownmiller in *Against Our Will* deals with the historical and anthropological aspects of rape.[10] These works are especially recommended for emergency room and police personnel and for anyone who is still not convinced that rape is a serious crime and that the time to end all jokes about rape is now. MacDonald and Selkin have worked not only with rape victims, but also with rapists.[11,12] While rape is a crime that should be prosecuted, rapists nevertheless need help as well. Many rapists are not one-timers. More effective laws as well as counseling help for rapists could reduce this steadily increasing crime.

Telephone Crisis Counseling for the Rape Victim

Case Example

Characteristics of crisis and intervention techniques	Telephone interview between Elaine and crisis counselor
	Counselor: Crisis Center, may I help you?
	Elaine: I just have to talk to somebody.
Establishing personal human contact	*Counselor:* Yes——my name is Sandra——I'd like to hear what's troubling you. Will you tell me your name?
Upset, vulnerable, trouble with problem solving	*Elaine:* I'm Elaine——I'm just so upset I don't know what to do.
Identifying hazardous event	*Counselor:* Can you tell me what happened?

Characteristics of crisis and intervention techniques	Telephone interview between Elaine and crisis counselor
	Elaine: Well, I was coming home alone last night from a party——it was late——(chokes up, starts to cry)
	Counselor: Whatever it is that happened has really upset you.
	Elaine: (continues to cry)
Empathy, encouraging feeling expression	*Counselor:* (waits, listens——Elaine's crying subsides) It must be really hard for you to talk about.
Self-blaming	*Elaine:* I guess it was really crazy for me to go to that party alone——I should never have done it ——on my way into my apartment this man grabbed me——(starts to cry again)
Identifying hazardous event	*Counselor:* I gather he must have attacked you——
Self-blame and distorted perception of reality	*Elaine:* Yes, the beast! He raped me! I could kill him!——but at the same time I keep thinking it must be my own fault.
Encouraging appropriate expression of anger instead of self-blame	*Counselor:* Elaine, I can see that you're really angry at the guy——and you *should* be——any woman would feel the same——but Elaine, you're blaming yourself for this terrible thing instead of him.
Self-doubt, unable to use usual social support	*Elaine:* Well——deep down I really know it's not my fault, but I think my parents and boyfriend might think so.
Obtaining factual information, exploring resources	*Counselor:* In other words, you haven't told them about this yet, is that right?——is there anyone you've been able to talk to?
	Elaine: No——not anyone. I'm too ashamed (starts crying again)

Characteristics of crisis and intervention techniques	Telephone interview between Elaine and crisis counselor
Empathy	*Counselor:* (Listens, waits a few seconds) I can see that you're really upset——
Failure in problem solving	*Elaine:* (continues crying)——I just don't know what to do——I feel like maybe I'll never feel like myself again.
Empathy Lethality assessment Feels isolated from social supports	*Counselor:* This is a really heavy thing that's happened to you, Elaine——I really want to help you ——considering how upset you are, and not being able to talk with your family and your boyfriend, is there a possibility that you've thought of hurting yourself?
Suicidal ideas only, is reaching out for help	*Elaine:* Well, the thought has crossed my mind, but no, I really don't think I'd do that——that's why I called here——I just feel so dirty and unwanted——and alone——I know I'm not really a bad person, but you just can't believe how awful I feel (starts crying again)
Empathy Involving Elaine in the planning	*Counselor:* Elaine, I can understand why you must feel that way——Rape is one of the most terrible things that can happen to a woman (waits a few seconds)——Elaine, I'd really like to help you through this thing——can we talk about some things that you might do to feel better?
Feels distant from social resources	*Elaine:* Well, yes——I know I should see a doctor ——and I'd really like to talk to my boyfriend and my parents, but I just can't bring myself to do it right now.
Supporting Elaine's decision, direct involvement of counselor, exploring resources	*Counselor:* I'd recommend, Elaine, that you see a doctor as soon as possible——do you have a private doctor?
Decision	*Elaine:* Yes——I'll call and see if I can get in.

Characteristics of crisis and intervention techniques	Telephone interview between Elaine and crisis counselor
	Counselor: And if you can't get in right away, how about going to a hospital emergency room as soon as possible . . .?
	Elaine: OK——I'll do that.
Obtaining factual information	*Counselor:* Elaine——I gather you didn't report this to the police, is that right?
Helplessness, feeling isolated	*Elaine:* I didn't think it would do any good—— and besides, just like with my boyfriend, I was too ashamed.
Obtaining factual information	*Counselor:* Were your clothes torn and do you have any bruises from the rape?
	Elaine: No, not that I'm aware of——I just feel sore all over, so maybe I do have some bruises I can't see——I probably shouldn't have taken a bath before going to the doctor, but I felt so dirty, I just couldn't stand it.
Reinforcing decision, suggestion to reconsider reporting	*Counselor:* It's really important, Elaine, that you see your doctor soon——You may also want to reconsider reporting the rape to the police.
	Elaine: I guess maybe you're right.
Exploring continued crisis counseling possibility	*Counselor:* Elaine, considering how badly you feel about this and that you don't feel up to talking with your parents and your boyfriend yet—— would you like to come in to see a counselor and talk some more about the whole thing?
Needs help in reestablishing contact with significant people in her life	*Elaine:* Not really——anyway I really feel better now that I've talked with you——but I still can't really face my parents and boyfriend.

Characteristics of crisis and intervention techniques	Telephone interview between Elaine and crisis counselor
Encouraging further expression of feeling with significant others; paving way for this through crisis counseling	*Counselor:* This is a really big thing to handle all at one time——I'm sure you're going to have more upsets about it——especially until you're able to talk with your boyfriend and parents about it——that's one of the things a counselor can help you with—— A counselor can also help you take a second look at the pros and cons of reporting or not reporting the rape to the police.
Mutually agreed upon plan Still very vulnerable Break in normal routine	*Elaine:* I guess maybe it's a good idea——I do feel better now——but I've been crying off and on since last night——and maybe I'll start crying all over again after I hang up——besides I called in sick today 'cuz I couldn't face going to work——so I guess I'll stay home tomorrow too and come in and talk to somebody——what time?
Concrete plan mutually arrived at by Elaine and counselor	*Counselor:* How about 10 o'clock?
	Elaine: That's OK I guess.
	Counselor: How are you feeling right now, Elaine?
	Elaine: Like I said before, quite a bit better.
Reinforcement of plan	*Counselor:* Elaine, I'm really glad you called and that you're going to see a doctor and come here to see someone too——Meanwhile, if you get upset and feel you want to talk to someone again, please call, as there's always someone here——OK?
	Elaine: OK, I will——thanks so much for listening.

CHILD AND SPOUSE BATTERING

Domestic violence, particularly wife beating, is considered by U.S. law enforcement officials the most unreported crime in the country. Yet child and wife abuse is a crime in each of the fifty states. Laws protecting children from abuse are more frequently enforced than laws protecting wives.[13,14] Perhaps this is due, in part, to the natural helplessness of children which inspires most adults to aid and protect them.

However, this was not always so. Lloyd DeManse has written that the "helping mode" in caring for children is of very recent origin, and was preceded historically by infanticide and rampant cruelty toward children.[15] The historical turn away from such practices as a norm has resulted in the "Good Samaritan" laws. These laws protect physicians, nurses, and social workers from prosecution for slander when they report suspected child abuse to authorities.

Child Abuse[16,17]

Child abuse can be physical, emotional, verbal, or sexual. It happens in financially well-to-do and in poor families, in cities, suburbs, and on farms. Child abuse results in part from the cultural prerogative of parents to physically discipline their children.[18] Either or both parents, as well as older siblings, may be involved. Some serious effects of child abuse are: physical handicaps, emotional crippling (an abused child may have a poor self-image and never be able to love others), antisocial or violent behavior in later life, and death.

Everyone should be aware of the signs of possible child abuse:

- Repeated injury of a child with unconcern on the part of the parent(s) or with unlikely explanations.
- Aggressive behavior by the child which is really a cry for help.
- Generally neglected appearance.
- "Super critical" parental attitude.

Suspicions of child abuse should be reported, although we need to be cautious and not make unthoughtful false accusations. All parents make mistakes; it is the *pattern* of abuse that must be reported. The rationalization of "minding one's own business" makes neighbors and friends hesitant to report what they know about child abuse. Teachers also are in strategic positions to assist the abused child; the school is often the only recourse open to the child.[18] Although teachers are not trained to deal with disturbed parents, they *are* responsible for reporting suspected child abuse to child welfare authorities. Parents who think they are abusive or who are afraid of losing control should be encouraged to seek help on their own by calling "Parents Anonymous," a nationwide self-help organization in the United States and England.

Abuse of a child is a crisis for the parent as well as for the child. What is often forgotten is that the abused child is sometimes one whose behavior and problems cause extreme stress for even the most forbearing parent. Parents-in-crisis are, unfortunately, sometimes overlooked by health personnel attending the battered child. The tragic situation of the helpless beaten child makes it very difficult for nurses and physicians to recognize the equally great need of the battered child's parents. Whether parents bring the abused child to the hospital themselves, or whether they are found out and reported by nurses, teachers, or neighbors, they are usually guilt-ridden and shaken by the experience. In most cases, they are fearful for the child's life, remorseful about their uncontrolled rage, fearful of their own treatment at the hands of the law, and fearful of future outbursts of uncontrollable anger displaced to the child.

If nurses, physicians, and social workers can overcome their own aversion and feelings of rejection for these parents, this crisis can become a turning point in the adults' lives. Understanding the emotional needs of abusive or neglectful parents is an important base for doing crisis intervention with them. Work with parents of battered children reveals the following characteristics:

- Emotional immaturity.
- A generally disturbed life.
- Unhappy marriage.
- Feelings of inadequacy in their role as parents.
- Frequent life crises plus drug and alcohol problems.
- Deprived or abused childhood.
- Unrealistic and rigid expectations of their children.

Crisis intervention in instances of child abuse includes:

1. Encouraging the parent to express feelings appropriate to the event.

2. Actively engaging the parent to participate in planning medical care for the child. This is a corrective emotional experience moving the parent in the direction of doing something constructive for the child.

3. Enlisting the parents' cooperation with child welfare authorities who have been appropriately informed by the nurse or physician. This includes correcting the parents' probable perception of child welfare authorities as only punitive. In reality, the people representing such authorities are concerned and will help parents to carry out their parental responsibilities.

4. Referring the parent to self-help groups such as "Parents Anonymous" or "Parents in Crisis." In these groups they can share their feelings and get help for their problem from other parents in similar situations.

Follow-up of child abusing parents should include referral to a counseling agency where they can receive more extensive help concerning the underlying emotional problems leading to the crisis. Hopefully child welfare departments will facilitate this kind of parent counseling if they do not offer it themselves. Role modeling, home supervision, and parent-effectiveness training are other facets of help that should be available to these parents.

Wife Beating[13,14]

Wife battering is much more common than either men or women care to admit. Mental health agencies in the process of routinely assessing clients regarding feeling management, ways of expressing anger, and history of assaultiveness, have found that wife beating is not specific to social class or education level.* Although laws specifically forbid such action, many men have been socialized to believe that physical expression against women of their pent up rage is somehow acceptable as part of the masculine mystique. A second contributing factor is the centuries-old view of women as men's property.

---

*Physical abuse also occurs among unmarried women, though less frequently. Psychological conflicts usually account for a single woman's failure to break out of such a destructive relationship, especially when there are no children involved.

Many women put up with physical abuse because the alternatives available to them seem as bad or worse than the battering. For example, they cannot imagine the burden of supporting their children financially. Or they do not have the strength and support to follow through on a criminal complaint. This latter difficulty is complicated by the fact that in the U.S. a woman must wait until the next day (most beatings occur at night) to file a complaint. By that time she has overcome her initial shock and pain and may have been threatened with more battering if she files charges. Further threats usually occur when the police have been called, either by observing children or a neighbor.

Earlier in this chapter the numerous consequences of alcohol were noted. In Ann Arbor, Michigan, the NOW (National Organization for Women) Wife Assault Project reports that alcohol is present in 60 percent of assaults, and in 90 percent of all crisis calls received.[14] Unfortunately, as is often the case when alcohol is involved, the opportunity for positive change is frequently missed at the crisis point of wife beating. Two of the major reasons for this are:

1. Police who intervene initially in these assaults have usually not been trained in family crisis intervention. As a result, the only alternative routinely presented to the battered woman is to file a criminal complaint. Ideally, these couples should be referred to family counseling agencies as recommended in the work of Morton Bard and colleagues associated with New York police.[19,20] In one Puerto Rican community in Buffalo, New York, the routine approach used by police is to drive the man around the block and to drop him off again at the house. As one might expect, there are many repeats of this kind of call.

2. Alternative housing and child care facilities for battered wives are lacking in most communities. The first "Women's Aid" Center was opened in London in 1971 and was soon overcrowded with battered wives seeking refuge.[14] In the absence of such alternatives, an abused wife concludes that she is only exchanging one horror for another if she leaves her husband. Most women are reluctant to leave or to fight back physically. Although women do manage to physically abuse men, in most instances a woman's lesser physical strength rules out any retaliation short of murder with a weapon such as a gun or knife. In many cases experience has taught the battered wife that she will be more severely beaten

if and when she retaliates. The women are also humiliated by the experience and hate to acknowledge that their husbands have beaten them. The majority of women were brought up to believe that they must make their husbands happy. Often they put up with the abuse for years. If and when they do finally retaliate, it is often tragically, in the extreme form of murder. A NOW report reveals that in one Michigan county 33 percent of murders involved women who had "had it," and killed their husbands after years of physical abuse.[14] Crisis intervention would in many instances prevent such an outcome.

The problem of wife battering is complicated further by the lack of crisis clinics in many communities. Or, when police are trained to make referrals to clinics, some family agencies with long waiting lists are unready to accept them. Hopefully this situation will change with the development of crisis clinics in every community. In London, a Men's Aid Center has been started recently to help men who want to change their abusive behavior pattern. Marital counseling is also offered to couples who wish to maintain and improve their marriages. In the United States the NOW National Task Force on Battered Women/Household Violence is actively working to set up more shelters for battered women. In England the National Women's Aid Federation sponsors 100 Women's aid groups and 73 refuges; all London boroughs now have refuges for battered women. The aims of the National Women's Aid Federation are:

1. To provide temporary refuge, on request, for women and their children who have suffered mental or physical harassment.

2. To encourage the women to determine their own futures and to help them achieve their goals, whether this involves returning home or starting a new life elsewhere.

3. To recognize and care for the emotional and educational needs of the children involved.

4. To offer support, advice and help to any woman who asks for it, whether or not she is resident, and also to offer support and aftercare to any woman and child who has left the refuge.

5. To educate and inform the public, the media, the police, the courts, social services, and other authorities about the

battering of women, mindful that this is a result of the general position of women in our society.[21]

These efforts, along with crisis counseling emphasizing decision-making, should help increasing numbers of battered women to make choices in the direction of self-assertion, freedom, and independence.

Case Example

Mrs. Marguerite Ballard, age 31, was married for 11 years and had 5 children ages 10, 8, 5, 4, and 2. Her husband, Richard, age 30, worked in an auto factory and maintained a steady income, but drank heavily on weekends and occasionally during the week. Marguerite and Richard had frequent fights when Richard drank. It took very little to set Richard off—a wrong word by one of the children or Marguerite, or his desire to be waited on which Marguerite sometimes refused to do. Richard's battering took the form of throwing Marguerite to the floor, kicking her, and punching her in the face. Occasionally he would unclothe her and bite her to the point of bleeding. Once Marguerite threatened Richard with a knife. He said he would strangle her if she ever tried it again.

One night Marguerite left and checked herself in at the Salvation Army mission house, but after one day there, she felt guilty about leaving her children and returned home. The battering continued, often in the presence of the children. One day Marguerite was beaten unconscious. Her husband left the house and her oldest child called the police who in turn sent an ambulance. The police also called the emergency division of the local child protection agency. When Marguerite regained consciousness in the hospital, she was informed of the whereabouts of her children (in foster homes) and was offered counseling service through the hospital's social services department. Marguerite finally made the decision to divorce her husband, apply for welfare assistance, and rebuild a life for herself and her children free of the terror of physical abuse.

BIRTH OF A HANDICAPPED CHILD

Parenthood can be a crisis point even if everything occurs as expected. The type of crisis associated with role change will be dealt with in the next chapter on Transition States. The birth of a handicapped child, however, presents a serious threat to the parents' image of themselves as successful parents. Frequently the parent asks: "What did I do wrong?" "What have I done to deserve this?" Parents conclude mistakenly that something they either did or did not do is responsible for their child's handicapped condition. The degree of handicap and the parental level of expectation of a normal child are the key factors influencing the likelihood of crisis for the concerned parents. Handicaps vary greatly. Down's syndrome is a mental deficiency with distinctive physical signs: slanting, close-set, deep eyes which are often crossed; flattened nose; loose muscles; thick stubby hands; and short stature. Hydrocephalus is characterized by an enlarged head containing excess fluid. In addition to Down's syndrome and hydrocephalus, the range of handicaps varies from gross deformity, to minor physical deformity such as a sixth toe, to developmental disabilities which surface later, for example, a learning disability or hypothyroidism.[22]

Initial Crisis Point

In many instances birth defects are obvious to anyone immediately after birth. Sometimes, however, the handicap is not noticed until later when the child is obviously lagging in normal development. Whenever the handicap becomes known to the parents, the usual response is anger, disbelief, a sense of failure, numbness, fear for the child's welfare, guilt, and an acute sense of loss—loss of a normal child, loss of a sense of success as parents. The parents' initial reactions of disbelief and denial are sometimes aided and abetted unnecessarily by medical personnel who withhold the truth from them. Seventy to 80 percent of mentally retarded children also have physical disabilities, but parents should not be encouraged in the belief that when these physical conditions are remedied, the mental condition will be cured as well.

Case Example

Edward and Jane took their six-year-old girl, Anna, for a kindergarten evaluation. They were told bluntly that she required special education. They were shocked by the news. No psychological or social services had been made available to these parents. Edward and Jane had tried to ignore their daughter's obvious differences and had not questioned their physician who was noncommittal. Finally the grandparents and a sister convinced them to seek guidance from the local Association for Retarded Children.

Successive Crisis Points

Parents of children who are developmentally disabled or otherwise handicapped can experience crisis at many different points. The most common times of crisis are:

- When the child is born.
- When the child enters and doesn't succeed in a normal classroom.
- When the child develops behavior problems peculiar to his or her handicap.
- When the child becomes an adult and requires the same care as a child.
- When the child becomes an intolerable burden and parents lack the resources to care for him or her.
- When it is necessary to institutionalize the child.
- When institutionalization is indicated and parents cannot go through with it out of misplaced guilt and a sense of total responsibility.
- When the child is rejected by society and parents are reminded once again of their failure to perform as expected.

The classic signs of crisis are easily identified in most parents of handicapped children:

FEELINGS: They deny their feelings and may displace their anger on doctors, nurses, or each other. They feel helpless about what to do. Essentially, they feel they have lost a child as well as their role as successful parents.

THOUGHTS: Expectations for the child are often distorted. The parents' problem solving ability is weakened; they lack a realistic perception of themselves as parents and sometimes expect the impossible. In short, they deny reality.

BEHAVIOR: Sometimes parental denial takes the form of refusing help. Sometimes help is not readily available, or parents are unable to seek out and use available help without active intervention from others.

The following case illustrates these signs of crisis and the manner in which a maternity nurse successfully intervened.

Case Example

Mona Anderson, age 31, was married for 10 years and finally became pregnant after many years of wanting a child. Her baby girl was born with Down's syndrome. When Mona was tactfully informed of this by the physician and nurse in the presence of her husband, she became hysterical. For four days she refused to look at the baby. Whenever the nurse attempted to talk with her about the baby's condition, she denied that she could give birth to a "defective child." The nurse allowed her this period of denial, but gradually and consistently informed her of the reality of her child's condition. During this time, her husband was also very supportive. Neither he nor the nurse insisted that she see the baby before she was ready.

Four days after the delivery, she asked to see the baby. When the nurse brought the baby in, she broke down, crying "All I wanted was a normal baby—I didn't expect a genius." Mona continued to grieve over her loss of a normal child. Gradually she was able to talk with the nurse about her hopes for her child, her sense of loss, and what she could and could not expect of her baby girl. While the nurse could not answer all of Mona's or her husband's questions, she referred them to a children's Institute for Genetic Counseling.* They were also given the name and number of a self-help group of parents of children with Down's syndrome.

The nurse was helpful also to Mona's family who were drawn into the crisis orbit. Mona's sister had had a baby two months previously. She concluded, wrongly, that she should not come to visit Mona with her normal baby because such a visit would only remind Mona again of her "abnormal" baby. The nurse counseled the family members against such a move as it would only support Mona's denial of the reality of her child's condition.

The nurse, in the course of her ordinary work in a maternity ward, practiced successful crisis intervention by supporting Mona through her denial and mourning periods, offering factual information about the reality of Down's syndrome, and actively linking Mona to her family as well as to outside resources who could continue to help in the future.

Giving birth to a premature infant is another crisis affecting a mother's self-image. She often feels a sense of failure in not producing a full-term infant. The parents' crisis responses and the recommended intervention techniques are similar to those described above. The reader is referred to Parad and Aquilera and Messick for further details regarding response to this crisis situation.[24,25]

SUMMARY

One's image of self is part of the very self itself. A person's body—its appearance, wholeness, and beauty—cannot be separated from the

---

*Opinions differ about the value and ethical implications of genetic counseling. For a fuller discussion of this point see Restak's "The Danger of Knowing Too Much."[23]

way one perceives of the self. Mutilation of the body by accident burns, or surgery, slow destruction of the body by chemicals or a wasting disease, attack of one's body by rape or other crime, or failure of our body to produce as expected, are crisis points so very close to home because they touch our very selves. Most of these crises do not occur in mental health or crisis clinics but out in the world of the police officer, in hospitals, in dark alleys or in people's homes. Much can be done for people in these crisis states if the right kind of help is available at the right time.

References

1. Grace, Helen K., ed. "Crisis Intervention." In: *Nursing Clinics of North America*. Philadelphia: W. B. Saunders Company, March 1974.

2. McCloskey, Joanne Comi. "How to Make the Most of Body Image Theory in Nursing Practice," *Nursing 76*, 6:68–72, May 1976.

3. "The Concept of Body Image." In: *Nursing Clinics of North America*, Ruth L. E. Murray, ed. Philadelphia: W. B. Saunders Company, December 1972.

4. Kuenzi, Sandra Hicks, and Mary V. Fenton. "Crisis Intervention in Acute Care Areas." *American Journal of Nursing*, 75:830–34, May 1975.

5. Polak, Paul. "A Model to Replace Psychiatric Hospitalization," *Journal of Nervous and Mental Disease*, 162:13–22, No. 1, 1976.

6. Shannon, Joseph. "Politics of Heroin and Alcohol." Workshop: Role of the Suicide Prevention Center in Substance Abuse Treatment. Ninth Annual Meeting, American Association of Suiciodology, Los Angeles, April 1976.

7. Rogers, Maurice J. "Drug Abuse: Just What the Doctor Ordered." *Psychology Today*, 5:16–24, September 1971.

8. Yankelovich, Daniel. "How Students Control Their Drug Crisis." *Psychology Today*, 9:39–42, October 1975.

9. Burgess, Ann Wolbert, and Lynda Lytte Holmstrom. *Rape: Victims of Crisis*. Bowie, Maryland: Robert J. Brady Company, 1974.

10. Brownmiller, Susan. *Against Our Will*. New York: Simon and Schuster, 1975.

11. MacDonald, John M. *Rape Offenders and Their Victims*. Springfield, Illinois: Charles C Thomas, 1971.

12. Selkin, James. "Rape." *Psychology Today*, 8:70–76, January 1975.

13. Gingold, Judith. "Most American Violence Happens in the Home." *Ms.*, 5:51–54, 94–95, August 1976.

14. "Do It NOW." Bulletin of the National Organization for Women, 9:3–8, June 1976.

15. DeMause, Lloyd. "Our Forbears Made Childhood a Nightmare." *Psychology Today*, 8:85–88, April 1975.

16. "What Everyone Should Know About Child Abuse." Greenfield, Massachusetts: Channing L. Bete, Co., Inc., 1976.

17. Carter, Bryan D.; Ruth Reed; and

Ceil G. Reli, "Mental Health Nursing Intervention with Child Abusing and Neglecting Mothers." *Journal of Psychiatric Nursing and Mental Health Services,* 13:11–15, September–October 1975.

18. Manley-Casiner, Michael E., and Beth Newman. "Child Abuse and the School." *Canadian Welfare,* 52:17–19, September–October 1976.

19. Bard, Morton, and B. Berkowitz. "Training Police as Specialists in Crisis Intervention," *Community Mental Health Journal,* 17:315–17, Winter 1971.

20. Baracos, Harvey A. "Iatrogenic and Preventive Intervention in Police-Family Crisis Situations." *International Journal of Social Psychiatry,* 20:113–21, Spring-Summer 1974.

21. "National Women's Aid Federation." London, England, 1976.

22. Hutt, Max L., and Robert Gwyn Gibby. *The Mentally Retarded Child, Development Education and Treatment.* 3rd ed. Boston, Massachusetts: Allyn and Bacon. Inc., 1976.

23. Restak, Richard. "The Danger of Knowing Too Much." *Psychology Today,* 9:21–23, 88–93, September 1975.

24. Kaplan, David M., and Edward A. Mason. "Maternal Reactions to Premature Birth Viewed as an Acute Emotional Disorder." In: *Crisis Intervention: Selected Readings.* Howard J. Parad, ed. New York: Family Service Association of America, 1965.

25. Aquilera, Donna C., and Janice M. Messick. *Crisis Intervention.* 2nd ed. St. Louis: C. V. Mosby Company, 1974.

CHAPTER 8

Crises of Transition States

INTRODUCTION

In transition states we move from one stage of development to another, from one physical settlement to another, or from one role to another. Throughout this book, maturational crises are presented as a normal part of human growth and development. When unanticipated hazardous events occur at the same time, or when anticipated moves or role changes produce added stress, our potential for crisis increases.

In some societies, for example, in the Cherokee Nation of Native Americans, women past menopause acquire a role of special status and esteem. Cherokee women look forward to transition through menopause and the special privileges that will follow this stage of development.[1] In contrast, white Western attitudes toward middle age devalue people who no longer have the cherished signs of youth.

Transition states which are frequently the occasion of crisis are:

Parenthood
Adolescence and Young Adulthood
Mid-life
Promotion and Success
Migration
Retirement
Death.

During these and other transitional situations, the person experiences a loss of familiar, secure routines and supports. He or she also faces a challenge to perform equally well in the new anticipated role. Sometimes the challenge becomes a real threat: Will I succeed or fail? What will people think if I fail? I think I'd just as soon stay where I am . . . keep on doing what I'm doing.

Parents must adjust themselves to include a third, fourth, or fifth member in their family group. Such adjustment is especially difficult for parents of first-borns. Adolescents and young adults must give up the security of dependence on parents and accept new roles in society: responsibility in the work world, and achieving a capacity for intimacy in one's chosen sex role.

Midlife is the occasion of crisis for many. Familiar parenting roles may no longer fill one's day. Some are threatened in their sexual roles. Both men and women may perceive their lives at middle age as quickly slipping away before they have achieved what they wanted for themselves. The O'Neills in *Shifting Gears*,[2] and Gail Sheehy in *Passages: Predictable Crises of Adult Life*[3] present useful insights for people in this transitional stage.

The person who is promoted to a more prestigious position may feel incapable of performing as expected in the new role. Suicide studies reveal that a number of individuals kill themselves after a long awaited promotion rather than face possible failure in the new role.

Moves across country or to a different continent require leaving familiar surroundings and friends for a place with many unknowns. Even though the would-be mover may have many problems in the place called "home," at least he or she knows what the problems are. Pulling up stakes and starting over can be an exciting venture for some; others find it an occasion of crisis.

Some people anticipate retirement as a high time of life. For most in the West, however, retirement signifies loss of status, a reduced standard of living, and a feeling of being discarded by society. The experience, is even more pronounced when one is forced to retire at an early age due to illness or other disability. It is a time of considerable stress not only for the retired person, but also for family members, especially wives who do not work outside the home. Suddenly a homemaker has to adjust to having at home all day a husband who often feels worthless and who may have developed few outside interests or hobbies apart from work.

Death is not so much a crisis in itself, but becomes one for the dying person and survivors because of the widespread denial of death as the final stage of growth. Through the work of Elizabeth Kubler-Ross and many others, we have made some inroads in dealing with death openly.[4] However, ours is still very much a death denying society. Thousands of physicians, nurses, and families still refuse to discuss the subject openly with the dying person.

As in the previous illustrations of crises threatening health and self-image, people experiencing transition state crises rarely come to the attention of mental health or crisis specialists in the early stages of stress. Much more frequently, they are seen initially by individuals in the following roles:

1. Teachers, pastors, school guidance and residence counselors who see troubled parents, young people, and newlyweds.

2. Nurses in maternity wards caring for the new mother and, hopefully, father, too.

3. Caseworkers in the Travelers' Aid Association who help travelers in distress.

4. Employers and industrial nurses who notice the depression and poor performance of a newly promoted or transferred worker.

5. Public health and nursing home staff who work with retired or disabled older people.

6. Physicians, nurses, and ministers.

Crisis intervention is, of course, already being practiced by these helpers, with or without the assistance of mental health or crisis specialists. The case examples which follow are intended to enhance the crisis intervention function of workers in settings where crises of transition states often have their beginnings.

PARENTHOOD[5,6]

The state of parenthood places continuous demands on a person from the time of an infant's conception until at least the child's eighteenth birthday. Many people assume the role of parenthood willingly. Such parents regard their children as a welcome burden. The unique pleasure and challenge of bearing a child and nurturing her or him through the hurdles of childhood into adult life outweigh for many the ordinary problems of parenthood.

Some parents fall into their role unwillingly or as an escape from other less tolerable roles. Consider, for example, the adolescent who is seeking relief from a disturbed family home and uses pregnancy as a means of trying to force an early marriage. Or the woman who may have many more children than she can properly care for emotionally and physically. Some women have been socialized to view themselves as having no other significant role than mother and wife. Others do not limit their pregnancies because of religious beliefs forbidding artificial contraception. Still others lack knowledge and means of limiting their pregnancies, even if they chose to do so. Unwanted children and their parents are more crisis-prone than others. Emotional, social, and material poverty are important contributors to their crisis vulnerability.

Stresses and Crisis Points of Parenthood

All parents—whether their children were wanted, or not—are under stress and strain throughout their parental lives. Parenthood is a state requiring constant giving of self. Except for the joy of self-fulfillment and watching a child grow and develop, the parent-child relationship is essentially nonreciprocal. Infants, toddlers, and young children need continuous care and supervision. In their natural state of dependency they give, in return for their parents' caring, the love of a child, a needy love which says, in effect, "I am helpless without you, take care of me, protect me."

Some children, in fact, are not only dependent and needy, but, for various reasons, are a source of grief to their parents. Their difficult behaviors, for example, trouble at school or drug abuse, usually signal that there is trouble in the parents' marriage or in the entire family system.

Sometimes parents try to deal with these troubles by themselves, struggling for a long time with whatever resources they have. Often, they are ashamed to acknowledge that there is a problem with the child. They view any problem as a reflection of self-failure. Still other parents may not have access to child and family resources for help, either because the resources do not exist or because they cannot afford them.

Chronic problems of parenthood often persist until a crisis occurs and finally forces parents to seek outside help. Common examples of such ongoing problems are a child's getting into trouble with the law; running away from home; becoming pregnant during adolescence; expulsion from school; or making a suicide attempt.

Parents usually seem surprised when these problems occur, but evaluation of the family system often reveals signs of trouble that were either unobserved or ignored. Teachers, recreation directors, and guidance counselors who are sensitive to the needs of children and adolescents can help prevent some of these crises. They should urge parents to participate in a family counseling program *early,* at the first sign of a problem. It is important for counselors and parents to keep in mind that even if preventive programs are lacking, it is never too late to act. An acute crisis situation provides, once again, the opportunity for parents and child to move in the direction of growth and development, and for fulfillment of the parents' needs for generativity.

Common crisis points for some parents are:

DIVORCE: The parent gaining custody of the children has the responsibility of childrearing alone, at least until remarriage; the other parent experiences a loss of his or her children. The loss is more acute if the divorced parents live in different cities or different parts of the country. If the loss is accompanied by a sense of relief, guilt usually follows. To assuage guilt, the relieved parent may shower the children inappropriately with material gifts or accuse the other parent of being too strict, inattentive, or uncaring. This crisis point of parenthood can be anticipated whenever the divorce itself is a crisis for either parent. Divorce counseling can help avoid future crises.

SUDDEN INFANT DEATH: This is also known as crib death. The exact cause of these deaths is still unknown, hence the medical designation: Sudden Infant Death Syndrome.[7] The parent or baby sitter finds the infant dead in its crib with no warning signs. They bring the infant to the hospital emergency room in the desperate but futile hope of reviving it. The parents or caregiver have fears and guilt that they may somehow have caused the death. Complicating this crisis is the fact that emergency room staff may look suspicious or blaming of the parents. And, indeed, the emergency staff must rule out the possibility of child battering, which they cannot do without examination.

In either case, emergency personnel should withhold judgment. Parents in both instances are in crisis and need understanding and support. Those in crisis over sudden infant deaths should be offered the opportunity to express their grief in private and with the support of a nurse. Hospital chaplains can often assist during this time and should be called in accordance with the parents' wishes. Parents should also be given information about self-help groups of other parents whose infants died suddenly in their cribs. (See Chapter 11 for case example.)

ILLNESS OF A CHILD: Similar intervention is indicated for parents whose children are seriously ill, have had a serious accident, or are dying. The modern, relaxed visiting regulations in most hospital wards for children has reduced the crisis possibility at this time for both parents and child. Parents are encouraged to participate in their child's care, so that the child feels less isolated and anxious about separation from parents, and the parents feel less threatened about their child's welfare.

BIRTH OF A STILLBORN CHILD: The response of a mother at this crisis point is similar to that of mothers giving birth to a handicapped child: anger, loss, guilt, questioning "Why did this have to happen to me? What did I do wrong? What did I do to deserve this?"

Grief Work

Case Example

Gerry Henderson, age 29, gave birth to a stillborn child. Immediately after delivery the child was taken out of the delivery room and never shown to Gerry who was asleep from the anesthetic given her. The obstetrician told Gerry's husband Tom that the child was stillborn and convinced him not to see the baby though Tom asked to do so. Together with hospital authorities, Tom, who was numb and frightened, made immediate arrangements to cremate the baby without consulting Gerry. The baby was not given a name. No one from the family attended the burial service which was handled completely by hospital authorities. Tom was convinced that this was the best way to spare his wife any unnecessary grief.

When Gerry woke up, these facts were announced to her by her husband and the nurse. She was beside herself with shock and grief, but Tom thought it best not to talk about the matter. Gerry was essentially alone in the hospital with her grief. The nurses had a hard time handling their own grief, so were unable to offer Gerry support.

When Gerry returned home from the hospital, her cousin invited her to come for a visit. Gerry's cousin had just had a new baby herself. Gerry felt she could not possibly face seeing another woman's live and healthy baby without breaking down. She was urged, however, to make the visit by her mother-in-law and husband who said, "After all, you have to face reality sometime." Gerry refused to go to her cousin's house, though this caused further strain between her and her husband. Gerry's pent up grief and tension reached such a point that she began hearing the sound of a baby crying at various times during the day and during her sleepless nights. Since she knew there was no baby, Gerry was afraid she was going crazy. She was barely able to complete simple household chores.

After one week of this lonely agony, Gerry walked into a nearby crisis clinic, where she cried inconsolably and poured out the above story to a counselor. Gerry's husband Tom was asked to come in as well. Through several crisis counseling sessions, it was learned that Tom was as shocked and grief-stricken as his wife, but believed that the only way to handle the infant's death was to "act like a man," not talk about his grief, and try to keep going as though nothing had happened. The cremation and not naming the baby were Tom's symbolic way of trying to wash (or burn) away the problem. Gerry's mother-in-law and cousin joined in one of the counseling sessions. They were helped to understand the importance of not forcing Gerry to relate to another child while she was actively grieving over the loss of her own.* Their support was enlisted in ways that Gerry decided would be helpful to her at this time.

After Gerry and Tom did their "grief work" with the help of the counselor, Gerry was able to resume a normal life without the child she had anticipated. Eventually she was also able to relate to her cousin and her cousin's child without hostility.

Normal "grief work," as defined by Erich Lindemann, consists of:[8]

1. Acceptance of the pain of loss. This means dealing with the memory one has of the deceased. In Gerry's case she had to openly discuss what she had anticipated in her child, but lost forever.

2. Open expression of pain, sorrow, hostility, and guilt. The person must feel free to mourn openly his or her loss, usually by weeping, and to express feelings of guilt and hostility. For example, Gerry was angry with her cousin for having a healthy child; she felt guilty about her anger and blamed herself for giving birth to a stillborn infant.

3. Understanding the intense feelings associated with the loss, for example, fear of going crazy, as a normal part of the grieving process. When these feelings of sorrow, fear, guilt, and hostility are "worked through" in the presence of a caring person, they gradually subside. The ritual expression of grief, as in funerals, greatly aids in this process.

4. Eventual resumption of normal activities and social relationships without the person lost. Having worked through the memories and feelings associated with one's loss, a person

---

*Note, in contrast, that Mona Anderson (Chapter 7) was encouraged to see her sister's child after grieving and accepting the reality of her own child's condition; whereas Gerry's loss was denied and, unlike Mona, she was unsupported in her grief and pressured with a reality she was unready to accept.

acquires new patterns of social interaction apart from the deceased.

When people do not do "grief work" following any profound loss, serious emotional, mental, and social problems can occur. All of us can help people grieve without shame over their losses. This is possible if we are sensitized to the importance of expressing feelings openly in order to prevent serious psychological damage later.

A Family in Crisis

The following example illustrates several intervention techniques for parents and children in crisis.

Case Example

Donald Page, 44, and Ann Page, 39, have been married for 20 years and have four children: Alice, age 20; Michael, 18; Betsy, 14; and Gary, 9. Donald worked in a local steel mill and was drafted into service at age 26. Two years later he returned home as a disabled war veteran. Ann worked as a secretary prior to their marriage and returned to work when her husband was drafted into the service. When her husband returned, Ann continued to work in spite of her husband's objections. The Pages moved to a small farm on the outskirts of a large city. They leased the farm land and Donald stayed at home most of every day doing odd jobs around the farm. He did little by way of routine house chores, even though Ann worked full time outside the home. The Pages had a bleak social life and, in general, their marriage and family life was strained.

The Page children felt isolated because it was difficult to see their friends except during school hours. Alice had a baby at age 17 and dropped out of school during her junior year in high school. She and her mother quarreled constantly over responsibility for the baby who lived in the family house. After two years of their fighting, Alice's parents asked her to find a place of her own, which she did. Meanwhile, Ann threatened to report Alice to child welfare authorities if she didn't start assuming more responsibility for her child. Ann really wanted to keep Alice's baby herself, for she had wanted another child. Alice also talked about giving her baby away to her mother.

Meanwhile, Betsy was reported to be having problems in school, and teachers suspected her of taking drugs. Betsy had been belligerent at home for a long time, refusing to do any chores and staying out late. Finally, Betsy ran away from home and was returned by police after having been gone three days. Donald and Ann were advised by police and school authorities to seek help for Betsy. They did not follow through and continued alone in their struggle to control her behavior. Michael tried to help both Betsy and his parents, but felt pulled between the two parties. Gary was the "spoiled" child, and occasionally asked why everyone was fighting all the time.

Betsy's school problems heightened, she was threatened with expulsion and a week later ran away again. This time when police found her, she threatened suicide if she was taken home. Police therefore took her to a community mental health emergency service. Betsy was seen by a crisis counselor; she begged to be placed in a detention center rather than go back home.

After several hours with Betsy, the counselor was able to persuade her that she could help Betsy and her family make things more tolerable at home and that a detention center was no place for a girl her age—at least not until other alternatives had been tried.

Meanwhile, Betsy's parents were called and asked to come to the crisis clinic. Betsy felt hopeless about anything changing at home, though she expressed the wish that somehow things could get better. Two situations she particularly hated were (a) her father and mother fighting about what she, Betsy, could and couldn't do, whom she could and couldn't see; and (b) her mother's and Alice's constant fighting about Alice's baby. If these situations at home didn't change, she said she just wanted to die.

The Pages agreed to a contract for eight crisis counseling sessions which were to involve the entire family, including Alice. One of the sessions was with the parents, Alice, and Betsy only. Another session was with the parents, Betsy, the school guidance counselor, principal, and home room teacher.

Goals of the counseling sessions were:

1. Improve communication among all members of the family and cut out the contradictory messages Betsy was receiving.

2. Help family members detect signs of distress among themselves and learn to listen to and support one another when troubled.

3. Work out a mutually agreeable program of social outlets for Betsy.

4. Work out a plan to divide the chores in a reasonable and consistent way among all family members.

5. Arrive at an agreeable system of discipline which included rewards and punishments appropriate to various behaviors.

6. Help Alice make some satisfying decisions regarding herself and her baby.

7. Develop a plan to work cooperatively with Betsy's teachers and the guidance counselor to resolve Betsy's problems in school.

Family members agreed on various tasks to achieve the above goals. For example: Donald and Ann would set aside some private time each day to discuss their problems and disagreements about discipline out of the children's hearing. Betsy agreed to carry through on certain chores around the house. If she failed to do so, Ann agreed *not* to pick up after her and to discuss disciplinary measures with Donald. Alice would seek individual counseling to assist her in making a decision about herself and her child.

Two of the counseling sessions were held in the home which was observed to be quite crowded. One result of this meeting was helping the family to work out ways of assuring individual privacy in spite of cramped quarters.

The threat of Betsy's suicide attempt and school expulsion were crisis points which moved Donald and Ann to work on underlying problems in their marriage. These problems made parenthood more difficult than it might otherwise have been. After eight crisis counseling sessions, the Page family existence was much less disturbed but by no means tranquil. However, Betsy was no longer in danger of being expelled from school, and she at least preferred her home to a detention house. Donald and Ann Page agreed to marriage counseling for themselves after termination of the crisis counseling contract. Hopefully, their future years as parents will be less burdensome as a result.

ADOLESCENCE AND YOUNG ADULTHOOD[9,10,11]

Opinion regarding the age span of adolescence varies in different cultures and according to different theorists. The Joint Commission on Mental Health of Children in the United States considered youth up to age 25 in the program it recommended for youth in the 1970's. The extent of adolescence is influenced by such factors as: (a) length of time spent in school; (b) age at first marriage; (c) parenthood or the lack of it; (d) age at first self-supporting job; and (e) residence: with or apart from parents. In general, adolescence can be considered in two stages—early and late. Late adolescence overlaps with young adulthood, particularly for those who prolong vocational and educational preparation into their early and mid-twenties.

Developmental Challenges and Stresses

During early adolescence the major developmental task is achievement of "ego identity." The adolescent struggles with the issue of independence and freedom from his or her family. On the one hand the young person is very much in need of the family's material and emotional support. On the other hand, he or she may resent the continued necessity of dependence on parents. Interdependence, a balance between excessive dependence and independence, is a mark of growth during this stage.

Developmental tasks during late adolescence include finding and adjusting to a place in the world apart from immediate family, and developing a capacity for intimacy in one's chosen sex role. These tasks may involve finding and holding a satisfying job; succeeding in college, technical training, or graduate school; and choosing and adjusting to a life style such as marriage or communal living.

Success with the developmental tasks of adolescence depends to a great extent on what happened during one's infancy and childhood. An unhappy childhood is the usual precursor to unhappiness for an adolescent or young adult. Successful completion of the tasks of adolescence or young adulthood can be accomplished only if parents know when to "let go," and do not prevent the young person from making decisions he or she is capable of making independently.

Our society has been described as youth-oriented. This description cannot be interpreted to mean that we particularly value younger people. Rather, it speaks to our devaluation of older people. In fact, the necessary services for both normal and troubled young people are grossly lacking in many communities.[12] For example, many schools do not have guidance counselors or school social workers. The youthful population in every community should have access to emergency hostels where young people abused by their parents or seeking refuge from conflict can go. There should be housing for youthful offenders in special facilities with a strong community focus (*not* with hardened criminals).

Young people today simultaneously have golden opportunities and face terrifying threats, often with insufficient support in either instance. Suicide is the second leading cause of death among teenagers, second only to accidents. This fact is a powerful indicator of the stresses today's youth experience in facing both the challenges and threats they encounter.

Helping Young People

Parents, teachers, pastors, youth directors, guidance and residence counselors, and school nurses are in powerful positions to help or hinder young people in their quest for identity and a meaningful place in society. Help may mean simply being available and attentive when a young person is upset and wants to talk; offering information the young person needs in order to make decisions about career, education, marriage, etc.; guiding young people in the use of counseling and other resources when they find themselves in a crisis; or acting as a youth advocate in instances of neglect, abuse, or other injustice.

The crisis intervention principle of doing things *with* rather than *to* and *for* troubled people is particularly important to remember when trying to help the young. Since a major developmental task is finding their own unique way and achieving healthy interdependence, a counselor's inattention to this principle can defeat the purpose of the helping relationship. Certainly a young person in trouble may be in need of a caring adult to make certain decisions *for* him or her. But the same principle applies here as in work with troubled adults: The troubled person should participate in any decision affecting him or her unless it is evident that the young person absolutely cannot make certain decisions. Then an adult should be ready and available to act on his or her behalf. Some adults assume automatically that young people are incapable of making any decisions or of accepting any responsibility. In contrast, others force the adolescent to make decisions and assume responsibilities he or she may not be ready for. Either attitude spells trouble for the adolescent or young adult. Crises and on-going problems such as drug abuse and delinquency can often be avoided when young people have the support they need in weathering the storms and meeting the demands of this phase of development.

Case Example

Nora Staples, age 17, and her sister Jennifer, age 16, moved to a large city 300 miles from their home in order to get away from their abusive father. Their grandparents, the elderly Staples, invited Nora and Jennifer to stay with them although their living quarters were cramped, and they were not well off financially. Nora's and Jennifer's parents divorced when the children were eleven and ten, respectively. Their mother left the area after the divorce, and the girls have not seen her since. For four years afterwards Nora and Jennifer stayed with an aunt and uncle who lived near their father's home.

When Nora was 15 and Jennifer was 14, their father insisted that they live with him. He expected them to cook and keep house, which they did without complaint; they were afraid of what he would do if they rebelled. On weekends their father went on drinking binges. Every month or two when he came home late at night he would put both girls out of the house and lock the door. At these times they would go back to their aunt and uncle's house for a couple of days until their father insisted they come home again. The aunt and uncle were finally threatened by the father if they ever took the girls in again. When they heard this, Nora and Jennifer hitchhiked the 300 miles to their grandparents' home.

Two weeks after arrival at her grandparents' home, Nora began talking about shooting herself. The grandmother called a local crisis clinic. The counselor and Nora's grandmother talked for about fifteen minutes, after which her grandmother was able to persuade Nora to talk with the counselor. Indeed, Nora had obtained a gun and was seriously considering suicide. She felt angry with her father, though she had never let him know. She also felt guilty about leaving him, although she couldn't bear being with him any longer. Now she felt she was a burden to her grandparents and saw no point in going on. Nora agreed, however, to come in to the crisis clinic for counseling to deal with her problem. She also agreed to a plan to dispose of the gun with the help of her grandparents and the police. The counselor learned that Nora's grandparents were also angry and disgusted with their son for the way he had treated Nora and Jennifer, but that they, also, had felt helpless until now.

In spite of her problems, Nora managed to graduate from high school with honors at age 17 and was offered a scholarship from a nearby private college. She was undecided about whether to accept the scholarship or get a job to help support herself while living with her grandparents.

The service plan for Nora and the grandparental family included the following:

> 1. Individual counseling sessions for Nora: to deal with her anger and misplaced guilt regarding her father, to help her make a decision about college or work, to explore alternatives other than suicide as a way out of her despair.
>
> 2. Family counseling sessions for Nora, her grandparents, and her sister Jennifer: to help them deal together with their feelings about the situation, to find ways of supporting one another, and to find a solution to the problem of crowded living quarters.
>
> 3. Collateral conferences with the Child Welfare Department to obtain financial support for Nora and Jennifer and to enable the grandparents to find a larger residence.

Nora, Jennifer, and their grandparents were also advised of their rights and the resources available to them to press charges of neglect against the father if he came to take the young women away with him, as they suspected he would do within weeks.

By the end of eight individual counseling sessions and six family sessions Nora was no longer suicidal. She had learned that the scholarship would be available to her the following year if she chose to delay going to college. She therefore decided to stay with her grandparents for a year and get a job to help support herself. One factor in this decision was Nora's realization, through counseling, that she was very resentful of having had to assume so much responsibility for her father and his needs. She said she wanted the chance to live in peace and quiet with a family for a while. Also, she felt deprived, as a result of her disturbed home situation, of the opportunity to live the way most teenagers do.

She also gained the strength and courage to follow through on charges filed against her father when he came—demanding that she and Jennifer return to his home. A restraining order was obtained against the father, and he was directed by family court to make regular support payments to Nora and Jennifer while they continued to live in their grandparents' home. Custody of Nora and Jennifer was vested with their grandparents.

A six month follow-up contact revealed that Nora was much happier and had decided to go ahead with college plans. She was advised of college counseling services available to her should she become upset and suicidal again.

INTIMATE RELATIONSHIPS: BEGINNINGS AND ENDINGS

Throughout this book we have noted the importance of intimate relationships and how a break in intimate attachments can lead to crisis. In this section, the beginnings and endings of intimate relationships are discussed briefly as one of the major transition states.

An intimate relationship refers to any close bond between two persons in which there is affection, reciprocity, mutual trust, and a willingness to stand by each other in distress without expectation of reward. The emphasis in this definition is on psychological and social intimacy, though a sexual relationship may also exist. Sexual relationships, on the other hand, do not necessarily imply intimacy as here defined.

Intimate relationships are essential to individuals and as such comprise part of the basic fabric of society by forming social bonds between people. Some of the more common relationships of intimacy are: (a) courtship, (b) marriage, and (c) deeply committed friendships outside marriage. Entering into such a relationship is a major event with important social-psychological ramifications. Some of the more common endings of intimate relationships are by divorce or widowhood (see pages 94 and 188). While divorce and widowhood are highly visible endings of intimate relationships, other less official disruptions of close bonds can be equally traumatic and crisis-producing for the individuals concerned.

Since intimacy with others is such an integral part of our lives, deep emotion and importance are attached to intimate relationships. Our feelings about these attachments affect, in turn, our thoughts and behavior in regard to the people concerned. For example, we may have unrealistic expectations of those we love, and we may behave in unusual ways when the bond between those we love is threatened or severed. Also, some people have such deep fear of possible rejection by others that they repeatedly resist offers of friendship, love, and intimacy. Crisis can occur at the beginning of such attachments or when the intimate relationship is disrupted for some reason, such as divorce, death of a spouse, or betrayal by a friend.

At both the beginning and ending of an intimate relationship the persons involved undergo a change in role and status: from single state to married, from spouse to divorcee, from associate to friend, or from friend to forgotten one. When beginning a new intimate relationship, old secure roles must be abandoned and replaced by a new unfamiliar role. If the person changing roles is lacking in personal and social resources, the taking on of a new role, such as that demanded in courtship and marriage, may be the source of crisis. Often a role change results in feelings of loss and the mourning of what one has given up. When the familiar role of lover, spouse, or trusted friend is ended, a person may lose his or her sense of security and experience crisis because a basic needed attachment is severed, and the person again faces the challenge of role and status change.

Thus transitions into and out of intimate relationships are among the more common occasions of crisis for many people. For case examples, see pages 13, 39, 128, and 283.

PROMOTION AND SUCCESS
Promotion and success would not seem to be hazardous events or occasions of crisis. And for many these events aren't. Yet suicide

studies reveal that promotion is the apparent "last straw" which leads some people to the decision to commit suicide. An anticipated promotion can also be a crisis point. The new position in a company brings with it higher rank and status as well as increased responsibility. It also requires a change in role relationships among peers. If the move is from ordinary staff worker to a management position, the person may fear loss of acceptance by the peer group he or she leaves.

The combination of loss of familiar supportive relationships at work and the challenge of an uncharted territory becomes too much to handle. A person's vulnerability to crisis in these circumstances is affected by several factors:

1. The general openness of communication channels within the company or human service agency.

2. The person's ability to openly discuss his or her questions and fears with a trusted confidante. If the person's work performance evaluation and outside evidence indicates his or her ability to do the job, the problem is probably one of self-confidence which can often be boosted by a friend or counselor. Confiding a lack of self-confidence to the "boss" at this stage might cost one the promotion.

3. The person's perception of self and how one *should* perform in a given role. People who experience promotion as a crisis are often perfectionistic; they become impatient with themselves when they make the smallest mistake.

A crisis stemming from promotion has also been called the "success neurosis." Success neurosis is frequently seen in women who are accustomed to viewing themselves in what they perceive as second-rate or second-best positions. Or if they have been socialized to view themselves primarily in the role of housewife and mother, they may become suddenly immobilized when other opportunities knock at their door. This can happen even when they have openly expressed a desire for these new horizons all their lives.

Case Example

Angie, age 37, had been doing volunteer work with the mental health association in her local community. One of her special projects was helping handicapped people run a confection stand for local Parks and Recreation Department events. Because of the high quality of her work—which she could only acknowledge self-consciously—her friends urged her to open and manage her own coffee house. She finally did so, and the project was a glowing success. Angie suddenly found herself in the limelight, a situation she had not anticipated. She couldn't believe it would last. After a few months, she began feelings tense and depressed and thought vaguely about suicide. She talked with her physician about her problem and was referred to a psychiatrist for help.

Crises associated with promotion and success are usually "quiet crises." People in this kind of crisis are not acutely upset, but feel generally anxious and depressed, and express bewilderment about being depressed. They feel disappointed that they can't measure up to their own expectations because, in light of their anticipated or actual promotion or success, they have "every reason to be happy." They are unable to sort out and relate their feelings of depression to their underlying lack of self-confidence and rigid expectations of themselves. A deep fear of failure may lead to the idea of suicide, in the event that the person really does fail.

Anxiety, depression, and suicidal thoughts may move a person in this kind of crisis to seek help. Usually he or she will go to a local crisis clinic or private therapist. Several crisis counseling sessions are often sufficient for the person to:

- Express his or her underlying fears, insecurity, and disappointment with self.
- Gain a realistic perspective concerning one's actual abilities.
- Grow in self-confidence and self-acceptance.
- Use family and friends to discuss feelings and concerns openly rather than viewing such expression as another failure.

Short-term crisis counseling may reveal deeper problems of low self-esteem, rigid role expectations, inflexible behavior patterns, and habitual reluctance to communicate feelings of distress to significant people. Psychotherapy should be offered and encouraged, for these people are high risks for suicide if other crisis situations arise.

WORK DISRUPTION
Just as promotion and success can be a source of crisis, so can work disruption or change in one's work role. In Chapters 1 and 4, involvement in meaningful work was cited as one of the basic attach-

ments necessary for personal and social well-being. Western society's value system concerning work, especially in the United States, is highlighted by a tendency to value people and to offer them respect in proportion to how much money they earn and the socio-economic status they derive from such earnings.

Conversely, the unemployed or those receiving public assistance are generally devalued. A deeply ingrained value system regarding work tends to evoke a suspicion on the part of the "haves" that the "have-nots" are ultimately responsible for their misfortune and, indeed, could remedy that misfortune if only they "tried harder." Yet social problems such as unemployment are very complex and not readily solved by simplistic answers such as "trying harder." For example, unemployment can be related to discrimination because of race, sex, age, or ill health. Usually, the unemployed are deeply regretful of their position.

Thus standards of personal success for most of us hinge on our involvement in work that is personally satisfying and of value to the external community. For example, a middle-aged woman who finds that her wife and mother roles are not enough to meet her work needs may experience crisis with repeated failure in her job hunting efforts. Or a 55-year-old man in a middle management position who is prematurely retired may begin to drink or may attempt suicide as a way of dealing with the crisis of job disruption. These and other crises related to work are within the common province of personnel directors, occupational physicians and nurses, or anyone the would-be worker turns to in his or her distress.

Case Example

Russell Owens, age 52, was a civil engineer employed for 20 years as a research consultant in a large industrial corporation. When he lost his job because of a job market surplus of engineers with his qualifications, he tried without success to find other employment, even at less pay if necessary. Family financial needs forced Jenny, his wife, age 47, to seek full-time employment as a biology instructor. She had worked only part-time before. Jenny was grateful for this opportunity to advance herself professionally. She had always resented the fact that she had made little effort previously to excell at a job, partly because Russell did not want her to work full-time. Gradually, however, Jenny became resentful of having to support herself, her husband, and their 16-year-old daughter, Gwen, plus assuming all responsibility for household tasks. She therefore urged Russell to do at least some of the housework. Since Russell had never before helped in this way, except for occasional errands and emergencies, Jenny's expectations struck an additional blow to his masculine self image beyond the sense of failure and inadequacy he already felt from his job loss.

Russell also found it difficult to follow Jenny's advice that he seek help about his problem of depression and increasing dependence on alcohol. The strain in their marital relationship increased. Jenny eventually divorced Russell, and Russell committed suicide.

Russell's drinking problem and eventual suicide might have been avoided if immediate help had been available to him at the crisis points of job loss and threat of divorce. Such help might also have resulted in a constructive resolution of Jenny's resentment of Russell concerning the housework problem.

MIGRATION

Moving can be an occasion of joy, of gaining a new lease on life or it can be a challenge and, for some, a source of deep distress. Consider the young woman who grew up in the country or a small town moving to the big city for the first time. She asks herself: Will I find a job? Will I be able to make friends. Will I be unbearably lonely? Will I be safe? Or put yourself in the position of the career person looking for bigger and better opportunities: Will things, in fact, be any better there? I wonder how I'll manage not seeing my family and friends very often? Lastly, imagine the immigrant from another country: How will those foreigners accept me? Will I ever be able to learn the language so I can get along? Who will there be to help me if things go wrong? What if I want to come back and don't have the money?

Anticipated Moves

These are a few of the many questions and potential problems faced by people who consciously plan a move with the hope that the move will improve their situation. Even in these instances, moving is a source of considerable stress. It takes courage to pull up stakes from familiar territory, even when the move would free one from many negative situations. No matter what the motive for the move, and despite the anticipation of better things to come, people in this transition state experience a sense of loss.

To prevent a crisis at this time, the person planning and looking forward to a move should avoid denying the feelings of loss that are always present. Even when a person is moving to much better circumstances, there is usually the loss of close associations with friends or relatives. As in the case of promotion or success, the would-be mover often does not understand his or her depression, which is probably related to denial of feelings and guilt about leaving friends and relatives. Understanding and expressing these feelings will help the person keep an open relationship with friends left behind, and will free the person to use and enjoy new opportunities to a fuller extent, unburdened of misplaced guilt or depression.

People who plan and look forward to a move are vulnerable to other crisis points. Once they reach their destination, the situation may not work out as anticipated: The job may be even less enjoyable than the one left. The person may lack the gregariousness to seek out and find new friends. Envisioned job opportunities may not exist. The latter was frequently the case when U.S. blacks moved from the South to the North—hoping for better employment and fairer treatment.

Migration, Isolation, and Singles

Social opportunities, especially for the single person who has moved recently to a new community, are often lacking. In many communities social events are organized around "couple relationships." Consequently, a single person may find it extremely difficult or impossible to "break in" to a tightly knit society which demands a "date" in order to participate. Many communities now have various "singles" organizations where single people of any age can make friends and enjoy a wide range of social activities. However, reports reveal that, despite the existence of these clubs, it is still difficult for a single person to establish satisfying social relationships in a new community. Fortunately, the single state is now being accepted by many as a fulfilling life style. This should make it easier for the single person to establish social contacts in a new community.

Crisis workers should always remember that social isolation and the inability to establish and maintain satisfying social attachments make one vulnerable to crises and even suicide. In general, the risk of isolation for the single person is even greater when the person is single because of divorce, separation, or widowhood. If a person is single *not* by choice and is also *not* able to make friends easily, he or she is likely to be more crisis-prone. People who have satisfying supports can do much to prevent crises among those who have moved recently and who have not yet established a reliable social support system.

Unanticipated Moves

The potential for crisis is even greater for those who do not want to move but are forced to for one reason or another. Consider the family uprooted to an unknown place because of a job transfer; the inner city dweller—especially an older person—dislocated because of urban renewal; the victims of disaster—moved from a destroyed community; political or war refugees who must leave their homeland; or the migrant farm workers who move each year in the hope of earning a marginal subsistence. Then there are the thousands of teenagers and young people who are either running away from home or simply "on the move" trying to find a niche for themselves. Often they lack housing, food, and money. Finally, there is the ordinary traveler simply enroute from one place to another, who loses money or belongings, or is victimized.

Helping the Migrant

Where is help available for the numerous people in crisis related to migration? Crisis centers and mental health agencies are appropriate for people who are under great stress before a move as well as those who are anxious and upset after the anticipated move. Social service agencies and services for aging persons should provide anticipatory guidance and crisis counseling to all groups forced to move because of a planned project such as urban renewal. Unfortunately, such support and counseling is not available or is not given in many instances.

Case Example

Mrs. Noreen Anderson, age 61, was confined to her apartment with a serious muscle disease. She was forced to retire at age 58 and had felt lonely and isolated then. She did not have family in the area but did have many friends. However, they gradually stopped visiting her after she had been confined for a year. Now her apartment building was being demolished. The heat had been turned off in March (in a cold northern U. S. city). Everyone in the building had moved out except Noreen, who was unable to move without help. Fortunately, Noreen's phone was not disconnected. She called various social service agencies for help, including the government funded Welfare Department. Finally, she was referred to a local crisis center.

An outreach crisis counselor went to Noreen's apartment. She expedited an application through HUD (Housing and Urban Development—a Federal agency) for a place for Noreen in a senior citizen's housing project. The counselor also engaged an interfaith volunteer agency to help Noreen pack, and processed a request for immediate physical supplies through Catholic Charities. Noreen was grateful for the help received after her several desperate telephone calls, but by this time she was depressed and suicidal. The crisis counselor saw her in her new apartment in the senior citizen's housing project for several counseling sessions. She helped Noreen get in touch with old friends again. The counselor encouraged Noreen's friends to visit her on a regular basis. R.S.V.P. (Retired Senior Citizen Volunteers) also visited Noreen, which helped relieve her isolation and loneliness. Noreen was no longer suicidal at termination of the counseling sessions.

Travelers' Aid Society

The Travelers' Aid Society has been doing crisis intervention work with people in transit for years. Caseworkers of this agency see travelers at the peak of their distress. The traveler who calls the Society is often without money, without resources, or fearful in a strange city. In the most extreme cases, the person may be beaten or raped. The Travelers' Aid Society caseworker gets in touch with identified relatives; assures emergency medical services, food, and emergency housing; provides travel money; and assures the traveler a safe trip home. Unfortunately the Travelers' Aid Society is poorly linked to other crisis services in most communities. It has low visibility as a social service agency and is often poorly funded. For these reasons the Society does not operate on a 24-hour basis in most places. A close working relationship with a 24-hour crisis service could remedy this situation. The relative isolation of this agency often results in the Travelers' Aid staff handling suicidal or emotionally upset travelers by themselves, without the support of crisis specialists who should be available. (See Chapter 10, Developing Community Crisis Programs.)

International Institute

The International Institute also helps people in crises related to migration. The Institute's unique contribution is crisis work with refugees and immigrants who do not know the local language. Inability to speak a country's language can be the source of acute crises related to housing, employment, health, welfare, and legal matters. Institute workers, all of whom speak several languages, assist refugees and immigrants in these essential life areas. There is an International Institute in nearly all major metropolitan areas, where most refugees and immigrants first settle. The language crisis is so acute for some immigrants that they are mistaken as insane and taken to a mental hospital. Intervention by a multilingual person is a critical part of care in such cases.

As is the case with the Travelers' Aid Society, this important social service agency has low visibility in the community and is not linked adequately with 24-hour crisis services. Hopefully, such arrangements will become routine as crisis services become more comprehensive and cosmopolitan (see Chapter 10, Developing Community Crisis Programs).

RETIREMENT[13,14]

Some people look forward eagerly to retirement. Others dread it. Much depends on the situation one retires *to*. The pleasure or pain of retirement is also influenced by the person's life style as a whole. Some key areas of concern in evaluating a person's retirement situation are:

1. Does he or she have any satisfying interests or hobbies outside of work? For many work has been the main focus all of their adult life, and most of their pleasures are essentially work related.

2. Does the person have a specifically planned retirement project? For example, one scientist known to the author wants to get a Bachelor of Arts degree when she retires.

3. Does the person have a comfortable place to live?

4. Does he or she have enough retirement income to manage without hardship?

5. Is the person in reasonably good health and free to manage without hardship?

6. Has the person been well adjusted socially and emotionally before retirement?

Even if the retired person's circumstances are favorable in all or most of these areas, retirement is still an occasion of stress. We live in a youth-oriented society. Retirement signals that one is nearing or has already reached old age; and after that, death.

Attitudes toward Older People

Old people are not highly valued in our society as they are, for example, in some Native American and Chinese communities.

Recent social emphasis on the small nuclear family has virtually displaced the extended family arrangement in most Western societies. Grandparents, aunts, and uncles are no longer an integral part of the familial scene. Today's children therefore routinely have only two adults (their parents) as role models and supporters. In cases of death, desertion, or divorce, children are even more deprived of adult models.

Older people experience even greater hardship by their relative exclusion from the nuclear family. They feel—and often are— unwanted. Often they are treated as guests, and have no significant role in matters of consequence in their children's families. When older people, because of health or other problems, do live with their grown-up children, additional tensions arise. The older person may become impatient and irritable with the normal behavior of the grandchildren. Space is sometimes insufficient to give everyone some privacy. Or the old person may seem demanding and unreasonable.

Services for the Elderly

Stress can be relieved and crisis situations prevented when special public health and social services are available to families caring for an older person. In some U. S. areas, outreach workers from the public office for aging make regular contacts with older people in their homes. Names of needy older people are obtained from pastors, welfare, and mental health workers.

Outreach service such as this is very helpful in preventing crises. Where such public services are lacking, the lives of many older people can take on a truly desperate character. The situation is particularly acute for the older person living alone who is also unable for physical or psychological reasons to get out. Senior citizen centers now exist in nearly every community. Every effort should be made to encourage older people to use the services of these centers. This may be their only real source for keeping active physically and for establishing and maintaining social contacts. Such physical and social involvement is essential to prevent emotional, mental, and physical deterioration. Some people will need help in order to use these services: money and transportation to get there, or counseling to convince the desolate why they should use the service.

Other crisis prevention services for the elderly in the U. S. are:

• R.S.V.P.—Retired Senior Citizen Volunteers—available for various kinds of volunteer tasks.

● Phone Lines, which maintains a roster of names of shut-in people (elderly or disabled) and calls to assure the person's safety and contact with a helping agency.

● Meals on Wheels, an organization making and delivering hot meals to the incapacitated.

● Help Your Neighbor and similar public and private organizations available to the isolated and distressed.

Public health nurses are another key resource. Often a visiting nurse can detect stress or suicidal tendencies. In addition to these crisis preventing services available for older people, all agencies for the aging should maintain active contact with the local crisis center. Workers from the center should assist in acute crisis situations.

Case Example

Mr. Antone Carlton, age 77, lived with his wife, Martha, in a run-down section of the city. Antone was nearly blind and had had both legs amputated, a medical necessity due to complications of diabetes. Antone and Martha survived on a poverty-level income. Martha, age 68, was able to take care of Antone. Then she was hospitalized and died of complications following abdominal surgery. Antone was grief-stricken; he and Martha were very close, and of course he was dependent on her. After Martha's death a public health nurse came regularly to give Antone his insulin injection. The nurse arranged for Antone to get help with meals through the food and nutrition service of the Welfare Department. However, this service did not meet the many needs Antone had. Within weeks the apartment became infested with roaches.

One day Antone's house was broken into, and he was beaten and robbed of the few dollars he had. This happened a few hours before the nurse's visit. She found Antone with minor physical injuries, but he was depressed and suicidal. The local crisis center was called and an outreach visit made. The crisis outreach team assessed Antone as a very high risk for suicide. Antone, however, insisted on remaining in his own home. The services of Help Your Neighbor were enlisted for Antone, especially to provide for an occasional visitor. Homemaker services from the Welfare Department were also arranged. A week later, Antone was beaten and robbed again; but he still refused to move out of his home. The public health nurse inquired about a senior citizen housing project for Antone. They refused to accept anyone as handicapped as Antone, although he did consider going this time. After a third robbery and beating a few weeks later, Antone agreed to move to a nursing home.

Institutional Placement of the Elderly

In Antone's case a nursing home placement was a means of resolving a crisis with housing, health care, and physical safety. However, admission to a nursing home is the occasion for another crisis for nearly every resident. A new nursing home resident will invariably mourn the loss of his or her own home or apartment and whatever privacy it afforded—no matter how bad or difficult the old circumstances were. New residents resent their dependence on others, regardless of how serious their physical condition may be. These problems are less acute for those who need intermediate-level care; their health status does not require such complete dependence. In domiciliary-level care, residents remain independent and are much less subject to crisis.

If a person has been placed in a nursing home by family members, he or she may feel unloved and abandoned. And some families do, indeed, abandon the old parent; often not by choice, but because they cannot handle their own guilt feelings about placing the parent in a nursing home, no matter how necessary that placement might be.

The most stressful time for a nursing home resident is the first few weeks after admission. The new resident's problems are similar to those of people admitted to other institutions: hospitals, detention facilities, or group homes for adolescents. Crisis intervention at this time will prevent many later more serious problems such as depression, suicidal tendencies, withdrawal, refusal to participate in activities, and an increase in physical complaints. Studies reveal that a significant number of elderly people simply give up after retirement or admission to a nursing home and die very soon thereafter.[15] Hopelessness in these cases is the forerunner to death. Elderly people admitted to nursing homes should also be routinely assessed for suicide risk.

Besides the feelings of loss, resentment, and rejection, some people placed in nursing homes do not get a clear, honest statement from their family about the need for and nature of the placement. This contributes further to the person's denial of his or her need to be in the nursing home.

Nursing staff who are sensitive to this crisis of admission to a nursing care facility are in a key position to prevent the negative outcomes noted above. The newly admitted resident—*and* his or her family—should be provided ample opportunity to express their feelings associated with the event. Family members should be persuaded to be honest with the resident about the *reality* of the situation. Family members will feel less guilty and more able to maintain the social contact so needed by the resident if they do not deny the situation. Staff should actively reach out to family members, inviting them to participate in planning for their parent's or relative's needs in the nursing care facility. This will greatly relieve the stress experienced by an older person during the crisis of admission and adjustment. It will also reduce staff crises. When families are not included in the planning and have no opportunity to express their own feelings about the placement, they often handle their stress by blaming the nursing staff for poor care. This is a desperate means of managing their own guilt as well as their parent's complaints about the placement.

Besides the crisis of admission, other crises can also be prevented when nursing care facilities have: (a) activity programs in keeping with the age and socio-cultural values of the residents; (b) programs involving the residents in outside community events, and (c) special family programs.

Unfortunately, the quality of nursing care facilities frequently reflects our society's devaluation of older people. Funding is often inadequate, which prevents employment of sufficient professional staff.

Retirement and the realization of old age are indeed times of stress, but need not be sources of the crises they often are. Hopefully societal attitudes toward old age will change so that this stage of life can be anticipated by more and more people as another opportunity for human growth. The United States might use as an example Denmark, a country in which retired people are called on regularly to work several weeks a year when full-time workers go on vacation.[16] There are many other opportunities in Danish society for older people to remain active and involved. Many crises in the lives of elderly U.S. citizens could be avoided if our society accorded them more honor and some post-retirement responsibilities.

DEATH
Death is the final stage of growth.[17] It marks the end of life and is the most powerful reminder we have that we have only one life to live. The beauty, rather than the horror, of this message is that, if heeded, it moves us to not waste the one and only life we have.

Vast and important as the subject of death is, consideration of it here is limited to its crisis aspect for health and human service workers.

Attitudes toward Death

Death in itself is not a crisis. As Tolstoy wrote so eloquently in *The Death of Ivan Ilych*,[18] the real agony of death is the final realization that we have not really lived our life, the regret that we did not do what we wanted to do, that we did not realize in and for ourselves what we most dearly desired. This fact was born out in research by Lisl Goodman who compared attitudes towards death of top performing artists and scientists with a group who were not performing artists or scientists, but similar in other respects.[19] She found significant evidence that the performing artists and scientists were less fearful of death, more accepting of death, and much less inclined to want to return to earth after their death, if they had a chance. They had led full and satisfying lives and were thus able to anticipate their deaths with peace and acceptance.

The denial of death, so common in our society, is a far greater enemy than death itself. It allows us to live our lives less fully than we might with an awareness and acceptance of death's inevitability.

Death has been a favorite topic of writers, poets, psychologists, physicians, and anthropologists for centuries. Volumes have been written by authors such as Feifel,[20,21] Kastenbaum,[22] Kubler-Ross,[4,17] Glaser and Strauss,[23] and others. There is even a science of Thanatology (study of death and dying). Yet, death is still a taboo topic for most people. This attitude is unfortunate. It means the loss of death as the "friendly companion" to remind us that our lives are finite. And such denial is the root of the crisis situation that death becomes for many.

Denial and Its Impact on the Dying

Many problems and crises associated with death, dying people, their families, and those who attend them in their last days might be avoided if death were not denied. Elizabeth Kubler-Ross has done pioneering work to help nurses, physicians, and ministers in becoming open, communicative companions to dying people. However, it is still an everyday occurrence in hospitals that nurses and physicians avoid talking openly with dying people about their condition. The numerous examples of avoidance cited in Kubler-Ross's classic book *On Death and Dying*[4] still apply in many situations unless the staff has had extensive sensitization concerning the practices recommended by Kubler-Ross and others.[21,24]

In our society most people whose deaths are anticipated die in institutions such as hospitals or nursing homes, not in their own homes. Ted Rosenthal, a young poet dying of leukemia, struck out against the coldness and technology that awaited him along with death in a hospital. He tells his remarkable story of facing his death and living fully until that time in a poetry book entitled *How Could I Not Be Among You?*[25] Rosenthal, on learning of his imminent death from leukemia, checked out of the hospital, moved to the country and did the things he wanted to do before dying.

Many others are not able to die in such self-chosen circumstances. Most people will continue to spend the last phase of their lives in hospitals or nursing homes. These dying people deserve to have the shock of their terminal illness tempered by those who tend them. Nurses and physicians are, of course, technically efficient and generally compassionate. However, their own denial of death often blocks them from dealing with dying patients in an honest, open manner. As a result, they may not be helpful in their interaction with dying patients and their families.

Helping a Person through the Stages of Dying
Crisis intervention for a person who has learned of a diagnosis of fatal illness begins with awareness of one's own feelings about death. This is essential if one expects to be a source of support to a dying person. Next in the helping process is understanding what the dying person is going through. Family members and everyone working with the dying should be aware of the five stages of dying described by Kubler-Ross in her book *On Death and Dying*.[4] (Her findings are based on interviews with over two hundred dying patients.):

1. *Denial:* Typically denial is expressed with "No, not me," on becoming aware of a terminal illness. People deny even when they are told the facts explicitly. Denial is expressed by disbelief in X-ray or other reports, insistence on repeat examinations, or "shopping around" for other doctors. It is the basis for the amazing continuance of various "quack" remedies. Denial is necessary as a delaying mechanism so the person can absorb the reality of

his or her terminal illness. During this phase, the person is also isolated and often refuses to talk. Nurses, physicians, ministers, and social workers must wait through this phase and let the person know that they are still there whenever he or she is finally ready to talk.

2. *Anger:* When denial finally gives way, it is often replaced by anger, "Why me?" This is even more difficult for hospital staff and family to deal with than denial as the person often expresses the anger by accusations against the very people who are trying to help. The person becomes very demanding. No one can do anything right. He or she is angry at those who can go on living. Nurses are frequently the targets of anger. It is important for them to understand that the anger is really at the person's unchosen fate, not at themselves. They must stick with the patient and not retaliate or withdraw—recognizing that the anger must be expressed and will eventually pass.

3. *Bargaining:* With the evidence that the illness is still there in spite of angry protests, the person, in effect, says, "Maybe if I ask nicely, I'll be heard." This is the stage of bargaining. The bargaining goes on mostly with God, even among those who don't believe in God. Bargaining consists usually of private promises: "I'll live a good life," "I'll donate my life, my money to a great cause." During this phase it is important to note any underlying feelings of guilt the person may have, or regrets about a life not lived as idealized for oneself. He or she needs someone who can listen to those expressions of regret.

4. *Depression:* During this stage of dying people mourn the losses they have born—body image, financial, people they love, job, role of wife, husband, or parent. Finally, they begin the grief of separation from life itself. This is the time when simple presence or a touch of the hand means much more than words. Again, acceptance of one's own eventual death and the ability to "be" in silence with another is the chief source of helpfulness at this time.

5. *Acceptance:* This follows when anger and depression have been worked through. The dying person is becoming weaker and may want to be left alone more. It is the final acceptance of one's end that is awaited quietly with a certain expectation. Again, quiet presence and communication of caring by a touch, a look are important at this time. The person needs to have the assur-

ance that he or she will not be alone when dying. Messages of caring will give such assurance.

Awareness and understanding of our own and of the dying person's feelings are the foundation of care during the crisis of a terminal illness and death. Crisis intervention with families of dying people will also be greatly aided by such awareness and understanding. Since dying alone is one of the fears of the dying person, communication with families is essential. Families should not be excluded from this final phase of life by machines and procedures which unnecessarily prolong physical life beyond conscious life. Family members who help the dying person by their presence will very likely become more accepting of their own future death. Denial of death and death in isolation does nothing to foster growth.

SUMMARY

The stages of dying described by Kubler-Ross—denial, anger, bargaining, depression, and acceptance—apply to all major changes or transition states. In each of these crisis situations we must leave something cherished and familiar for something unknown and threatening. We must mourn what is lost in order to move without terror to whatever awaits us. Preparation for transitions—whether from one role to another, one place to another, or from life to death—is always helpful in overcoming such crisis points. The best assurance for growing with each of life's moves—whether unexpected or planned—is to have lived our lives each day, at whatever age, to the fullest extent possible.

References

1. Hutchison, Sara. "Workshop: Suicide Among Minorities." Ninth Annual Meeting, American Association of Suicidology, Los Angeles, April–May 1976.

2. O'Neill, Nena, and George O'Neill. *Shifting Gears.* New York: M. Evans and Company, 1974.

3. Sheehy, Gail. *Passages: Predictable Crises of Adult Life.* New York: E. P. Dutton and Co., 1976.

4. Kubler-Ross, Elizabeth. *On Death and Dying.* New York: MacMillan Publishing Co., Inc., 1969.

5. Donner, Gail J. "Parenthood as a Crisis: A Role for the Psychiatric Nurse." *Perspectives in Psychiatric Care,* 10:84–87, No. 2, 1972.

6. LeMasters, E. E. "Parenthood as Crisis." In: *Crisis Intervention: Selected Readings.* Howard J. Parad, ed. New York: Family Service Association of America, 1965.

7. Marx, Jean L. "Crib Death: Some

Promising; Leads but No Solutions Yet." Clark, Ann. "Nursing Implications," *Nursing Digest,* 4:12–15 Summer 1976.

8. Lindemann, Erich. "Symptomatology and Management of Acute Grief." *American Journal of Psychiatry,* 101:101–48, September 1944.

9. Monea, Helen Pazdur. "Developmental Reactions in Adolescence." In: *New Dimensions in Mental Health-Psychiatric Nursing.* 4th ed. Marion Kalkman and Anne J. Davis, eds. New York: McGraw-Hill Book Company, 1974.

10. Erikson, Erik. *Childhood and Society.* 2nd ed. New York: W. W. Norton Co., 1963.

11. LeVeck, Paula J. "Developmental Reactions in Young Adulthood." In: *New Dimensions in Mental Health-Psychiatric Nursing.* 4th ed. Marion Kalkman and Anne J. Davis, eds. New York: McGraw-Hill Book Company, 1974.

12. Joint Commission on Mental Health of Children. *Crisis in Child Mental Health: Challenge for the 1970's.* New York: Harper and Row, Publishers, 1970.

13. Busse, Ewald W., and Eric Pfeiffer, eds. *Behavior and Adaptation in Late Life.* Boston: Little, Brown and Company, 1969.

14. Gubrium, Jaber F., ed. *Time, Roles and Self in Old Age.* Part IV: Retirement Roles. New York: Human Sciences Press, 1976.

15. Seligman, Martin E. P. "Giving Up on Life." *Psychology Today,* 7:80–85, May 1974.

16. Evans, Frances Monet Carter. *Psycho-Social Nursing.* New York: The MacMillan Company, 1971.

17. Kubler-Ross, Elizabeth. *Death, the Final Stage of Growth.* Englewood Cliffs, New Jersey: Prentice-Hall, Inc., 1975.

18. Tolstoy, Leo Nikolaevich. *The Death of Ivan Ilych.* New York: New American Library, 1960.

19. Goodman, Lisl Marburg. "Winning the Race with Death." Symposium: Fear of Death and Creativity, American Psychological Association Convention, Chicago: September 1975.

20. Fiefel, Herman, ed. *The Meaning of Death.* New York: McGraw-Hill Book Company, 1959.

21. Feifel, Herman. *New Meanings of Death.* New York: McGraw-Hill Book Company, 1977.

22. Kastenbaum, Robert, and Ruth Aisenberg. *The Psychology of Death.* New York: Springer, 1972.

23. Glaser, Barney G., and Anselm L. Strauss. *Time for Dying.* Chicago: Aldine Publishing Company, 1968.

24. Epstein, Charlotte. *Nursing the Dying Patient.* Reston, Virginia: Reston Publishing Company, 1975.

25. Rosenthal, Ted. *How Could I Not Be Among You?* New York: G. Braziller, 1973.

CHAPTER 9

Crises of Disaster

INTRODUCTION

"My wife has never gotten over the shock of the flood . . .
for a while I thought I'd lose her."

"I saw what a flood did to my father years ago and I made up
my mind I wasn't going to let it ruin my life."

"You'd think I'd be able to talk about it without crying."

"My uncle has never been right ever since the flood. . . ."

"A retired priest I know still wakes up in the middle of the
night with nightmares. He woke up and stepped into water up
to his knees; he saw the water was rising and his house was
floating; he hung to the ceiling on a light fixture for hours
until he was rescued from the house which had landed on a
higher spot."

"It's a very sobering experience to see that much humanity
stretched out before you. It really drives home the point
about the frailty of life."

"It's the largest fire I ever saw."

These are a few of the reactions of disaster victims and survivors
of floods in Rapid City, South Dakota, Buffalo Creek, West Virginia,
and Wilkes-Barre, Pennsylvania in 1972, and of the Beverly Hills
Supper Club fire in 1977. Floods of similar proportions occurred in
Idaho and Colorado in 1976 and aroused similar reactions.

One can only guess at the extent to which a disaster such as a
flood, fire, or earthquake affects the people who go through it. The
depth of the tragedy is very private and hardly measurable. Since formal crisis intervention is a new field, there is even less known about
its application to the crisis of disaster. Rescue operations and assistance with physical necessities occur in all disaster stricken communities throughout the world. Foreign countries may even assist in this
aspect of disaster work. For example, many countries sent aid to
Mexico and Rumania following recent earthquakes.

Project Outreach—Wilkes-Barre, Pennsylvania

Much less has been done to attend to the psychological needs of
disaster victims. James Tyhurst studied individual and social reactions
to natural disasters in Canada during the 1940's and 1950's.[1,2,3] In the
United States, disaster-stricken communities have for years received

federal aid for physical reconstruction. However, it was not until 1972 that the National Institute of Mental Health (NIMH) was prepared, organizationally, to provide disaster victims with emotional first aid services as well: that is, crisis intervention. Consequently, the community of Wilkes-Barre, Pennsylvania through its Luzerne-Wyoming County Mental Health-Mental Retardation agency received financial aid to assist in offering crisis services to flood disaster victims through Project Outreach.[4,5] The NIMH grant included funds for the training of indigenous crisis workers and for evaluation of the program. Richard McGee of Community Crisis Corner, Inc., Gainesville, Florida, headed up the training project, and Jack Zusman of Community Mental Health Research and Development Corporation, Buffalo, New York, directed the evaluation program.

The significance of this project is threefold:

1. It was the first of its kind in the United States although other disasters occurred within the same two years: The California San Fernando Valley Earthquake in February 1971; the Buffalo Creek, West Virginia flood in February 1972; and the Rapid City, South Dakota flood in June 1972.

2. It demonstrated the need for outside mental health assistance in times of disaster to supplement local resources. Local mental health workers may be disaster victims themselves and would, therefore, be temporarily unable to help others in distress.

3. It confirmed that the ability of people to help others in crisis was strongly influenced by their prior skill or training in crisis intervention.

In the Wilkes-Barre community the special federal aid for crisis intervention was a supplement to crisis services offered by other groups. For example, Jewish social services from New York deployed social workers to Wilkes-Barre to assist disaster victims.[6] Other religious groups as well—Amish, Catholic, the Salvation Army, Protestant, Mennonite, and others—traditionally offer help to disaster-stricken communities.

It is probably impossible to have an oversupply of crisis intervention services for people struck by a disaster. Norma Gordon of San Fernando notes that community mental health agencies must have prior crisis intervention skills in order to mobilize the resources necessary when a disaster occurs.[7] Health and mental health workers,

along with other community caretakers, must be prepared and know
how to put their crisis intervention skills to use when a disaster
strikes. Since there is little or no time to prepare for the disaster,
there is no time to prepare oneself, as a crisis worker, once a disaster
is imminent. Workers must be ready to apply their knowledge,
attitudes, and skills in crisis intervention.

The Rapid City Tragedy

What, then, do we need to know about disaster and its victims in
order to help? The very nature of a disaster affects the victims'
response. A disaster usually occurs very rapidly and is therefore
completely unexpected and shocking. The following account by Dana
Kizzier portrays vividly the depth of terror and destruction of life and
property that resulted from the Rapid City flood.[8]

> *And then it happened. The raging, silt-filled water burst*
> *through Clerghorn Canyon, loosening everything in its way*
> *and pushing it miles downstream, sucking human lives into its*
> *muck with no more respect than it had for cars and houses*
> *and bridges. The entire canyon had become its creek bed.*
>
> *When the people of the upper canyon heard this news, they*
> *were afraid and many of them left their homes to move to*
> *higher ground, but still some stayed, clinging to the protec-*
> *tive knowledge that it could not happen to them. They sat by*
> *their radios and waited and listened, unable to see any dis-*
> *tance because of the darkness. They could only hear the*
> *noise, the roaring constant noise as if a huge train was*
> *rumbling through their valley. By seconds, the water was ris-*
> *ing and then it battered against doors and windows. Fear*
> *rose as panes of glass shattered, followed by the rushing*
> *water, and then the people raced to second floors, attics and*
> *rooftops. It was too late to get out, they had to stay together*
> *and remain calm. Surely the house would not break away*
> *from its foundation. And then they saw a house, an entire*
> *house, bobbling past them. They heard pleading voices and*
> *turned their flashlights toward the sound. People, people they*
> *knew, were clinging to the roof, panic stricken and scream-*
> *ing, wasting the little strength they had left. "Don't you know*
> *no one can get to you, my God, don't you know?"*

*And then there were screaming voices all around them,
young voices and old voices and the brief, chilling howl of a
baby. They saw friends and neighbors struggling against this
overpowering force; grabbing onto anything that could steady
them long enough to gasp for air.*

*And then they heard it, the cracking noise of the timbers
tearing loose with the growing force and weight of the water.
They saw their car smash through the garage wall and spin
out of sight. With a sucking noise, the garage followed and
the house rocked back and forth on its foundation before it
finally broke loose, pitching on its side and dumping its riders
into the greedy river.*

*Some survived. It was probably fate that saved them, or
sheer super human strength, or anger, or revenge, or the gut
determination to live–but some did survive . . . somehow,
some way, they lived to tell about Rapid City's cold and
chilling night of terror . . . a memory that will plague them
for the rest of their lives, a lesson that taught them how precious and fragile life itself is, a constant fear of the seemingly
harmless stream where fishermen wade and children splash
and ducks paddle about contentedly.*

Fortunately, tragedies like this happen very rarely—or perhaps
not at all—in the lives of most people. Most of us are, therefore,
unfamiliar with a disaster and do not know what to expect. Our famil-
iarity is usually of an intellectual nature—not from personal experience. Moreover, the speed, the unexpectedness, and the lack of
experience with disaster greatly reduce a person's opportunity for
escape and effective problem solving.

Denial Responses to Disaster Warnings

Because a natural disaster is a dreaded experience, most people deny
the possibility that it could ever happen to them, even when they live
in high risk areas for floods, tornados, or earthquakes. Such denial is
the means people employ to go on living otherwise normal lives while
under more or less constant threat of disaster.

Escape and problem solving are also affected by the extent of a
person's denial. Jerry Jefferson in Wilkes-Barre ignored the flood
warnings and convinced his wife that they should go to bed as usual

because "it will never get so high that we'll have to move." His wife Ann was unconvinced and kept watch on the rising water during the night. Each new warning from Ann left Jerry unconvinced that the flood could really hit them. When the water reached the second floor of their house, Jerry finally gave up his denial. Fortunately this couple was rescued and did not lose their lives. Francis Kane in Wilkes-Barre absolutely refused to leave his home despite all warnings. Eventually he clung to a telephone pole and was rescued by helicopter.

In Rapid City, Davis Heraty said: "When we heard the warning we thought he (the mayor) was kidding. We just sat there, and pretty soon this big bunch of water came down the creek. We ran next door and suddenly the water was up to my neck. The top of a house came floating by and we grabbed on to that. A little way downstream we got off and climbed on the roof of a neighbor's house. We stayed there until the flood began to fall on Saturday."[9] This family was lucky to come out alive in spite of their denial.

Others may be in special circumstances that prevent them from hearing the warnings. Evelyn Schoner, age 68, was driving to and from the hospital in Wilkes-Barre to visit her husband and bring him some personal supplies. She had not listened to the car radio and therefore missed the warnings until her phone rang at 5:00 a.m. A friend advised her to pack a bag and move quickly. (This case is discussed in detail at the end of the chapter).

It is difficult for anyone who has not experienced a flood to imagine that heavy rain alone can produce enough water to flood out a whole city, or that high, tornado winds can sweep a house away. People are used to associating certain results with certain causes. When cause and effect are not familiar, it is easy to deny. For example, the individual flood victim could not imagine the results of the breaking of a dam in the Rapid City flood. Suddenly people were surrounded by huge amounts of water which could not be accounted for by the heavy rain alone. The broken dam plus the spring thaw from the nearby Black Hills produced such sudden torrents that many people were unable to escape. At least 227 people died in the Rapid City flood; it was one of the worst natural disasters in the United States.

INDIVIDUAL RESPONSES TO DISASTER

Reactions to the stress and trauma of a disaster are not unlike reactions to transition states, such as migration, or loss of a loved one through death. James Tyhurst has identified three overlapping phases in disaster reaction.[1,3] These are similar to the four phases noted by Caplan (see Chapter 1) in the development of a crisis state:

1. Impact: This is the period during which the person is hit with the reality of what is happening to him or her. In catastrophic events, the impact period lasts from a few minutes up to one or two hours. The concern of disaster victims during the impact phase is with the immediate present. An automatic stimulus-response reaction occurs—with the catastrophe as stimulus. Victims are struck later with wonderment that they were able to carry on as well as they did, especially if they break down under the full emotional impact of the experience. During the impact phase, individual reactions to the disaster fall into three main groups.

a. Ten to 25 percent of the victims remain calm, cool, and collected. They do not fall apart. On the contrary, they assess the situation for what it is, develop a plan of action, and carry through with it.

b. Seventy-five percent of the victims are shocked and confused. They are unable to express any particular feeling or emotion. The usual physical signs of fear are present: sweating, rapid heart beat, upset stomach, trembling, etc. This is considered the most "normal" reaction to a disaster.

c. Another 10 to 25 percent become hysterical or confused, or are paralyzed with fear. These victims may sit and stare into space or start running around wildly. The behavior of this group has the greatest implication for rescue workers and crisis counselors who may be on the scene during emergency operations.

Evelyn Schoner, caught in the Wilkes-Barre flood because she did not hear the warnings, fell into the first group of victim reactions during the impact phase. When she finally received the warning telephone call from a friend, she packed her bag at 5:00 a.m. and drove herself to safety to her friend's house on a hill. She had no difficulty doing this, even though, ordinarily, she depended heavily on her husband when in distress. (Her husband, as noted, was in the hospital.) Evelyn stated: "It really only hit

me afterward . . . that everything I treasured was lost . . . I just
had to drive away and leave everything behind . . . you don't
know what that's like—saving precious things all your life, then
all of a sudden they're gone—even the photographs of our
family.''

There is no research to identify or predict which people will
fall into the last group of reactors to disaster. However, prediction criteria (see Chapter 2, Predicting Crisis) indicate that the
following types of people are particularly vulnerable to crisis or
emotional disturbance following acute stress from a disaster:

- The elderly who have few physical resources and a reduced
capacity to adapt to rapid change.

- Those who already are coping with stress in self-destructive
or unhealthy ways. Some people in Wilkes-Barre just kept
drinking throughout the flood in an effort to escape the reality
they could not face.

- Those who are alone and friendless and who lack physical
and social resources they can rely on in an emergency.

During the San Fernando Valley earthquake, mental health
staff at the Los Angeles County-Olive View Medical Center
observed that some acutely disturbed mental patients reacted
more rationally than usual during the acute phase of the quake.
For example, they helped to rescue fellow patients.[10] In Rapid
City, Gertrude Lux, 71, stood for five hours in shoulder deep
water balancing her disabled grandaughter Vicki on a foam mat-
tress floating in the room where they were trapped. Many survivors in Rapid City described the horror of listening to screams,
of watching people being swept past them to their deaths, and of
being helpless to save them.[9] These incidents speak to the commonly observed heroism and humanity of disaster victims despite
personal pain and loss. People rise dramatically to the occasion
and mobilize resources to help themselves and others.

2. Recoil: During this phase there is at least a temporary suspension of the initial stresses of the disaster. Lives are no longer
in immediate danger though other stresses, such as cold or pain
from injury, may continue. In Rapid City there was the threat of

another flood a day later. During the recoil phase, survivors are typically enroute to friends' homes or have found shelter in community facilities set up for the emergency, for example, in college dormitories. They may mill around looking for someone to be with. They want to be taken care of—to receive a cup of coffee or a blanket. The disaster experience leaves survivors with an almost childlike dependency and need to be with others. At this phase, survivors gradually become aware of the full impact of what they have just been through. It is the time when both women and men may break down and weep. This is also when they have their first chance to share the experience with others. Their attention is focused on the immediate past and how they managed to survive. This phase has the greatest implication for crisis workers helping the survivors.

3. Post-Trauma: During this period, survivors become fully aware of what occurred during the impact phase: loss of home, financial security, personal belongings, and, particularly, loved ones who may have died in the disaster. One woman in the Wilkes-Barre flood collapsed and died in her flooded, damaged house when she went back to see it. This is the phase—as Jane Cantor, a Wilkes-Barre survivor put it—during which much depends on one's age and general condition: "A disaster can bring out the best and the worst in a person." Those who are too old to "start all over again" find their loss of home and possessions particularly devastating. Older people who prize the little reminders of their children and earlier life feel robbed of what they have worked for all their lives. Anger and frustration follow.

If loved ones have died in the disaster, grief and mourning predominate. Some survivors of the Rapid City flood had overwhelming guilt reactions to the death of loved ones: "Why me . . . why was I spared and not she (or he)?" Lifton and Olson have described this reaction as "death guilt."[11] Survivors somehow feel responsible for the death of their relatives or others whom they were unable to save. They can't quite forgive themselves for living, for having been spared. At the same time, they may feel relief at not being among the dead. This, in turn, leaves them feeling guiltier.

During this third phase survivors may have psychotic episodes, reactive depressions, anxiety reactions, and dreams in which they relive the catastrophic experience. Father Benedict Pfaller, chaplain of St. John's Hospital (now the Rapid City Hospital, amalgamated with another city hospital which was wiped out by the flood) observed that for several months afterward there were numerous hospital admissions for emotional disturbances related to the flood. Staff of the Child Guidance Center in San Fernando Valley counseled hundreds of parents and children following the earthquake. Children, typically, were afraid to be alone and afraid to go to sleep in their own beds.[12] Bennet, in his study of survivors of the 1968 floods in Bristol, England, found that twelve months after the disaster the health of flooded people was worse than the general health of those not in the flood and that the likelihood of older people dying within twelve months was increased.[13] Lifton and Olson report that when survivors perceive the disaster as a reflection of human callousness—rather than an act of God or nature—the psychological effects are more severe and long lasting.[11] Effects of man-made disasters are discussed later in this chapter.

This post-traumatic phase may last for the rest of one's life, depending on a person's predisaster state, the help available during the disaster and whether the disaster was natural or man-made. Evelyn Schoner said: "I don't think I'll ever be the same . . . I just can't get over it . . . I live in constant fear that there might be another flood . . . there's just no guarantee that there won't be another one."

Rescue and crisis workers have the most influence during the impact and recoil phases, while mental health workers play a key role during the post-traumatic phase. As noted throughout this book, crisis intervention—available at the right time and in the right place—is the most effective means of preventing later psychiatric disturbances. As Evelyn Schoner said: "If only I would have had someone to talk to when it happened."

COMMUNITY REACTIONS TO DISASTER[2]

The most immediate social consequence of a disaster is the disruption of normal social patterns upon which all community members depend.

In short, the community suffers a social paralysis. People are separated from family and friends and spontaneously form themselves into other groups out of the strong need to be with others.

When disaster strikes, large numbers of people are cut off from public services and resources which they count on for survival. These can include water (one of the first resources to go in the event of a flood), electricity, and heat. People are scrambling for shelter, food, and water. Traffic controls are out, so accidents increase. Heavy demands are made on local hospitals to care for the injured. In Wilkes-Barre, many people fell in the slippery mud and broke limbs, thus placing more demands on hospital staff. In Rapid City, one of the city's two hospitals was flooded out, so that all patients had to be transferred to other facilities. In flooded communities, mass inoculations are ordered to protect against disease from polluted water. Schools and many businesses are closed, creating further strain and chaos in homes and emergency shelters.

As noted, a disaster can bring out the best and the worst kinds of human behavior. Some people take advantage of the disorder and chaos to loot and steal. Citizens in disaster-struck communities noted that some businesses took advantage of the occasion to make a large profit from others' misfortune.

Normal communication networks are either destroyed or are very limited in scope. Rumors grow, in turn increasing panic and chaos. Residents not even on the scene of the disaster can be affected. Jane Cantor of Wilkes-Barre was traveling abroad and saw television pictures of dead bodies, described as flood victims, floating down the Susquehanna River. She was unable to make telephone contact with relatives and feared that they were perhaps among the dead. It was a few days later when she learned that the bodies were, in fact, from a local graveyard which was washed away in the flood. Communication problems also result in uneven distribution of information about relief benefits available from the Federal government or from other sources. This in turn causes resentments among those who feel they did not receive a fair share of the benefits.

The Schoners in Wilkes-Barre observed that the flood was instrumental in bringing the people of their neighborhood closer together. Professional evaluators observed the same phenomenon.[4] During the impact period of a disaster, there is greater cohesion among community members; later, people focus again on their individual concerns. People have to rely on one another for help and support during a disaster in a way that was not necessary before. This was illustrated dramatically in Rapid City. During the flood a group of professionals were attending a conference on death and dying. A call was put out to the conference participants to assist families in identifying members who had died. The helpers reported that many friends had already turned out to help the bereaved families.

A small group of disaster survivors gives up. These people remain despondent and hopeless for the rest of their lives. Most survivors, however, gather together and reconstruct their lives, their homes, and their community. While a number of people in Wilkes-Barre moved to higher elevations, many others rebuilt their homes on the same location, even though there is no guarantee against further flooding. This was particularly true for older people who found it too costly to "start all over" and who wanted to keep at least the comfort of a familiar neighborhood, even though they had lost everything else.

During the impact and recoil stages of a disaster, community control usually passes from elected government officials to professionals who direct health, welfare, mental health, and public order agencies. This occurs out of necessity and because of the reactions cited above. Elected officials have the important function of soliciting assistance for the community from state and federal resources. The community's priorities are rapidly redefined by professional leaders, and an emergency health and social system quickly established. This emergency network focuses on:

- Preservation of life and health: rescue activities, inoculations, treatment of the injured.
- Conservation and distribution of resources: organization of emergency shelter, distribution of supplies such as water, food, and blankets.
- Conservation of public order: police surveillance to prevent looting and accidents rising out of the chaos and scramble for remaining resources.
- Maintenance of morale: dispatching mental health, welfare, and pastoral counselors to assist the panic-stricken and bereaved during the acute crisis phase.

In summary, a community's response to disaster is poignantly revealed in the following description by Dana Kizzier of Rapid City:[8]

With all of this help from private, city, county, state and federal funds and with the compassion and support offered from an entire nation, Rapid City is restoring and rebuilding with a new appreciation for life. It has pulled together for a purpose before, but never before has it become a pulsating, throbbing being as it is now, in the aftermath of a flood.

Not one person has been untouched by the drama of the recovery. Through the silent heartache and compassion, we again remember what it is like to be patient with each other. There is a need for the comfort of physical contact as we greet each survivor with a thankful hug.

We are more aware of the things we take for granted, like the utility companies, bridges and the National Guard. We now look at the police with new respect, feel thankful for the closeness of the air force base and vow never again to pass the ringing Christmas bells of the Salvation Army without dropping in a coin. We marvel at the strength of our young Mayor and we tremble with held back tears when we see him weep for his city.

We no longer look down at the long haired so-called hippies who have worked right along side the clean cut looking men, wading in muck up to their waists in the rescue operation. We pull to the side of the road when we hear the warning of a siren and we stop a whole line of traffic to let a city truck pass on its route to the dump. We wait our turn in one long line after another. We empty our food closets and our clothes closets in an attempt to lend a hand to someone who was left with nothing. We shake our heads in dismay as the big scoops move in on the destruction to clear away the mess. We smile with pride as we see the city mowing machines, dodging in and out of the debris, clipping what is left of the grass. We are amazed at the human survival instinct as new cars are being unloaded at what remains of the car dealerships. We wonder how small children can be so untouched by the horror of disaster as we watch them laugh and run circles around their grim faced parents, and we thank God.

We go to the city-wide memorial service on Sunday, feeling sad and empty and discouraged after being threatened by another torrent of rain the night before. We see people there

*who have lost far more than we have, bearing their burden
with surprising spirit. We let some of our emotion escape
when we join in the shouting voices to sing "Battle Hymn of
the Republic." We listen to the comforting sermons, tense up
when the memorial wreath is put in its place and feel a sur-
ging love for all of the people around us. We want to cry with
all the pent up emotion, but we are being told that we must
overcome our grief, rejoice and sing and carry on with life.
And so we will, just like everyone around us will, because
people need to laugh or they will break. We come from the
memorial service feeling renewed and we try laughing and it
makes us feel warm inside and a little lightheaded.*

*On the way home, protruding from the debris and twisted
car bodies wrapped around its base, we see a billboard and
we can read only the words, "Have a nice day." We are
determined, after we swallow hard, that we will go home and
have a nice day!*

HELPING SURVIVORS OF A DISASTER

Factors Affecting Recovery

Tyhurst notes that the nature and severity of reactions to disaster
and the process of recovery are influenced by several factors:[2]

1. The element of surprise. If and when warnings are given
they should be followed by instructions of *what to do*. Warnings
followed by long silences and no action plan can heighten anxiety
and lead to the commonly observed denial of some residents that
a disaster is imminent.

2. Separation of family members. Children are particularly
vulnerable to damaging psychological effects if separated from
their family during the acute period of a disaster.[12] Therefore,
families should be evacuated as a unit whenever possible.

3. Outside help. Reasonable recovery from a disaster
demands that aid must be provided from areas not affected by the
disaster. Since military forces possess the organization, discipline,
and equipment necessary for dealing with a disaster, their instruction should include assisting civilians during disaster.

4. Leadership. As in any crisis situation, a disaster demands
that someone have the ability to make decisions and give direc-

tion. The police, the military, and physicians have "built in"
potential for leadership during a disaster. Their training should
include preparation to exercise their leadership potential appropriately.

5. Communication. Since failures in communication give rise
to rumors, it is essential that a communication network and public
information centers be established and maintained as a high prior-
ity in disaster work. Much impulsive and irrational behavior can
be prevented by the reassurance and direction that a good communication network provides.

6. Measures directed toward reorientation. Communication
lays the foundation for the reidentification of individuals in family
and social groups. A basic step in reorientation is the registration
of survivors, so that they can once again feel like members of
society. This is also critical as a means of relatives and friends
finding each other.

7. Evacuation of populations. In any disaster there is a spon-
taneous mass movement to leave the stricken area. Planned evacuation will prevent panic, especially if escape is blocked and
delayed. A failure to attend to the psychological and social problems of evacuation can result in serious social and interpersonal
problems.

Help During Impact, Recoil and Post-traumatic Phases

The helping process during disaster takes on distinctive characteristics during the disaster's impact, recoil, and post-traumatic phases.
Figure 9–1 illustrates the kind of help needed and who is best suited
to offer it during the three phases of a disaster. The figure also suggests the possible outcomes for disaster victims if help is not forth-
coming in each of the three phases.

Although disasters are unexpected, in most cases there is sufficient warning to allow people to escape even though their homes and
possessions are destroyed. This was not, however, the case in Rapid
City where 227 people lost their lives in spite of organized rescue
efforts supplemented by support from the National Guard and a
nearby air force base. In Wilkes-Barre, state mental hospital personnel were called in from outside the area to assist during the recoil and
post-traumatic phases. Federal assistance included a corps of crisis
counselors specially trained for the occasion. The Rapid City commu-

Figure 9–1. Assistance During Three Phases of Natural Disaster

	Help needed	Help provided by	Possible outcomes if help unavailable
Phase I: Impact	Information on source and degree of danger Escape and rescue from immediate source of danger	Communication network: radio, TV, public announcement system Community rescue resources: Police and Fire Companies, Red Cross, National Guard	Physical injury or death
Phase II: Recoil	Shelter, food, drink, clothing, medical care	Red Cross Salvation Army Voluntary agencies such as colleges to be converted to mass shelters Local health and welfare agencies Mental health and social service agencies skilled in crisis intervention Pastoral counselors State and federal assistance for all of above services	Physical injury Delayed grief reactions Emotional or mental disturbance later
Phase III: Post-Traumatic	Physical reconstruction Social re-establishment Psychological support concerning after-effects of the event itself; bereavement counseling concerning loss of loved ones, home, and personal property	State and federal resources for physical reconstruction Social welfare agencies Crisis and mental health services Pastoral counselors	Financial hardship Social instability Long-lasting mental or emotional problems

nity received crisis counseling assistance from community mental health agencies in nearby Denver, Colorado. Survivors of the San Fernando earthquake and the Beverly Hills fire were helped by local and neighboring social and mental health services.

Crisis Intervention
The basic principles of crisis management should be applied on behalf of disaster victims. During and following a disaster, people need an opportunity to:

- Talk out the experience and express their feelings of fear, panic, loss, and grief.
- Become fully aware and accepting of what has happened to them.
- Resume concrete activity and reconstruct their lives with the social, physical, and emotional resources available.

To assist victims through the crisis, the crisis worker should:

- Listen with concern and sympathy and ease the way for the victims to tell their tragic story, weep, express feelings of anger, loss, frustration, and despair.
- Help the victims of disaster accept in small doses the tragic reality of what has happened. This means staying with them during the initial stages of shock and denial. It also may mean accompanying them back to the scene of the tragedy and being available for support when they are faced with the full impact of their loss.
- Assist them to make contact with relatives, friends, and other resources needed to begin the process of social and physical reconstruction. This could mean making telephone calls to locate relatives, accompanying someone to apply for financial aid, giving information about social and mental health agencies for follow-up services.

In the group setting where large numbers are housed and offered emergency care, the panic-stricken should be separated and given individual attention to avoid the contagion of panic reactions. Assignment of simple physical tasks will move the panic-stricken in the direction of constructive action. Any action that helps victims feel valued as individuals is important at this time.

In spite of massive efforts to help survivors of disaster, it seems almost impossible to prevent life-long emotional scars among the people who live through the experience. It is important to make crisis and bereavement counseling services available to *all* disaster survivors so that the damaging effects of the experience can be reduced as much as possible.

One lesson learned in the Wilkes-Barre Project Outreach was the necessity of actively seeking out those in need of crisis counseling.[4] Crisis workers got acquainted with residents on a block by block basis, and were thereby able to assess needs and make crisis services available to people who otherwise might not have used them.

No local community can possibly meet all of the physical, social, and emotional needs of its residents who are disaster victims. The Wilkes-Barre experiment of providing federal funds for crisis services as well as for physical reconstruction should set a precedent for the kind of assistance necessary for every community that is disaster-struck in the future. This will be true even when local mental health, welfare, and health workers are better trained in crisis intervention. In most disasters the need is too great for the local community to respond to alone, especially since some of its own human service workers (e.g., police, nurses, clergy, and counselors), will themselves be among the disaster victims.

Preventive Intervention

It is, of course, impossible to prepare for the crisis of disaster the way one can prepare for transition states such as parenthood, retirement, or death. However, we can act on a community-wide basis before a disaster strikes. This is particularly important in communities at high risk for natural disasters. Such preparation is a form of psychological immunization.

There are several things a community might do to prepare for possible disaster:

1. Public service announcements during spring rains or tornado seasons urging people not to ignore disaster warnings.

2. Educational programs on TV dramatizing crowd control techniques and what to do with a panic-stricken person or one who is in shock.

3. Review of public safety codes to assure adequate protec-

tion against fire in public gathering places such as restaurants, theaters, and hospitals.

4. Public service announcements urging people to take first aid courses with local Red Cross and fire departments.

5. Educational programs on radio and TV to acquaint people with social agencies and crisis services available to them in the event of a disaster.

6. A program of crisis intervention training for mental health and social service workers as an addition to their traditional skills.

7. An upgraded program of disaster preparation by medical, health, and welfare facilities, including mechanisms for community coordination of disaster rescue services. It was apparent after the Rapid City flood that the community had an excellent medical disaster plan. As a result, survivors did not lack adequate medical and health care during and after the flood.[9] This is remarkable, since medical disaster plans sometimes are not well enough organized to be practical during an actual disaster.

These preparations will not avoid the devastating effects of a disaster, but may be effective in reducing the impact of the trauma and in equipping people with some additional personal tools for living through the experience with less physical, social, and emotional damage than they might otherwise suffer.

Case Example: Wilkes-Barre, Pa., 1972

Martin Schoner, age 69, and his wife Evelyn, age 68, had lived in Wilkes-Barre all their lives in an intimate neighborhood in the "valley." The Schoners had both been retired for several years, Martin as a men's clothing merchant, Evelyn as a nurse. They were enjoying the activities of their retirement years which included occasional babysitting of their five grandchildren in two neighboring towns. They and their two children exchanged visits frequently. Evelyn was not as well adjusted to retirement as was Martin. Through the years she had managed to maintain a spotless house while working full-time as a nurse. Now she did not have enough to do. Her hobby of crocheting could not fill all the hours. Martin, on the other hand, had cabinet-making skill and solicited enough business to keep himself busy for many hours each day. However, he still found himself bored at times and not as busy as he wanted to be.

The evening before the flood Martin was admitted to the hospital for chest and stomach discomfort. There was some suspicion and fear that his symptoms signaled a problem with his heart. When Evelyn left her husband at the hospital that evening, they still did not know his diagnosis. Nor did they have any suspicion of an imminent disaster.

Meanwhile, numerous flood warnings were being broadcast by radio and TV. Evelyn, however, heard none of these. She went to bed as usual, only to be awakened at 5:00 a.m. by a telephone call from a friend advising her of the flood and the need to leave her house quickly. She heeded the warning, immediately packed a bag, and drove from her home to her friend's house. A few hours later, she learned on radio news that houses in her neighborhood were filled with water up to the second floor. She tried to reach her husband but could not; the hospital was also flooded and the patients evacuated. Both Martin and Evelyn were beside themselves with fear and worry, for each had no idea of the whereabouts of the other.

One of Evelyn's special concerns was Martin's medical condition. She still did not know if his symptoms signaled heart trouble. As it turned out, Martin's symptoms were from food poisoning. He had been moved to a local college which was converted into a temporary shelter. Seriously ill patients were moved to another hospital. Martin, however, was so upset and worried about his wife, Evelyn, that rescue workers finally sent a hospital chaplain to talk with him. Martin stated afterwards that he found it a tremendous relief to pour out his worry and fear to a sympathetic listener—in this case a Catholic priest. The chaplain helped him through the "good cry" he seemed to need without embarrassment or shame.

Evelyn had no way of knowing these facts because public communication networks were not operating. Her main support at this time was the friend she was staying with. Meanwhile, her elderly cousin, Helen, who was a houseguest with the Schoners when the flood came, fell and broke her arm. Evelyn succeeded in getting Helen to the hospital for treatment.

Two days later, Evelyn finally learned from a friend that she—the friend —had located Martin at the college emergency shelter. Evelyn went to the college to pick up Martin. They stayed for a few days together at their friend's house before returning to their neighborhood to assess the damage.

When they returned, they were grief-stricken over the loss of their possessions and destruction of the home they had treasured. Evelyn was particularly upset. She kept repeating: "If only I had known that this was going to happen, I would have moved at least some of our precious things upstairs or packed them up to take with me."

Martin and Evelyn, with the help of their friend, decided to stay in the neighborhood and rebuild their home with federal aid. In the aftermath of the crisis, Martin, despite the tragedy, gained a new lease on life. He no longer had any empty hours in his days; he single-handedly took on the job of repairing the flood damage and refinishing the house. He became a source of support and encouragement for others in the neighborhood. Evelyn feels the flood left an indelible mark on her. She seems unable to stop grieving over the loss they suffered. Evelyn also states, "If only our minister hadn't been out of town at the time, I would have had someone to talk to when it happened . . . Maybe things would be different now . . . if only he had been there."

Martin and Evelyn said they did not know that specially trained crisis counselors (Project Outreach) were available to survivors of the disaster. This highlights the fact that communication in a disaster-stricken community is often inadequate.

Martin, Evelyn, and all their neighbors live in fear of another flood; they have no assurance that adequate precautionary measures have been taken to prevent a recurrence. They decided, however, to take a chance and live their last years in the neighborhood they dearly love, with the resolution that, should another flood occur, they will move away once and for all.

MAN-MADE DISASTERS

A special note is in order about causes, effects, and prevention of man-made disasters since these are among the most destructive experiences recorded. The world at large knows about the Nazi holocaust and the bombing of Hiroshima. War is a man-made disaster which brings about physical, social, and emotional destruction of immeasurable proportions. In Western industrial societies, man-made disasters have also occurred because of careless development, handling, distribution, or disposal of drugs and other potentially harmful substances. Examples in the recent past include: explosion of a chemical plant in Northern England killing several people; escape of dangerous gases in Italy causing suspected damage to unborn children; sale and prescription of an inadequately tested drug, Thalidomide, to pregnant women—resulting in thousands of deformed babies; and floods in Wales and West Virginia occurring because of carelessly dumped coal waste which formed artificial dams that eventually broke, and resulting in dozens of deaths.

In the last instance cited, residents in Buffalo Creek, West Virginia knew that the dam was considered dangerous and that the mining corporation neglected to correct the danger.[11] Thus, when loved ones, homes, and the natural environment were destroyed, survivors concluded that the mining company regarded them as less than human. (One of the excuses offered by the company for not correcting the dangerous waste disposal method was that the "fish" would be harmed by alternative methods.) The survivors' feeling of devaluation was confirmed by their knowledge of the coal company's proposal of hasty and inadequate financial settlements. Also, the physical damage to the community was never repaired by the responsible company or through outside assistance. Thus residents are constantly reminded of the disaster.

Unlike the Rapid City community described above, Buffalo Creek survivors have *not* responded to the disaster with community rejuvenation born out of the tragedy. Lifton and Olson attribute this tremendously different response to the disaster's human (rather than natural) origin.[11] Even though the mining company was forced to pay 13.5 million dollars in a psychic damage suit, Buffalo Creek residents seem to feel that they and their community will never be healed.

Reactions of Buffalo Creek survivors are similar to those observed among survivors of Hiroshima and the Nazi holocaust. Lifton and Olson state: ". . . as the source of stress shifts from indiscriminate violence by nature to the discriminate oppression by man, the damage to human personality becomes less remediable."[11] Survivors of man-made disaster—including war—feel that their humanity has been violated. Their psyches are bombarded to such a degree that their capacity for recovery is often permanently damaged. Rakoff notes similar long-lasting effects of destructiveness toward fellow human beings among the children and families of concentration camp survivors.[14]

Many people earn their living amidst daily exposure to dangerous materials; all of us live in the shadow of potential destruction. It is important, therefore, not to lose sight of the fact that man-made disasters are preventable; that the destruction of our very lives and of the natural world can rest with ourselves and our fellow human beings.

SUMMARY

Disaster is a crisis unlike any other a person will ever live through. Victims may experience a threat to their lives, may lose loved ones, home, and personal belongings. Many spend the rest of their lives mourning these tragic losses and trying to rebuild their homes and lives. Rescue services, crisis intervention, and follow-up care for physical, emotional, and social rehabilitation are necessary for all survivors. While financial aid for physical restoration and rehabilitation has been available for years, crisis counseling services are a newer phenomenon on the disaster scene. Communities will be better equipped to handle the emotional crisis related to the disaster experience when mental health and social service workers, as well as other caretakers, are prepared in advance with skills in crisis management. The urgency of preventing man-made disasters is self-evident.

References

1. Tyhurst, J. S. "Individual Reactions to Community Disaster," *American Journal of Psychiatry,* 107: 764–69, April 1951.

2. Tyhurst, J. S. "Psychological and Social Aspects of Civilian Disaster," *Canadian Medical Association Journal,* 76: 385–93, March 1957.

3. Tyhurst, J. S. "The Role of Transition States—Including Disaster—in Mental Illness." Symposium on Preventive and Social Psychiatry. Walter Reed Army Institute of Research and The National Research Council, Washington, D.C., April 1957.

4. Zusman, Jack; Robert H. Joss; and Peter J. Newman. *Final Report: Project Outreach.* Luzerne-Wyoming County Mental Health/Mental Retardation Joinder. Buffalo, New York: Community Mental Health Research and Development Corporation, December 1973.

5. Okura, K. Patrick. "Mobilizing in Response to a Major Disaster." *Community Mental Health Journal,* 11: 136–44, No. 2, 1975.

6. Birnbaum, Freda; Jennifer Coplon; and Ira Scharff. "Crisis Intervention After a Natural Disaster," *Social Casework,* 54: 545–51, November 1973.

7. Workshop: "Disaster: Research, Training, Service." Ninth Annual Meeting, American Association of Suicidology. Los Angeles, California: April–May 1976.

8. Kizzier, Dana. "A Chilling Night of Terror." In: *The Rapid City Flood, June 9, 1972.* Lubbock, Texas: C. F. Boone, Publisher, 1972.

9. "The Rapid City Journal." Rapid City, South Dakota: June 26, 1972.

10. Koegler, Ronald R., and Shelby M. Hicks. "The Destruction of a medical Center by Earthquake," *California Medicine,* 116: 63–67, February 1972.

11. Lifton, Robert J., and Eric Olson. "The Human Meaning of Total Disaster. The Buffalo Creek Experience." *Psychiatry,* 39: 1–18, February 1976.

12. Blanford, H. and J. Levine. "Crisis Intervention in an Earthquake," *Social Work,* 17: 16–19, July 1972.

13. Bennet, G. "Bristol Floods 1968. Controlled Survey of Effects on Health of Local Community Disaster." *British Medical Journal,* 3: 454–58, 1970.

14. Rakoff, V. et al. "Children and Families of Concentration Camp Survivors," *Canadian Mental Health,* 14: 24–26, 1966.

PART III

COMPREHENSIVE CRISIS SERVICES

CHAPTER 10

Developing Community Crisis Programs

INTRODUCTION

Everyone helping people in crisis must depend on others and on helping agencies in order to do the best job possible. The case examples in this book and the experiences of numerous crisis workers bear out this fact. Hopefully every community will someday assure its members that if they are in crisis, help is available *when* they need it and *where* it will do the most good—in their real-life setting. Crisis services should be taken for granted in a community, just as we assume the presence of police and fire protection, postal service, and schools.

Much has been written concerning various crises and what to do about them. Authors have described programs that fit specific communities—a large metropolitan area, a rural community, or a Native American community on an isolated reservation. Much less has been written about how crisis workers in the community relate to one another while helping people in distress. The question is, how does it all *come together* in a way that is practical and workable? What are the principles and guidelines that should characterize all crisis programs regardless of individual differences specific to certain settings?

Crisis specialists, suicidologists, U.S. Government agencies such as NIMH (National Institute of Mental Health), and the American Association of Suicidology, have set guidelines for the organization and delivery of suicide prevention and crisis services.[1,2,3,4,5] These guiding principles and the author's experience in implementing them are summarized in this chapter.

ELEMENTS OF SERVICE

A comprehensive crisis service should include several basic elements, regardless of organizational model. These service elements are:

1. Twenty-four hour telephone service.

2. Face-to-face crisis service: Walk-in service to crisis centers in local neighborhoods, and twenty-four hour crisis outreach to homes and other community settings.

3. Emergency medical/psychiatric service: Emergency assessment of suicide or other risk to life, and availability of emergency medication.

4. Linkage network with established community emergency services: Police and rescue squads, Travelers' Aid, and other community resources. The network should include standing

agreements and a procedure for convening emergency planning conferences when necessary to resolve a crisis constructively.

It is unnecessary and, indeed, impossible in most communities to administer these services through a single agency. The important requirement is that one element of service does *not* operate in isolation from the others. Now let us examine the four service elements in greater detail.

Telephone Service

Twenty-four hour telephone emergency service has had a major impact in launching the suicide prevention and crisis intervention movement in the United States. The phenomenal aspect of this backbone of the crisis intervention movement is that most telephone services are operated predominantly by lay volunteers, with consultation and supervision from professional crisis workers.

Important as the telephone service is, it is not adequate by itself. Volunteer telephone counselors must be able to put a caller in touch with a face-to-face counselor or mobilize an outreach team when more than telephone counseling is needed. Indeed, for two crisis-prone groups—the elderly and Native Americans on reservations—telephones are often not accessible.

Another limitation of twenty-four hour telephone service, if not linked with other elements of service, is that people at greatest risk are the least likely to use this service. If a telephone service is run largely to meet the needs of a white middle class population, the service will not help many high risk groups.

The telephone service has been expanded in many communities to include services to special groups. Some communities now have teen hotlines, drug hotlines, parents-in-crisis and rape crisis lines.

In St. Louis, Contact Teleministry has developed a telephone service for the deaf. This was made possible by the technical contribution of a physicist who, in 1964, linked the teletypewriter mechanism to the telephone.[7] As with suicide prevention and crisis telephone services, these special programs should not operate in isolation of other community resources.

One of the problems faced by all telephone services is that of the repeat caller. This is a complex problem for which there is no simple solution. However, the problem is most troublesome when telephone services are not effectively integrated with face-to-face counseling programs and other community services. Routine supervision and consultation for telephone counselors, including thoughtful service planning for the repeat caller, are strongly recommended. Without such an approach, it is all too easy to "write off" these callers as "not in crisis" and "wasting our time which should be spent on people in crisis." Many repeat callers are already beyond a crisis, or are simply lonely and want someone to "rap" with. Familiar examples of the repeat caller are people with sexual or chronic drinking problems. A well-trained crisis counselor should be able to link people with chronic problems to resources more appropriate for their needs than a telephone crisis service.

Face-to-Face Crisis Service
Face-to-face crisis service refers to the work of mental health crisis clinics that are designed specifically to offer assistance to people in crisis. This is done by specially trained crisis counselors. The term does not imply that face-to-face crisis services exist *only* in such agencies. The case examples in this book illustrate the role of health workers and community caretakers in face-to-face crisis work as well.

Crisis counseling centers can operate as an adjunct to a twenty-four hour telephone service or as an integral part of a community mental health center. People can "walk in" to the center or be referred by others. These centers are the chief resource that should be available to teachers, police, nurses, physicians, and ministers—all the people who most often have the *first* face-to-face contact with people in crisis.

CRISIS OUTREACH: Face-to-face crisis service should be organized so that counselors can go to a person's home or other community setting, if necessary, and intervene in acute crisis situations. Crisis outreach work is indicated in the following circumstances:

1. When a crisis situation cannot be adequately assessed by telephone. For example, the caller is being interrupted by an extremely upset family member, thus making telephone assessment impossible.

2. When the police or rescue squad are inappropriate, are refused by the caller, or are unavailable. For example, the

following tragedy occurred in one community that had no crisis outreach service: A mentally disturbed man was brought to a hospital emergency room by two police officers for psychiatric examination. On the way out of the car, the man grabbed the gun of one of the officers and shot him. The other officer in turn shot the patient. The patient died instantly and the police officer died a few hours later. While this man had a history of mental disturbance, he had no lethal weapons at the time of the police investigation. If crisis outreach workers had been available to this family, they might have prevented two unnecessary deaths.

3. When assistance is needed immediately to avoid acute family disruption and possible forced removal of a person from home.

4. When there is acute danger of suicide and the person cannot or will not come to a clinic or hospital for help.

5. When there is possible danger to others. The counselor should determine by telephone whether lethal weapons are involved. If so, the case should be handled collaboratively with police. This implies that prior working relationships with police have been developed to avoid crisis escalation by police presence.[8] At no time are crisis workers expected to place themselves in situations that are openly dangerous to their own lives.

People doing specialized crisis work should be skilled in assessing suicide risk and in working with police and other emergency services. They should also be capable of mobilizing emergency housing facilities and of making hospitalization arrangements when necessary. They also serve as consultants and supporters to front line crisis workers such as nurses, rescue workers, teachers, and police. A trained group of crisis workers capable of such community outreach work can prevent many destructive outcomes of crisis.

Emergency Medical/Psychiatric Services
The initial step in this element of service is carried out by the specialized crisis workers described above, and by rescue squads, volunteer fire departments, and police. Hospital emergency rooms and emergency services of community mental health centers also play a large

role in the complete delivery of this service element.[9] An effective crisis service must have reliable working relationships with psychiatric, medical, and hospital establishments. Physicians—preferably psychiatrists—should be available as part of the team, at least as consultants when medication and hospitalization are needed. Community crisis centers and hospital emergency rooms should have established agreements with crisis hostels as an alternative to psychiatric hospitalization whenever it is impossible to maintain a person in crisis in his or her natural community.[10] In those instances when medication and psychiatric hospitalization are indicated, neither should be delayed because of poor working relationships with the medical community.

Linkage with Other Community Services

It seems logical and natural that a crisis counselor would work with police and other emergency services in the community. Indeed, this should happen in a way that brings maximum benefit to the person in crisis. Effective and comprehensive crisis work in a community includes establishing clear working agreements and referral procedures with all agencies involved in crisis work. In practice this means that referral procedures and telephone numbers should be available mutually among all involved agencies. Also, in hospital emergency rooms and in doctors' offices, information cards describing local crisis counseling services and phone numbers should be made available to people in crisis. This is especially important for those who have made suicide attempts and still receive medical treatment *only* in many general hospitals. Police might also distribute such information routinely.

Certainly a formal written agreement is not a guarantee against interagency communication problems. However, such agreements provide a context in which workers can begin to resolve some of the problems and misunderstandings that can occur in crisis work. The larger the community, the more important formal agreements become. Bureaucratic red tape is by nature less complicated in smaller communities. Also, working relationships in smaller communities are usually more closely knit, thereby preventing the "systems" problems prevalent in metropolitan communities.

A "systems" problem occurs when the network of community agencies does not work together in a cohesive manner to help people in crisis. Formal agreements, which include a review process, can reduce this hazard to effective crisis work.

ORGANIZATIONAL MODELS

Service Models in the U. S.
Essential elements of a crisis service can and do exist in a variety of models. Several models are described by Richard McGee in *Crisis Intervention in the Community*.[4] Examples of different models in the United States include:

> 1. A suicide prevention and crisis center with its own policy board which provides all elements of service within its own program. This type of model often originates through the volunteer efforts of mental health associations, ministerial associations, or other voluntary citizen groups.

> 2. A twenty-four hour telephone service which relies on agreements with various private and public agencies to provide face-to-face, walk-in, and outreach service.

> 3. A community mental health program which provides face-to-face, walk-in, and outreach services; and has its own or relies on another local hotline for twenty-four hour telephone coverage. This model evolved from the Federal Mental Health legislation of the early 1960's mandating the delivery of emergency mental health services as a part of all community mental health programs.

> 4. A public health hospital or detention center on a Native American reservation which relies on police and community health workers for word-of-mouth contacts with people in crisis, since few of the residents have phones.[6]

Developing a Model
Each community should develop a model that suits its unique circumstances. Regardless of the model, however, the essential characteristics of a crisis service are these:

> 1. Various caretakers, such as police and rescue workers, health, and mental health workers, *coordinate* with one another to offer their services to people in crisis.

2. Local citizens/consumers have a voice in developing the service.

3. Service is relevant, available, visible, and accessible to the people it is intended to serve.

4. Consumers have a voice in monitoring whether their needs for crisis services are being met. They should be strongly represented on a Board of Directors.

5. Leaders in human service agencies assume responsibility for assuring that crisis services are delivered in a coordinated, effective manner.

We know a lot about what a comprehensive crisis service in a community ought to be, and in most communities one or more elements of service already exist. In a typical community, future efforts should be focused on:

• Community examination to learn what services do and do not exist. This can be done by a survey of social and mental health agencies to determine the extent of an agency's involvement in delivering crisis services. The examination should also include citizen surveys. One rural community in Vermont found that citizens in crisis usually called on registered nurses working part-time in the community. The nurses were then enlisted—on a voluntary basis—to receive training to increase their skills as crisis workers.[11]

• Development of crisis service elements that do not exist (e.g. twenty-four hour, 7 day-a-week outreach service), and evaluation and improvement of effectiveness of those elements that already exist.

• Development of a system for *maintaining* a high quality crisis service and for revising it according to the changing needs of consumers.

A crisis worker can possess all the knowledge and skills necessary for effective crisis management; but if individual workers feel forced to function in a vacuum, in isolation, without the support and help of a well-coordinated human service system, the worker's best efforts can be undermined. Individual efforts are also frustrated when administrators in specific agencies such as hospitals and mental health centers are unconvinced of the importance of crisis work. Commitment to crisis service probably does not exist if it is the last area to be adequately funded and staffed, or if workers are not provided the training and supervision they need to effectively help people in crisis.

The British Model—The Samaritans[12,13,14,15]

The Samaritans in the British Isles began in 1953 when the Reverend Chad Varah started a counseling service in his London church for despairing and suicidal people. His service became widely known and was used by increasing numbers of people. Friendly volunteers offered to help by chatting or having a cup of tea with clients waiting to see Reverend Varah. To his surprise, some people no longer needed his counseling after they had been helped informally by volunteers. Thus was born The Samaritans, a disciplined lay organization for befriending troubled and suicidal people. In 1963, Samaritans Incorporated, a national association, was formed to protect the name and basic principles of The Samaritans. Today, there are 165 Samaritan branches in Great Britain, with a total of 18,500 volunteers. There are branches on every continent.

Each Samaritan branch is represented on the national Council of Management which, through an Executive Committee, sets policy, appoints Branch Directors, offers direction, and holds educational conferences for the branches. Two members of the Council's Panel of Visitors site-visit and make reports on the branches during organizational phases and every 2½ years after a branch is fully established. A branch can be closed by the Council of Management if it is not operating according to Samaritan principles and policy, though such action has rarely been necessary. Otherwise, local branches operate independently and provide their own funding, which is from voluntary sources. All volunteers must successfully complete a preparation program and a probationary period before final acceptance into a Samaritan branch. With the exception of occasional part-time secretaries, Samaritan branches are operated entirely by volunteers— Samaritans who befriend lonely, isolated people; and select, prepare, and direct fellow Samaritan volunteers.

Samaritan befriending occurs in two senses: (a) It is a general relationship between any caller and the Samaritan volunteer who stands in for the person's best friend or relative who is not available or cannot help. (b) It is a relationship between a *particular* Samaritan called a "Befriender" who is assigned to help someone needing *more* than ordinary support.

"Befriending" in the second sense grows out of the first. When general befriending by the Samaritan on duty is not enough, the volunteer discusses the situation with a leader who suggests a particular "befriender" according to the needy person's individual circumstances.

Befriending is done by phone, in branch offices, by mail, in the client's home, or over a cup of tea in a restaurant—in any place that best suits the person's needs, but not in the Samaritan's home. Samaritan befriending is carefully supervised to protect against development of unhealthy dependency relationships or misuse of the service by people incapable of benefiting from it. Each branch can also dispatch a "Flying Squad," that is, a team of Samaritan volunteers who go to the scene of crisis when necessary. If clients need medical or psychiatric service, they are helped to obtain it through the National Health Service. Clients are also helped to obtain material aid from Social Services when necessary.

Samaritan philosophy emphasizes that befriending is a process of helping lonely and despairing people to see some purpose in life and re-establish broken social ties. It is *not* a form of therapy, and evangelizing of any kind is strictly forbidden.

The Samaritan movement appears to be related to a drop in the suicide rate in England and Wales from 12.7 per 100,000 population in 1963 to 7.7 per 100,000 in 1972. In contrast, suicide rates are rising in many other Western countries. The success of the Samaritans is attributed to several factors:

1. A publicity program which has made the Samaritans known to 92 percent of the population.

2. The Samaritan principle of ordinary people helping others in distress in an absolutely confidential relationship with no strings attached.

3. The Samaritans' independence from the official helping bureaucracy which is suspect to many people who fear they will be "put away" in hospitals if they seek help.

The Samaritans illustrate a basic principle of the crisis intervention and suicide prevention movement: One need not be a professional with years of training to help people who are despairing or suicidal. The work of Samaritan volunteers apparently makes a life and death difference to a significant number of people in the British Isles and elsewhere.

STAFFING PATTERNS

Staffing of human service programs should be determined by the kind and extent of service the agency intends to offer. People who do crisis work need the support of a clearly defined staffing arrangement. Crisis workers must know who their teammates are and who to call for consultation or other assistance. Crisis counselors and mental health professionals doing crisis work must possess an attitude of flexibility about hours they work. The need for crisis intervention cannot be confined to the traditional hours of nine to five. Workers responsible for consultation and outreach must be willing to be "on call." Mechanical devices such as a beeper system should be part of any well run crisis service. This increases the reliability of the call system as thereby workers need not remain beside a phone during the entire call period.

Staffing arrangements must also include provision for the staff to take time off when they have worked into the evening and night hours on crisis outreach calls. This is unnecessary in agencies that are sufficiently budgeted to pay staff for call-time, even when no calls are made. However, most crisis agencies do not have the budget for such reimbursement.

General hospitals which do not already have mental health specialists routinely available to emergency room staff should make every effort to develop such a program. Emergency room personnel who do not have this assistance will be less able to act as crisis managers in the emergency room.

Administrators of all crisis and emergency services should keep in mind that even with the best staffing arrangements, some people are unsuited for crisis work. There are many rewards, continuous excitement, and challenges in the crisis arena; but there is also a lot of stress and some danger. These factors must be kept in mind in the recruitment, training, and supervision of crisis workers. A person whose tolerance for stress is low and whose attitude is not suitable, or who feels forced into an unwanted assignment, will be part of the problem rather than the solution in acute crisis situations. If administrative policies and staffing arrangements are reasonable and supportive of crisis work and crisis workers, there will be enough people wanting to do the job without forcing it on those who do not.

TEAM RELATIONSHIPS IN CRISIS INTERVENTION
Team relationships are important in carrying out any human service function. In crisis work such team relationships are critical. The effective use of social network techniques in crisis intervention demands that we be able to relate with clarity and effectiveness to other people who are helping. Social systems techniques demand a minimum of two people for constructive outcomes. In high risk suicidal or homicidal situations in the home or elsewhere, the presence of at least two team members is essential as a resource and for safety.

When a person or a family in crisis comes to an agency for help, they should be informed that the entire agency team is available to them. The emergency telephone number of the agency, never the counselor's home number, should be given to the person. Giving someone a personal telephone number for emergencies implies that the counselor will, in fact, be available for possible emergencies. If a person in crisis calls and the counselor is not there as implied, a serious credibility problem can result. Counselors cannot and should not attempt to provide twenty-four hour crisis service singlehandedly. To do so may result in what has been called the "burn-out syndrome." That is, after six months or so, the exhausted and overspent counselor gives up and may abandon crisis work altogether. However, people in crisis do need twenty-four hour service available. This can only be provided by an agency or community plan designed for such continuous service. Twenty-four hour emergency coverage demands that all agency staff members collaborate as a team.

Teamwork is also a vital means of offering encouragement to one another while working with people in crisis. Strain is inevitable when one deals regularly with life and death matters and other traumatic life events. For example, if a person commits suicide despite a counselor's efforts to prevent the suicide, the counselor is one of the survivors who needs someone to talk with about the traumatic experience. Counselors are people. Their supply of energy is not inexhaustible. One of their sources of "refueling" for more crisis work is the support and active cooperation of fellow team members.

ROLE OF VOLUNTEERS

In spite of the fact that volunteers are the backbone of the suicide prevention and crisis movement, they are sometimes treated like second class citizens. For example, some volunteer telephone counselors are not allowed to see clients face-to-face for crisis counseling. The alleged reason for this staffing arrangement is that the telephone counselor is not sufficiently skilled for this task. This practice is ironic on several counts:

First, it implies that the caller is in worse shape *after* telephone intervention than before, when in reality the opposite is usually true. If people in crisis use the telephone at all, they usually use it at the peak of their crisis.

Second, helping a person in crisis by telephone often requires *more* skill than counseling on a face-to-face basis. The telephone counselor can rely only on verbal and voice cues and has less opportunity to "control" the counseling situation ("control" here is used in the sense of directing the counseling situation). The caller can always hang up, leaving the counselor very frustrated. In contrast, face-to-face counseling allows for many more situational supports.

Finally, crisis intervention is crisis intervention whether conducted over the phone or face-to-face. The telephone is only one of many devices available to a crisis worker. If a volunteer has mastered the basics of crisis intervention, he or she should be able to help a person in crisis either over the telephone *or* face-to-face. Volunteers who are trained to practice crisis intervention according to only one mode—the telephone—are only partially trained. If a crisis volunteer is trained to help people express feelings and understand their crisis situation, and to assess lethality and develop and implement a plan for crisis resolution over the phone, then there is no reason why the person cannot practice the same techniques face-to-face.

Perhaps one reason for not allowing telephone counselors to work face-to-face with clients is that such work in some settings is really psychotherapy rather than crisis intervention. Most crisis workers are not trained to do psychotherapy, and some professional psychotherapists are not trained to do crisis intervention. Optimally, helpers should do only what they are trained to do, but they should not be prevented from doing fully what they *are* trained to do.

All of us do crisis intervention in our everyday lives, either formally or informally. Throughout this book, people who formally help other people in crisis are referred to as "crisis workers" or "crisis counselors." No distinction has been made between those who do crisis work on a volunteer basis and those who do it to support themselves. Volunteer crisis workers are the thousands of women and men who staff (on about an 85 percent basis) the twenty-four hour telephone crisis services throughout the U. S. Some of these same volunteers do outreach work and face-to-face counseling with people in crisis. This army of crisis workers are often referred to as the "real professionals" in the field of crisis intervention.

Those who volunteer their time as crisis workers do so because of their dedication and interest in this work, as their chosen way of helping others. Most volunteers claim that the experience is personally growth producing as well. This often depends on the nature of team relationships and the quality of supervision they receive. Volunteer crisis workers earn their living as accountants, teachers, writers, psychologists, homemakers, nurses, secretaries, and in many other occupations. They work several hours per week or month as crisis service volunteers. They are not paid and do not rely on the work as a means of supporting themselves. "Paid" crisis workers may be full-time crisis specialists and should also include nurses, physicians, police, and rescue workers who are constantly in contact with people in crisis.

Another group of crisis workers are fire fighters and rescue workers, noted in various case examples. Their vital work in the community is often taken for granted. Although their immediate concern is to put out fires and provide physical support before the person is brought to a hospital, such workers are not included often enough in the development of a community's comprehensive crisis services. Yet fire fighters and rescue workers are called routinely in cases of suicide attempts. They are also left with the job of consoling the survivors of accidents or the relatives of a heart attack victim. Such situations certainly require crisis intervention skills. These volunteers should not be neglected as part of the total community "staff" of crisis workers.

STANDARDS FOR CRISIS SERVICES
Many of the issues discussed in this chapter will be less problematic if and when suicide prevention and crisis services in the United States are developed and operated according to the standards set by the American Association of Suicidology (AAS).[5] In 1974, a National

Task Force was appointed and convened for the purpose of defining standards for suicide prevention and crisis services in the United States.* At this time the standards have been officially adopted by the AAS Board of Directors and membership, and the process of certifying suicide prevention and crisis services has begun. The National Task Force has now become the AAS National Committee on Certification.

It is the hope of the AAS and the organization's Certification Committee that all crisis services in the U. S. will eventually seek and receive certification. Such certification will assure people in crisis that the services provided by a certified crisis program meet at least the minimum standards of service performance and program administration recommended by the AAS. In an age when consumers are increasingly conscious of the quality of service they receive, certification is a step in the direction of assuring such quality.

Briefly, the AAS certification process includes evaluation of a crisis program in seven areas:[5]

Administration

Training Procedures

General Delivery System of Crisis Services

Suicide Prevention Services

Ethical Issues

Community Integration

Program Evaluation

Programs are evaluated by examination of written materials describing the center's operation. Two Regional Certification Committee members make a site visit. The evaluation team rates the program on a scoring sheet according to predefined standards. Data is gathered about the program and forms the basis for the rating.

The certification process does more than give a "stamp of approval" to acceptable or high quality programs. The process also helps agencies improve services if they do not meet minimum standards. Consultation for program upgrading is available through the

*Members of the Task Force: Richard K. McGee, Chairperson; Bruce Danto; Lee Ann Hoff; Calvin Frederick; Charlotte Ross; Gwyn Harvey; Thomas Welu; and Consultants Norman Farberow, Leonard Linden, and Jerome Motto.

Certification Committee and other members of the American Association of Suicidology. Further information regarding AAS Certification and Standards is available by inquiring at the nearest crisis center which should have information on specific AAS resources.

COMMUNITY EDUCATION, CONSULTATION, AND TRAINING ABOUT PEOPLE IN CRISIS

Introduction
While people have been helping others in distress since the beginning of time, many still ask, "What should I do? How can I help?" Or they are concerned that they might make things worse by saying or doing the wrong thing. Others express fear of liability for helping another in distress. Who knows the motives that allowed 38 people to observe the attack and killing of a woman on the streets of New York City without a single one calling the police?[16]

Crisis intervention, protection from attack, and suicide prevention are everybody's business, not just the business of those who make these services a full-time job. Most European countries have laws requiring people to assist others in danger. Two dozen people were convicted for violation of such a law in France during 1975. Aside from laws requiring physicians, nurses, and social workers to report child abuse, there are no similar laws in the United States except in Vermont.[16]

Parts 1 and 2 of this book describe the serious consequences that can occur when people do not get help when they need it, and what we can do to help people in crisis. Now let us consider the community approaches to preventing destructive outcomes of crises and helping people to grow through a crisis experience.

Three functions are essential aspects of primary prevention. These are: (a) education about what to do in a crisis situation, (b) consultation with other human service or health workers, and (c) training in crisis intervention for everyone involved in human services. In the U. S. most public and many private dollars spent on mental health are used largely for secondary and tertiary, rather than for these *primary* preventive efforts. Certainly those who are disabled mentally and emotionally should have the public and private care they need. But there is a twofold irony in the wastefulness of a human service system that does not emphasize primary prevention along with other necessary care of the disabled. First, if community education, consultation, and crisis intervention were available to all, much human pain in the form of depression, drug and alcohol abuse, institutionalization, suicide, and homicide might be avoided. Second, the dollar costs per client of secondary and especially tertiary level of care is much higher than the cost of primary care. It may require several intensive hours of social systems intervention to help a worker stay on the job, a child to stay in school, or a person to stay in a home situation rather than be institutionalized. But such crisis service is still much less expensive than the alternatives of unemployment, individual child care, or institutionalization.

Community education, consultation, and training in crisis intervention should interface. For example, an education program for a parent-teacher association regarding crisis and drug use could result in the teachers' requesting regular consultation concerning crises among drug-involved children and adolescents. Or a public health nurse who receives consultation regarding a suicidal person may request inservice training in crisis intervention for the entire staff.

Let us now consider specific aspects of these three program elements—education, consultation, and training.

Community Education

Since each community member is bound to experience a crisis at one time or another or will be called on to help someone else in crisis, everyone should know where and how to get community crisis services. A comprehensive community crisis service has a public relations program that gives all citizens this vital information. There should be established channels of communication between community members and the service organizations. One of the AAS (American Association of Suicidology) standards for crisis services is that citizens have regular input to the board of control and administration.[17] This is one important way of determining how well informed citizens are about their crisis service. Do citizens know:

- What services are available.
- How they can get in touch with the crisis service.
- How long it takes to get help in an emergency.
- Who is eligible for the service.

• What—if anything—it will cost to use the service. (The service should be publicly supported).

• If the case will be kept confidential.

All citizens should know the answers to these questions. A public relations committee of the community crisis service has several avenues through which it can publicize these answers. At the same time, the committee can offer information to help people: (a) better recognize and understand the common signs of crisis; (b) learn how to better help themselves and others through new ways of problem solving; and (c) generally improve their mental health and avoid destructive ways of problem solving such as drug and alcohol abuse and suicide attempts.

Some of the basic tasks involved in a community education program are:

1. Appoint a director or coordinator of public relations with experience in crisis intervention and community education work. He or she should select committee members who are willing and able to work on behalf of the service.

2. Identify the specific education needs of the local community being served. This can be done by contacting board members, citizen advisory and planning groups, town boards, caretakers such as police, teachers, and rescue squads, service clubs (Lions, Elks, Rotary, etc.), churches, and other community groups.

3. Develop education materials such as brochures and posters which tell about crises in families, drug and alcohol use, aging, suicide, divorce, illness, and transition states.

4. Organize a systematic means of distributing these materials. For example, develop working agreements with physicians for making brochures available in waiting rooms and a routine mechanism for replenishing the supply. Churches and service clubs are also good places to distribute crisis information.

5. Organize a speaker's bureau with speakers who can discuss various topics pertinent to crisis intervention. Speakers could appear at service clubs, churches, and other community groups; on the local media; and before special groups such as

senior citizens, and school health and social science classes. Speakers bureau activities can often be developed cooperatively with the local Mental Health Association.

6. Develop a program of systematic and periodic contact with the media. Only 3 percent of the total U. S. population does not have television, and nearly everyone has a radio. The Public Relations Committee of the AAS has developed an impressive media kit for promoting public information about suicide and how to get help in a crisis. This is a valuable resource for every public relations coordinator of a crisis service.

7. Work with the local telephone company to assure listing of the suicide and crisis service number along with emergency numbers at the front of the directory, if this has not already been done. The AAS recently adopted a resolution supporting such action.

8. Develop a system for monitoring and evaluating the outcome of the public relations program. For example, conduct a random survey to find out what percentage of citizens have appropriate information about local crisis services.

A strong community education program not only gives people the information they need about crisis services, but also helps keep the program on a firmer financial foundation. Citizens who are informed and actively involved with a program important to them will make sure that they are not deprived of this vital use of their tax dollars.

Consultation

Consultation is an excellent means of assuring that clients do not suffer because a worker lacks extensive experience in solving complex human problems. In the medical field, consultation is an old practice that is widely used to bring the fullest possible range of knowledge to bear on a person's particular medical problem. In the community mental health movement in general and in Caplan's work *Principles of Preventive Psychiatry,* consultation is considered to have an equally important function in the mental health and crisis intervention fields.[18]

In crisis work, consultation can take place between a crisis counselor, who may be volunteer or paid, and a designated consultant; between a crisis counselor and his or her supervisor; or between a crisis specialist and another service worker such as a nurse, physician, police officer, teacher, pastor, or agency administrator. Many supervisors prefer to function in a consultative role with workers concerning clinical matters, rather than in their appointed authority role as supervisor. The exception to this usually occurs when the worker's level of skill is insufficient to allow complete freedom to accept or reject the recommendations of the supervisor, a freedom that characterizes the consultative relationship.

CRITERIA FOR USE OF CRISIS CASE CONSULTATION:

There are many reasons why counselors and community caretakers should seek consultation. The following instances illustrate some of these:

1. A particular human service worker may wish to provide a service for a person in crisis in which he or she is not particularly skilled.

Case Example

A police officer called a local crisis clinic from the Monet home when he saw that he was unable to handle Orville Monet's irrational, upsetting behaviour. Although Orville was violent—throwing things and breaking furniture—the police officer could tell that he was also mentally disturbed. (The man had mentioned being afraid that his wife and others were plotting against him.) The crisis counselor came to the home and acted as a consultant to the officer who, by this time, had established some rapport with the family. Together they convinced Orville to seek help at an emergency mental health clinic.

2. A crisis counselor wants to obtain a broader perspective and help with a complex crisis situation that involves many people.

Case Example

Janet, age 29, has diabetes but neglects to take her insulin; she believes it is contaminated after each use of the vial and refuses to let her mother or the public health nurse administer it. Janet is also picked up occasionally by the police for vagrancy and public intoxication. She has a crisis counselor who has assisted her through several stormy incidents, but without much change in her underlying life style. Janet refuses psychiatric treatment regarding her irrational ideas about the insulin. One day the nurse called the crisis counselor after discovering Janet in a diabetic coma. An ambulance was dispatched, and Janet was hospitalized. When Janet was over her medical crisis, the crisis counselor sought consultation from the program director of the crisis clinic concerning the next steps in helping Janet. Among other suggestions the supervisor made was an interagency planning conference—including Janet.

3. Someone in a supervisory position needs advice from a crisis specialist concerning a staff problem. For example, a hospital supervising nurse calls a crisis worker for help with a staff member who becomes suicidal. Since the supervisor is personally concerned about the staff member and has her own fears about suicide and death, she wants the help of an outside consultant to avoid an overly subjective approach to dealing with the problem.

4. A member of the community, perhaps a teacher or public health nurse, wants to gain a broader base of knowledge in working with someone who may be suicidal. A consultation session is arranged in which the case is discussed in detail and an agreement reached about the next steps to take. For example, the nurse or teacher may be given suggestions about how to respond to the person's suicidal talk so that he or she will feel more at ease discussing the problem openly. Subsequent steps for a referral process may be worked out, or the situation may be discussed in a follow-up consultation session depending on the particular circumstances of the case. Such determining circumstances might be: How much information does the worker already have? How much danger of suicide is there, based on the information available? What other information is needed and what is the best way of obtaining it in order to decide on next steps?

Case Example

Dennis, age 15, was referred to the school by a community mental health agency for disturbed children and adolescents. His grades were passable. He was physically abusive to other children and sometimes struck out at teachers as well. Dennis also had outbursts of uncontrolled behavior at home. During one of his fights with another boy he knocked out both the boy and the teacher who tried to intervene. Dennis was immediately expelled from school. While he was on home instruction, the counselor initiated consultation sessions with the school in an effort to get Dennis reinstated. In fact, Dennis' upsets in school coincided with his mother's hospitalization for heart disease.

Family crisis counseling sessions were held along with individual sessions for Dennis. He was able to verbalize many of his fears about his mother's illness and possible death from heart disease. Gradually he learned how to express his feelings in less destructive ways. After several conferences at school—including Dennis and his parents—Dennis was reinstated. Teachers and the guidance counselor stated that they had learned a great deal about adolescent behavior, and the role of the family—in this case, the mother's illness—in an adolescent's problems. The school decided to continue regular consultative sessions with the mental health agency, even though earlier attempts of the agency to establish a regular consultative relationship had been refused.

PROGRAM CONSULTATION: Most consultation occurring in crisis intervention and mental health fields concerns *individuals* whom the worker is concerned about helping. This is generally referred to as "case" consultation. "Program" consultation is also important but is practiced much less frequently.[19] There is a tendency to wait for a specific crisis before we examine an entire program and the institutions that contribute to individual crisis situations. For example, one public health nursing agency of the author's experience was instructed *not* to visit a mother if an infant was stillborn. Such a program directive defies the possibilities of crisis intervention on behalf of these distressed mothers. Many nursing homes have the practice of a "fruit-basket-upset" staffing arrangement in which staff switch ward assignments every two weeks. This kind of programming contributes to the adjustment problems of older people whose age makes it difficult to accommodate such rapid changes. It also prevents older people and staff from establishing stable relationships with one another, which in turn could prevent individual crisis situations.

The concept of program consultation is often resisted very strongly by the very institutions which could use it most productively—hospitals, nursing homes, and schools, for example. The most effective way to proceed in these circumstances is through community education efforts and the availability of consultation regarding individual crisis cases. When administrators can see the positive results of consultation concerning individual stress situations, they often are more open to the possibility of program consultation. For example, one crisis counselor assisted nursing home staff in understanding and helping a man who had attacked a nurse and another resident. Following this experience, the nursing home administrative staff arranged for a regular consultative program with the mental health agency in which the crisis counselor worked.

CONSULTATION AND SUPERVISION FOR CRISIS WORKERS:
Success in resolving certain crises often depends on the availability of consultation and supervision for crisis workers. Who, among crisis workers, requires supervision and/or consultation? Actually, everyone does. This is true at least inasmuch as all workers are accountable to someone:

- Executive Director to the Board of Directors.
- Crisis workers to a program or clinical director or appointed supervisor.
- All of us to the consumers (people in crisis) whom we serve.
- Agency or Board of Directors to a funding body or to legislators who in turn are accountable to the people who elected them.

In crisis work there will be many times when we need the support of a colleague, especially in very stressful situations. When dealing with a highly suicidal person, we should always work on a team or consultative basis, even if it is only with one's peer. The responsibility and risks involved in doing otherwise are too great.

People doing consultation and supervision should be employed in those roles because of their experience, knowledge, and skill in the field of crisis intervention. A professional degree in a mental health field may or may not be one of the qualifications of a good supervisor or consultant. It depends on whether the individual has expertise as a crisis worker. Unfortunately, consultants in some suicide prevention and crisis services have had no special training in crisis intervention or in lethality assessment and have never made a crisis outreach visit. Crisis workers and the people they serve are bound to be short changed by this kind of staffing and consultative arrangement. Supervision and consultation can be challenging and rewarding, but can also be taxing and riddled with problems. Extensive knowledge of and experience in the field are undisputed means of avoiding many problems in the consultative and supervisory process.

Training

The American Association of Suicidology standards for crisis services include the basics of how crisis workers should be trained.[20] The training of crisis workers, as considered in this book and by the AAS, does not defy the natural instinct and ability that most people have of helping others in crisis. Crisis training should build on human qualities and professional skills already possessed in order to enhance one's effectiveness as a crisis worker.

WHO SHOULD BE TRAINED: Everyone who does crisis work should be trained. The most obvious group needing crisis intervention training are those whose work brings them regularly into contact with people in crisis. Sometimes the assumption is made that mental health professionals—psychiatrists, psychiatric nurses, psychiatric social workers, and clinical psychologists—do not need specific training in crisis work because it is included in their professional training. This assumption is not shared by the American Association of Suicidology for good reason. Most schools that prepare mental health professionals do not, in fact, require formal course-work in crisis intervention with supervised crisis field experience. A number of schools are correcting this deficiency but such training is by no means common.

This is critical, as it is these very mental health professionals who will be called upon to act as consultants to crisis workers. A credibility problem, and a crisis in supervision and consultation for volunteers can result when the professional is inexperienced in crisis intervention. Certainly a mental health professional's knowledge of personality dynamics and psychopathology can be useful in certain crisis situations; but that knowledge is no substitute, for example, for the skills of lethality assessment or the ability to rapidly convene social and rescue resources in the community. When mental health professionals are also trained in crisis intervention, their knowledge of personality dynamics and their skills in psychotherapy are particularly helpful to the person who is crisis prone because of deep seated problems of adjustment, depression, self-destructiveness or neurotic patterns of behavior. A trained mental health professional will not confuse crisis intervention with psychotherapy. He or she can do crisis intervention and knows when it is needed in conjunction with psychotherapy.

Similarly, a well trained crisis worker who is not a mental health professional knows what crisis intervention is and is not. It *is* a helping technique focused on resolution of an immediate situational crisis through personal, social, and environmental problem solving mechanisms. It is *not* an occasion to delve into an individual's personality or long-term problems unrelated to the crisis. If and when these personality issues arise in the course of working toward crisis resolution, the crisis worker knows such issues are not the domain of crisis work. He or she acknowledges the existence of the issue and recommends a psychotherapy or counseling referral to help the client resolve the underlying problem contributing to crisis-proneness.

In comparing volunteers with mental health professionals Richard McGee found that unpaid volunteers scored higher than the professionals on warmth with callers. Volunteers scored equally with professionals in being direct and genuine in their work with troubled people.[21] A crisis counselor will not hesitate to go to the home of a person in suicidal danger or to provide transportation to a hospital in an emergency. Training in crisis intervention teaches the counselor how to make wise judgments in these situations and avoid "savior" tactics. Traditional psychotherapy training usually does not include such content.

Physicians, nurses, police, and rescue workers also have an advantage as crisis workers. Their basic training teaches them to do problem solving, to develop concrete, rapid solutions to life and death emergencies. Crisis intervention training added to this kind of background is a highly advantageous set of skills for doing effective crisis work.

CONTENT AND METHOD OF TRAINING: Having considered who should be trained in crisis intervention, let us look at what the training should consist of. The AAS recommends that those working in suicide and crisis centers and in mental health agencies as paid or volunteer staff should receive a minimum of 40 hours of training in crisis intervention.[20] The author recommends that this standard be extended to include nurses, physicians, psychologists, social workers, police, counselors, rescue workers, and clergy—the front line workers and consultants who most often see people in crisis or are called on by crisis counselors. This means that (a) crisis centers and community mental health agencies must develop inservice training programs in crisis intervention to meet these standards, if they do not already exist, and (b) educational and training institutions for physicians, nurses, police, clergy, psychologists, social workers, and counselors should develop and introduce formal courses which meet the minimum training standards of the AAS.

The knowledge, skills, and attitudinal content of crisis training programs and the methods of training are spelled out in the AAS Certification Manual, Section on Training. Any reader or prospective trainer interested in details of training content is advised to consult the AAS Manual.[20]

Before and during training, which includes supervised practice, trainees should be carefully evaluated for their potential as effective crisis workers. Those incapable of acquiring the necessary knowledge, attitudes, and skills of a crisis worker should be screened out and advised to seek other work. Not everyone is cut out to be a crisis worker. In fairness to the trainees themselves and to people in crisis, trainers should be clear, honest, and highly selective about whom they recommend to do crisis work.

Training should also include periodic updating in the form of inservice courses for crisis workers, as determined by the observed and expressed needs of the workers.

Who should do this crisis training? Ideally, according to AAS standards, a trainer should be someone with extensive experience as a crisis worker and with a record of above average job performance. The person should also have had training and experience in techniques of training others.[20] A knowledgeable and skilled worker is not necessarily a knowledgeable and skilled trainer. Those applying or selected for training positions should be evaluated for their skill as trainers as well as crisis workers.

SUMMARY

Crisis programs can be set up in a variety of ways. Administrative models, style and funding sources will vary from community to community. The specifics of a particular program should be determined by the imagination of its sponsors and the needs of the local people it serves. Most important is that those involved in delivering comprehensive crisis services collaborate and cooperate as fully as possible so that valuable financial and human resources are not wasted and people in crisis are served as they should be. Community education, consultation, and training are vital means of maximizing a community's total resources and of reaching large numbers of people who might otherwise not be reached. One of the best assurances of a coordinated community crisis service is adherence to the standards and guidelines set by the American Association of Suicidology. Thus, the uniqueness of individual community programs can be preserved while people in crisis have the advantage of service standards that have been tried and tested as most helpful and productive.

References

1. "Criteria for Defining Community Mental Health Centers' Emergency Services." *Bulletin of Suicidology,* National Institute of Mental Health, 1971.

2. Resnik, H. L. P., and Berkley C. Hathorne, eds. *Suicide Prevention in the 70's.* National Institute of Mental Health, 1973.

3. Motto, J. A.; R. M. Brooks; C. P. Ross; and N. H. Allen. *Standards for Suicide Prevention and Crisis Centers.* New York: Behavioral Publications, 1974.

4. McGee, Richard K. *Crisis Intervention in the Community.* Baltimore: University Park Press, 1974.

5. *Evaluation Criteria for the Certification of Suicide Prevention and Crisis Intervention Programs.* Prepared by Committee on Certification, The American Association of Suicidology, April 1976.

6. Shore, James H.; John F. Bopp; Thelma R. Waller; and James W. Dawes. "A Suicide Prevention Center on an Indian Reservation," *American Journal of Psychiatry,* 128: 1086–91, March 1972.

7. Metzler, Paul A. "A Telephone Service for the Deaf." *Proceedings, Eighth Annual Meeting, American Association of Suicidology.* St. Louis, Missouri, April 1975.

8. Danto, Bruce. "Management of the Man With the Gun." Workshop: Suicidologists on Violence. Ninth Annual Meeting, American Association of Suicidology. Los Angeles, April–May 1976.

9. Resnik, H. L. P., and Harvey L. Ruben. *Emergency Psychiatric Care.* Sponsored by the National Institute of Mental Health. Bowie, Maryland: The Charles Press Publishers, Inc., 1975.

10. Polak, Paul R., and Michael W. Kirby. "A Model to Replace Psychiatric Hospitalization." *Journal of Nervous and Mental Disease,* 162: 13–22, No. 1, 1976.

11. Marshall, Carlton, and John L. Finan. "The Indigenous Nurse as Crisis Counselor." *Bulletin of Suicidology,* National Institute of Mental Health, 1971.

12. Personal communication with David Evans, General Secretary, Council of Management, The Samaritans, London, England, December 1976.

13. Varah, Chad., ed. *The Samaritans in the 70's.* London: Constable and Company, Ltd., 1973.

14. Arthur, David. *The Samaritans, A Project.* London, Gatesbury Ltd., 1974.

15. Bagley, Christopher. "The Eval-

uation of a Suicide Prevention Scheme by an Ecological Method," *Social Science and Medicine,* 2: 1–14, December 1968.

16. Huston, Ted; Gilbert Geis; and Richard Wright. "The Angry Samaritans." *Psychology Today,* 10: 61–64, 85, June 1976.

17. "Standards for Administrative Structure." *Evaluation Criteria for the Certification of Suicide Prevention and Crisis Intervention Programs.* Prepared by Committee on Certification, The American Association of Suicidology, April 1976.

18. Caplan, Gerald. *Principles of Preventive Psychiatry.* New York: Basic Books, 1964.

19. Anderson, Luleen S. "The Mental Health Center's Role in School Consultation: Toward a New Model." *Community Mental Health Journal,* 12: 83–88, Spring 1976.

20. "Training Procedures." *Evaluation Criteria for the Certification of Suicide Prevention and Crisis Intervention Programs.* Prepared by Committee on Certification, The American Association of Suicidology, April 1976.

21. McGee, Richard K. and Bruce Jennings. "Ascending to 'Lower' Levels: The Case for Nonprofessional Crisis Workers." In: *Crisis Intervention and Counseling by Telephone,* David Lester, Gene Brockopp, (eds.). Springfield, Illinois: Charles C Thomas, 1973.

CHAPTER 11

Putting It All Together: Vignettes from the Lives of People in Crisis and Those Who Help Them*

*Material for this chapter was obtained from interviews and experiences with the following people: Gary Burdick, David Butler, Sally Dean, Charles Gambo, Mary Harris, Loren Keller, James Leuthe, "Lorraine," Daniel Morelli, Jean and Joe Oddo, "Ruth," Kay Sullivan, LeRoy Tudor, Howard Walter, and Jean Willis.

INTRODUCTION

This book is filled with examples of people in crisis and how they lived through or died from the experience. Perhaps you have identified with some of them. We have each had our own personal experiences with crises which we may or may not have shared with others. Hopefully the following narrations will strike a familiar chord and help us with our own crises and in our efforts to help others.

LORRAINE—WOMAN IN CRISIS

I can't begin to tell you what my life was like before Doris at our local counseling center helped me. Six months ago my second child died from what they call "crib death." She was two months old. When she (Deborah) stopped breathing at home I called the rescue squad. They resuscitated her and took her to the hospital. Deborah was kept in the intensive care unit for two months. Finally, the hospital and doctor insisted that we take her home. When we did, she died the very same day. I was completely grief-stricken, especially since I am 41 years old and had waited so long to have a second child. Our other child, David, is seven. I just couldn't accept the fact that Deborah was dead. My husband and the doctors kept telling me to face reality, but I kept insisting on an answer from the pediatrician as to why Deborah had died. I began having chest pains and problems breathing. Several times my husband called the ambulance and had me taken to the hospital. Once, after one of these attacks, I spent five days in the hospital for elaborate heart tests. My doctor told me there was nothing physically wrong with me.

I went home and things got worse. My husband became impatient and annoyed because I couldn't attend the usual cocktail parties with him. (He's an executive in a large company). I worried day and night about doing something wrong with David and eventually causing his death. The school principal finally called me to say that David was having problems at school. I realized I was being overprotective, but I couldn't help myself. The school recommended that we go to a child guidance clinic with David. I resisted and went back, instead, to my pediatrician and insisted once again on knowing the cause of Deborah's death. The pediatrician was apparently tired of my demands and recommended that I see a psychiatrist. I felt he was probably right, but felt we couldn't afford a psychiatrist; we had spent so much money on medical and hospital bills during the past year. I became so depressed that suicide began to seem like my only way out. One night, after an attack of chest pain and a crying spell, I was so desperate that I called the suicide prevention center. The counselor referred me to the local counseling center where I saw Doris.

At first I was terrified at the thought of coming to a public place to get help. Our family had always seen only private doctors. Except for our money problems, I would never have accepted the center's recommendation. But they assured me that the crisis and counseling center was for *anyone* who had a problem, not just for poor people. I can't begin to tell you how my life changed after a few weeks of help from Doris. We discovered together that I was suffering from a delayed grief reaction. Through several counseling sessions I was able to truly mourn the loss of my child which I had not really done through all those months of trying to keep a "stiff upper lip" and be "brave" as my doctor and husband wanted me to be. I also discovered that I was feeling regret and some guilt for becoming pregnant in the first place. My doctor had warned me of the dangers. I was forty-one and did have complications during the pregnancy. Doris and I included my husband in some of the counseling sessions. On her recommendation I finally joined a group of other parents whose infants had died of crib death. Actually, the hospital staff had recommended this earlier, but I was too upset and just couldn't believe a group like that would help me. I began to understand my fear of causing David's probable death and, finally, I could let go of my overprotectiveness of him. Doris arranged a consultation with a child psychologist who helped both me and my husband with David.

I didn't know that places like this crisis and counseling center existed. It helped me so much that I would never hesitate to recommend it to any friend of mine in trouble. I only wish I hadn't waited so long before I finally got help.

POLICE OFFICER (CAPTAIN)

We're sitting in an area of the world where, by midafternoon, we have reached the peak temperature and are tired. An officer reporting to work at this time is subject to the same stresses of climate as the average citizen. Hopefully he has enough discipline to control himself in dealing with the problems of others. The officer's family stresses are not that different either—a court appearance for a marital problem, a child's illness, or an operation.

The overall scope of an officer's job is so broad that it can be confusing and frustrating. He handles everything from minor traffic violations to serious crime.

Complaint from private citizen: "Somebody's riding a motorcycle (a dirt bike) on my property. It makes a lot of noise and I can't sleep." I investigate the complaint, apprehend the boy, and call his father. The boy is riding unregistered, uninsured equipment. His father says "It's *your* responsibility." This kind of call is really frustrating.

Missing person call: A mother, a widow, came home and found her 15-year-old son missing. Though he often stayed with his grandmother, he was not there this time. The mother noticed that his motorcycle was gone. We investigated and found that he had flipped his machine and died of injury and exposure to the elements—a real tragedy. I talked with the boy's mother and offered what sympathy I could.

The shopping mall: We get call after call from this location for merchandise stealing, shoplifting, and car theft. Sometimes I get impatient with this kind of thing and wonder what's happened to our values and family discipline.

Domestic call: The woman complained of being kicked by her husband and didn't want me to leave until she felt safe. I told the lady she could make a citizen's arrest if she wanted to. When she did, her husband struck me. The couple went to family court, but the woman dropped the charges. Two weeks later we were called again. The woman was unconscious and appeared beaten up. We called the rescue squad and had her taken to the hospital. She died. The medical examiner ruled that she died of heart failure. I guess her husband had an expensive attorney. This kind of case really gets me down . . . I wish these women would follow through. Now that we have a local counseling center, I always make referrals of cases like this.

Suicide call: A woman called, gave us her sister's name, and announced that she was going to kill herself. She said good-by and hung up. We tracked her down through her sister and went to the house. She was in the car—poisoning herself with carbon monoxide. We took her to the hospital immediately. After emergency treatment she went home and two weeks later died of carbon monoxide poisoning. This is really sad because I think maybe this suicide could have been prevented if she had been followed-up from the hospital.

Call for pedestrian accident: We found a man thrown to the side-walk. There was blood all over . . . he had been hit by an intoxicated driver and died on the scene of the accident. Sometimes I have a hard time controlling my feelings about drunk drivers.

One of the hardest things for us as officers is to go on a call and knock ourselves out to save people, and then they die in spite of our efforts. One recent case like that was a fire call. Two people died and the officer was really upset that he couldn't save them. Another case was a little five-year-old girl who dashed in front of a car and was killed. We spent time with her parents and the driver. Even though the driver was not at fault, he felt terrible and needed someone to talk to. In cases like this we always try to give officers a chance to talk things out later . . . sometimes they expect more of themselves than is humanly possible.

One of the things that helps me in police work is trying to remember the spirit rather than the letter of the law. I think com-passion for people is really important. I try to remind myself, ". . . there but for the grace of God go I."

RESCUE TEAM

No matter how long we work in the rescue business, there are still scenes we never get used to. One of the hardest things is the death of children. Lately it seems we've had so many calls for children . . . an eight-year-old killed on the expressway . . . a ten-year-old hit by a car. My heart really goes out to the parents . . . I'm a parent too, and it hurts to witness these tragedies.

One of the saddest things happened last night. We were called to the foster home of a child who had originally been abandoned. She died of liver cirrhosis in spite of the foster mother's efforts to make up for years of neglect. It's very sad to watch a child die . . . I thought about it all day.

Another scene that haunts me is the man we found yesterday in the driveway of the hospital when we pulled in with our ambulance. He was just standing there with tears rolling down his cheeks. We asked the hospital guards and EMT's (Emergency Medical Tech-nicians) what was wrong. They said they didn't know and just laughed. We had to go out on another call right away. It's hard to believe that our fellow EMT's and the guards wouldn't help the man. I probably should have called the hospital, but I got busy and didn't.

Now I can't get the man out of my mind . . . maybe I'll still call the hospital.

We had another sad experience one day at a hospital emergency room. We arrived with a woman who had made several suicide attempts. The staff greeted us with "Why didn't you save your gas?" We were shocked, and determined for ourselves that we'd try never to become hardened, no matter how many false alarms and unreasonable demands we're expected to answer.

One of our common calls is for overdose victims. A recent one was for a young woman with three small children. If her husband hadn't come home and found her, she might have died . . . but her husband seemed indifferent. She is like a lot of others who really don't want to die but are very desperate about their family situation.

There seem to be a lot of overdose cases at our local college dormitory. For this kind of call we need to know how to handle crowds. If there is an illegal drug involved, it's hard for us sometimes to carry out our life-saving procedures . . . Sometimes the other students interfere and even the residence counselor won't give us the information we need because of fear of getting someone in trouble. If residence counselors were trained better, they could help us a lot in this kind of emergency.

Another frequent call is to the scene where a death has already taken place. One call that I remember well was for an elderly woman who died of cancer. She had taken a bath and told her daughter to leave her alone . . . that she wanted to go to sleep. The daughter thought her mother was still alive when she called. From what the daughter said, it seems this lady knew her time was up and prepared herself to die. Often, the dying seem to be thinking more of those left than of themselves. Families have all kinds of different feelings about death: "Well, at last," . . . "It's best that all the suffering is over" . . . or some are very upset and can't accept the death. We try to talk with them as much as we can regardless of the reaction.

One of the hardest things to deal with is a call for a person with a chronic drinking problem. We take some people into the hospital a dozen times or more, and nothing seems to change. It's really discouraging, especially when we see so many accident victims of drunken driving. Usually it's the sober person who is hurt. There ought to be more treatment centers, but I also think that some drunk drivers ought to be locked up. There's just not enough attention paid to our country's alcohol and drug problem. Some parents simply deny that their child is drinking. One of the saddest cases was of a 14-year-old girl who died of alcohol poisoning.

A very dramatic first aid call was to a tavern where 200 kids had come after drinking all day at the beach. A teenager had been hurt in a fight. A big problem in our community is with kids on alcohol.

Rescue work is exciting . . . there's never a dull moment. The best thing about it is the opportunity to help people. But there's only so much we can do. In most cases it's up to the hospital emergency room staff to pick up where we leave off. Sometimes that doesn't happen, I'm afraid, and that's really sad.

FAMILY PHYSICIAN

I spend only one day a week working in the emergency room. Once in a while things are quiet, but most of the time I run into all kinds of crisis situations. Whenever there is a true emergency, there is almost always a crisis as well, because the person's body image is altered in a lot of cases. For example, if someone comes in with the symptoms of a heart attack, I tell the person the facts as gently as I can and try to minimize the negatives: "You may be having a heart attack . . . you have to be treated in the intensive care unit for a while."

Some people come to the emergency room because they *think* they have an emergency or are in crisis. One young man came in with a very unusual story regarding his operations and medicine. He thought he had appendicitis. We examined him and did various diagnostic tests. I assured him that he did not have appendicitis and referred him to his regular doctor. This young man was grossly overweight . . . it occurred to me that he was probably destroying himself by overeating. I hope that his physician helps him with his psychological as well as physical problems. Sometimes I think that we should make a mental health as well as medical referral for people like this.

Most of the people who make suicide attempts are not at high risk medically. But I carefully examine what led to the suicide attempt in each case; I assume it must be pressure of some kind. A sympathetic, supportive approach is really important. If the family is involved, I often get caught in between. Sometimes they get angry and ask, "Why are you keeping her here? . . . she'll never do it again!" I make a mental health referral in spite of the family's objections.

Besides believing the referral is best for the patient and family, I could get into medical-legal trouble if I didn't follow through.

A fairly typical crisis in the emergency room is the case of an accident victim. The magnitude of the crisis usually depends on the degree of injury. The family always needs help. In our hospital we take them to as private a place as we can find with our crowded conditions so that we can talk with them freely. Again, it's important to give them straight facts along with sympathy and support.

Another typical situation happened just last night. The volunteer fire department sent an ambulance to a home where someone was having a cardiac arrest. They also alerted the hospital emergency room. The man was dead on arrival and his wife was very upset. Besides her normal grief, she blamed herself for her husband's death because she didn't force him to follow his doctor's advice and go to the hospital when he first had symptoms. I asked the nurse to put the woman in a nearby room so I could talk with her. This kind of situation is never easy . . . words seem so hollow when confronted with the death of a loved one. I sensed disbelief and denial when I saw this woman. One way I've found to approach this sad situation is with the opener: "I have some very bad news to tell you." She cried . . . I stayed with her and listened to her story. At first she demanded that I bring her husband back to life. I told her that we couldn't bring him back, and gradually she accepted that. In a case like this, when the woman is blaming herself for her husband's death, I find it helpful to use my medical authority to assure the person that she and the rescue team did everything they could to save her husband. I also try to capitalize on the positive things people did do to help. During the ten minutes I spent with this woman, I learned that her daughter was at home. This was fortunate, because she seemed helpless to make arrangements by herself. Another thing I learned was that religion was important to her and her husband. Her involvement in the anointing helped her accept the reality of her husband's death.

One of the worst things I ever witnessed in the emergency room was the suffocation, gagging, and death of two students from one of our local colleges. When I first saw the victims wheeled into the emergency room, I wondered why they were tied up. Then I learned the gruesome facts about their murder. The scene was really terrible and I must confess my revulsion against the criminal who killed these students.

Another thing that's hard for me to deal with is the parents of child abuse victims. I try to control my revulsion and talk with them about what I've found in examining the child, and my obligation to report the facts. At first they deny, then they usually cooperate, maybe because I try to be supportive in spite of my feelings about this kind of thing.

There's a lot that can be done in the emergency room, if we only take the time to do it.

PASTOR

The best part of the ministry for me is working with people. Funerals and weddings symbolize the high points of my work—sharing people's joys and sorrows is very rewarding. Sometimes I wonder whether people come to me because I'm a person or a pastor. I guess it doesn't matter, as long as I help them.

A lot of my work is with parents and their teenage children. For example, if a youngster is caught shoplifting, parents send the child to me with the idea that I will reinforce their values around the commandment "Thou shalt not steal." Some parents just don't want to believe that their child did it . . . "we didn't bring her up that way. She has everything she wants." In trying to find out from the teenager what happened, I discover that it often happens with a peer group: "I wasn't thinking . . . I'd never do it again." Some kids claim "everybody does it . . . I just happened to get caught." When I ask the teenager about his or her value system, I sometimes hear: "My parents are always trying to rip somebody off . . . they're just more sneaky in how they do it." Parents often feel guilty and defensive regardless of the kind of role models they have been. Shoplifting, delinquency, and drug abuse are all occasions of crisis which I use to bring parents and teenagers closer together through better communication and more understanding.

Another common crisis I deal with concerns wives who are beaten up by their husbands. So often this is associated with abuse of alcohol. Sometimes the woman presents the problem to me as a religious one. For example, the husband does not attend church but is persuaded by the wife to join as a means of solving the problem. This is really just a cover-up of the problem. Or, the woman may say, "I've prayed a long time about this and have been going to church every Sunday, and he hasn't gotten better." It really disturbs me that people expect religion to cure their problems. Some people think that if they only had more faith, they wouldn't have so many problems. I wish, instead, that people would take the initiative themselves to do something about a problem like alcoholism—instead of expecting a miraculous cure from religion. In situations like this, I have to be very careful not to be judgmental when I offer guidance and direction about a problem. If I probe about why a woman waits so long to deal with a husband who drinks too much and beats her up, I often find that she is trying to maintain an image. She's afraid of what other church people will think if she admits the problem.

Some of my most satisfying work is done after a funeral service. I never consider my work done after conducting the funeral itself. People need an opportunity to express their feelings about the death of a loved one. I always make a personal visit to their home a week or two later. A lot of people are hesitant to say how they feel, but they really appreciate the personal interest I show.

The ministry is a tremendous way to help people . . . the home visits, counseling, hospital calls. Religion is important to many people who are reluctant to seek help from any other source. My biggest problem is not having enough time. I think if I had more time that I could reach more people and prevent such things as "shot-gun-marriages" because of pregnancy.

VOLUNTEER TELEPHONE COUNSELOR
Driving home at midnight from the Crisis Center, after a six-hour shift on the phones, I'm trying to sort out some of the things that happened. The place felt kind of lonely: just Tina, the other counselor, and me—both volunteers—in the silent, empty Center. Tina took the first call: "Crisis Services, may I help you?" and had barely started when another phone rang. I grabbed that one.

The call was from a young-sounding woman, who was crying hard and refused to give her name. "I don't want my husband to know I'm calling . . . he'd kill me if he found out." Her husband drinks a lot and is physically abusive to her and their children when he's drunk. They argued about it at dinner tonight; he'd gotten very angry and had driven off—to a bar, she was sure—and she had immediately phoned the center. What should she do? We talked about relatives or neighbors helping, but she rejected the idea. "I love him, and I don't want him to be embarrassed by having people find out." I tried to get her to put herself and the children first in her thinking. If she wanted him to stop abusing them, she might have to take serious steps. We explored alternatives—marriage counselors, family court, an outreach service, the police—and she seemed to feel less helpless. But she was still scared about tonight when he came home. Phones were ringing, and Tina had another call, so I asked the woman if she would hold on while I answered the next call.

It was a caller named Dave, who had called many times before. He didn't seem to have any urgent new problem, so I told him I was on a heavy call. He rather unwillingly said he'd call back later. There was still a phone ringing, so I took it. A teenager named Patti said calmly that she was pregnant and wanted some counseling about it. I told her I'd be glad to talk to her about her problem, but she said she thought she ought to go to an agency that specialized in problems of pregnant women. I gave the address and phone number of an agency where I knew she would not be "talked into" anything, either abortion or having the baby, but where all possibilities would be explored and the choice would be hers. She seemed pretty much "together," so I went back to the call from the abused woman. She had hung up while on hold. That bothered me a lot—I could imagine that her husband had returned drunk and was beating her right now—but there was nothing I could do. I did feel a little better knowing that we had discussed the various things she could do about her problem.

A period of silence descended again, giving us a chance to get our previous calls logged; but it felt strange and ominous after being so busy. Then the phones started ringing again. The only really suicidal caller tonight was Lana, whose husband had deserted her. She was planning to take an overdose, and she had plenty of sleeping pills to do it with. Lana had no family and no close friends. Her husband had been her whole world. At first I felt she was highly lethal, and even considered having the call traced; but she hadn't taken *any* of the pills yet, and the more we talked, the less I felt that she would. Finally she agreed to make an appointment tomorrow to see a counselor at an agency near her home. She took only her prescribed dosage, put the other sleeping pills away (although she refused to flush them down the toilet), and lay down. I prodded her to call me if she couldn't sleep, and to call for that appointment in the morning. She promised she would.

Dave had called back, and Tina had listened to his sad story, the one he always told about his sexual hangups and problems with women. There were other calls, but they're swimming together a little hazily in my memory. None were as heavy as the two long ones I'd spent so much time dealing with. I feel fairly good about Lana, because I think counseling will help her. But I'm still worried about the woman with the alcoholic husband. Right now, though, I have to get myself settled down and get a little sleep. I have to be at work at 8:00 this morning.

HOSPITAL EMERGENCY ROOM NURSE

What I like about emergency nursing is the chance to follow the patient and develop a relationship. Many people who come to the emergency room don't have a private doctor; they use the hospital emergency room as a family physician.

Any number of people come to the emergency room for social or psychological problems, which are covered over with complaints of abdominal pain, back trouble, or other aches and pains. We examine them and reassure them that nothing is wrong physically. Sometimes the reason for the complaint is to get a statement from the doctor as an excuse for missing work. Even though there's nothing wrong physically, we never take anyone's problem lightly. Sometimes we make a mental health referral when we sense that the person is troubled. In fact, at times I feel that I'm working in a mental health clinic rather than an emergency room. We have developed a referral system to a primary care clinic for minor medical complaints, so we can concentrate more on the *emergency* function of the emergency room.

In cases of true medical emergency, such as an accident, many people come in extremely upset. For example, if a child has been hurt, the parents need reassurance that everything possible is being done. I wish we had a private room for talking with people . . . usually we just have to hunt around for an empty office or treatment room. It's also important to let parents stay with an injured or sick child as much as possible.

In cases of serious injury or accident it's hard to keep in mind the family's state of emotional upset because we're so busy doing all the necessary procedures to keep the person alive. I think everyone understands and wants us to focus our efforts on necessary life saving procedures . . . but at the same time it's important to keep the family posted on the progress being made. I have to keep reminding myself of people's psychological needs in a busy place like this.

One of the hardest problems to deal with in the emergency room is the case of battered children. I remember a father who brought in his 4-year-old child. He had pushed her down the stairs when she wouldn't eat the steak he brought home. The question that kept coming to my mind was "Why didn't the mother intervene?" I have a hard time being helpful to parents like this, but I did make a social service referral.

Our emergency room is the scene of some fairly regular visitors. We have a nearby church where the Pastor apparently delivers "fire and brimstone" sermons. Every Sunday after services (except when the Pastor is on vacation) we have several parishioners come in with symptoms of hyperventilation (rapid, shallow breathing), fainting, and emotional turmoil. We examine them, talk with them, and sometimes prescribe a tranquilizer. I kind of wonder about that church sometimes.

Spouse abuse is another thing we commonly treat. It's unfortunate, but in most cases the beaten partner will not press charges. In many cases we see the other partner in the emergency room a few days later. Instead of doing something about their problems, they just seem to take it out on each other. One of the expressions around here is "It must be full moon time again," whenever the number of beatings goes up.

Even though this is an emergency room, you'd be surprised how many teenagers we see with venereal disease, pregnancy, or both. I know this is a sign that kids must really be troubled, and that social and other circumstances have to change. It's really too bad that a 16-year-old boy feels that he doesn't belong if he hasn't fathered a child.

Emergency nursing and all the nonemergency work we do with it is a real challenge. I've been an emergency room nurse for several years and like it better than any other area of nursing.

RUTH—WOMAN IN CRISIS

I called the Crisis Center because I was afraid I'd attempt to take my life again. All my suicide attempts stemmed from feeling rejected. As a child I always felt my father rejected me . . . Now I think this was just his way of punishing me. He picked on me and favored my older sister. I couldn't do anything right. Once I stole some money from my mother's purse so I could buy a gift for my friend (now I think I was trying to buy friendship). My father beat me so that my hands were bleeding; then he made me show my hands to my mother. My mother cried when he beat me, but I guess she was afraid to stop him. When my father died, he asked me to forgive him.

I dropped out of school after tenth grade and got a job in a stockroom and later worked as a bookkeeper. I got married when I was 19. Our first five years were beautiful. We had three boys. I loved my husband very much and waited on him hand and foot. We bought a home, and he helped finish it. During the second five years, he started changing and got involved with another woman. My family and everyone knew, but I kept denying it. Then he left for about four months. I made a suicide attempt by turning on all the gas. I didn't really want to die, I just wanted him to stop seeing the other woman and come back to me. He came to pick me up at the hospital, and two weeks later I went over to his girlfriend's house and beat her up one day. I could have gotten in trouble with the law for that, but she didn't press charges.

After that, we tried to patch things up for about four months, but it didn't really work. Then I started seeing other men. We had lots of arguments. I threatened divorce and he threatened to kill himself, but I didn't believe him.

One night he sat in his car and wouldn't come in to go to bed when I asked him. At 7:00 a.m. my oldest son reported finding Dad dead in his car. I thought it was my fault. Even today I still tend to blame myself. His parents also blamed me. My father was still alive then, and he and my mother stood by me. After his death, I made another suicide attempt. I was in and out of the hospital several times and received a lot of shock treatment. Nothing seemed to help in those days.

Three years after my first husband's death, I remarried. We argued and fought and again I felt rejected. When I was afraid of taking an overdose of aspirin, I called the Crisis Center and was referred to the local crisis and counseling center near my home. I can't say enough good things about how my counselor, Jim, helped me. After all those years of being in and out of hospitals, having shock treatments, and making several suicide attempts—I'm so glad I finally found the help I needed long ago.

I don't think I'd ever attempt suicide again. I still struggle with the problem of feeling rejected, which I think is the worst thing in the world to go through. But I can cope a lot better now and am not half as bad about condemning myself as I used to be. My counselor has really helped me to get to the place I am now. He keeps reminding me that I've done these things for myself, but I have a hard time giving myself credit for anything.

Even though I feel I'm on the horizon of something much better, I still have my down days and have to watch myself that I don't drink too much. But I don't think I'd ever let myself get as down and out as I've been in the past . . . I've seen that real help is available when I need it.

CRISIS COUNSELOR

There's never a dull moment at our Center—home visits, assessments, counseling sessions, and the continuous hassle of trying to work through the system for the kind of services people need.

When Darrell, age 20, finally decided to admit himself to the hospital for detoxification from Valium and sleeping pills, I was glad because for a long time I wondered if Darrell would ever change. He's from a drug abusing family so had a very hard time even thinking about kicking the habit. This is one of those cases that shows how important it is to keep in touch with someone even if it *appears* that nothing can be done. I helped Darrell sort out some of his financial problems, and later he *asked* for help with his emotional and social problems. Other members of his family will be working with him on the total family problem. When something finally works out in a very difficult situation like this, I feel some payoff for all my efforts.

Another big challenge I had recently was working with Joe, age 29. Joe is a little slow mentally and was in more or less constant danger of losing his job and going to jail for public intoxication. One day the nearby hotel-tavern owner called and asked us "to come and get Joe . . . we don't want him anymore." Joe had fallen and was bleeding, so we called the rescue squad. I went to the hospital, too. When we got there, Joe and I found ourselves in a Catch-22 situation. An alcoholism consult was requested. The Alcoholism Department said "He's drunk and we can't admit him unless he comes voluntarily . . . Besides, he's a retardation problem." The Psychiatric Department said "He's an alcoholism problem." The Medical Department said his condition wasn't serious enough for them to admit him. Emergency Housing for alcoholism also refused him. Four hours later, at about 10:00 p.m. a neurology resident said, "He hit his head, didn't he? We can admit him for observation." Sometimes I wonder what would have happened to Joe in that emergency room if I hadn't been there to advocate for him. It seems like people use their mandate sometimes to exclude service.

Things aren't always this frustrating. Last week another counselor and I made a home visit to a family that was very upset because they reported that their 22-year-old son Ray had "flipped out" on drugs. They called with the express purpose of getting their son into a psychiatric hospital, even though he had refused to go before. I told the family when they called that we would not automatically put Ray in the hospital, but that we would come over to assess the situation and help the entire family through the crisis. We worked out a strategy for telling Ray directly and clearly the reasons for our visit. Ray refused to come to the phone shouting, "They're the people who will take me to the hospital in an ambulance." When we got there, we had a family session which showed Ray up as the scapegoat for many other family problems. We worked out a crisis service plan and Ray started to show some trust in us after about two hours with the whole family. He could see that we didn't just come to whisk him off to a mental hospital, which was what he had suspected we would do. In the end, even Ray's family was relieved that he didn't have to go to the hospital. Before our home visit, they just couldn't see any other way out. They had talked with several psychiatrists before, but no one had ever come to the house or worked with the whole family. Working with families is a great thing, especially when they are so upset and, with a little help, can come around as far as Ray's family did.

Other members of the team helped me a lot with some of the questions I had about this family. I knew that even though things went very well in the first sessions with Ray and his family, they had had many disappointments with therapists before. So if we didn't plan carefully, things might not work out very well even though we had had a good beginning. Our case conferences are really helpful for this kind of thing.

Some of the problems I run into as a crisis counselor would be really tough to handle without the help and support of my supervisor. For example, my teenage client with the gun really worried me for a while. I always want to be able to tell myself that I've done everything possible for a person. I hate to think of how I might feel if I didn't have someone to talk with who is understanding and helpful.

A similar situation concerns the young man who has a drinking problem and had crashed his car 19 times. It's really surprising that he hasn't killed himself in one of those crashes. Originally he came in wanting to shoot himself. As I work with him it's sometimes very hard to control my feelings of helplessness and hopelessness. For example, when he says, "I don't think I'm ever gonna change . . .

one of these days I think I'll just crash my car." But in spite of how he talks, he has made some positive changes; and I know that I've been instrumental in this. So, even though some people live a pretty rough life, I keep reminding myself that "where there's life there's hope," and I try not to give up on people no matter how heavy their problems are.

That's one of the things I like about working here . . . I have a chance to learn and grow and improve my ability to help people. If things weren't set up the way they are—flexible, good team support, sharp supervision—I think this kind of work could get a person down. It's really frustrating in a job when you know how to do something but can't do it because of some rules and regulations of the bureaucracy that nobody understands.

PROGRAM DIRECTOR OF A CRISIS AND COUNSELING CENTER

In this job it seems like I'm struggling half the time between my preference for working directly with clients, and my awareness that *somebody* has to do the administrative work. But even though I'm not that turned on to administrative work, I'd rather do it myself than be in a situation with an incompetent director. Actually, there are some good things about a job like mine—being able to help other people improve their skills, working closely with them when they're in a really tough spot with a client, and organizing the program so that we can offer the best service possible with our limited budget and staff. These are some of the pluses of working as program director. But sometimes it's scary to me when I think of how much influence I have in other people's lives—the clients, the staff, the Board of Directors, and the community. I have to get away from it periodically so that I can keep myself together and remember why I work here.

I guess the only things I really don't like about my job are the paperwork and the constant coping with bureaucratic red tape and political in-fighting. As for the paperwork, I've resigned myself to the fact that it's a necessary evil. At least in this organization we have something to say about the kind of records we keep, and there's a real belief in client's rights and in not labelling people with a psychiatric diagnosis.

The political situation is much more frustrating. With the way we have to struggle to keep our program afloat financially, it's hard to believe sometimes that there's any real interest in providing service, especially at the top echelons. It's even worse when you know that the counselors are doing a good job and that a lot of people need our help pretty badly. One of the things that keeps me going is working with our Board of Directors. They are really interested in making sure that their community has the crisis and counseling services it needs.

All in all, I can say that my job as Program Director is interesting and challenging. I work with a good team and have opportunities for contacts in a lot of different directions.

Some typical scenes in my work as Program Director are:

Conference with my supervisor (Direct Services Manager): One of the problems we discussed during this meeting concerned a crisis counselor who tends to take on more work than she can handle. I picked up some useful ideas about reorganizing the staff assignments to capitalize on the unique talents of different people. Another problem we worked on was a client's threat to sue us after we reported her to child protection authorities for suspected child neglect due to her alcohol and Valium abuse. One result of this discussion was a plan to reinforce the staff's attention to our client grievance procedure.

Crisis outreach visit with a new counselor: This particular counselor had some doubts about his desire to do crisis work. After this experience, he was sure that he didn't want it. We (one of us black, the other white) went to the home of a man who was threatening to shoot himself and refused to come to the center to talk with anyone. As it turned out, there was a white and black team of suspected burglars who had been working over the area. The house was open; no one answered the door, so we went in and started looking for the suicidal man. The next thing I knew, the house was surrounded by police cars, my partner was handcuffed, and they were coming after me. It took some convincing to get the police to believe that we were not the suspected burglars since we matched the description: white and black team driving a blue car. Wow! What an experience. My teammate made up his mind after that . . . he definitely did not want to do crisis work on a full-time basis. Since then, I've learned a lot about staff selection and assignment, and I know for sure that some people just aren't cut out to be crisis counselors.

Meanwhile, I continued intensive crisis counseling with the suicidal man. He cooperated with me in getting rid of his guns. His wife had left him, and he had a hard time with that. It seemed like we were making a little bit of progress through the crisis. Then one day he went in for a medical checkup and was told he had a tumor on his testicles. He left the clinic, went out and bought another gun, and shot himself. This was my first experience with anyone who carried through with suicide. I really felt bad, but I didn't lay any big guilt trips on myself because I think we did everything we reasonably could for that man. The counselor who was seeing the man's estranged wife needed a lot of support in working through his feelings about the suicide. We had a team conference with the Direct Services Manager, and she helped us a lot in working with the man's surviving wife and small children. It was a loaded situation all the way around, but all of us came through it all right. Among the things we learned was the importance of a close working relationship with general physicians in the community who might be seeing the same people we see.

Consultation–Public Health Nursing Office: It's been difficult to really get this consultation program off the ground. For one thing, we don't have enough staff to do the kind of job we ought to for the public health nurses. The other problem is the various administrative changes in the public health office. But we've managed to have some useful sessions together anyway. One of the important points we discussed this week was a community systems approach to a person with both physical and emotional problems. The case involved a senior citizen. The nurses were concerned that the woman was taking too much medication. In reality, the lady was taking her medicine as prescribed, but was also making a lot of demands and complaining of pain that seemed to have no physical basis. The nurses asked for help in sorting out with this woman her various problems and working out a more satisfying approach to her.

Client Referral from Direct Services Manager: A family had originally contacted our Regional Mental Health Office because they didn't know where to get help for their son. He had been upset for a long time and then disappeared for two days. They had tried to get him admitted to a psychiatric hospital on an involuntary basis because they didn't know what else to do. Actually, it wasn't very difficult to work with this client using the family approach we emphasize here. What bothers me is that, in spite of our public relations program, some people living nearby still don't know that we exist and that our services are available for help with a crisis or other problems. It shows that we can never take anything for granted; public relations is a constant thing.

Consultation Call from a Drug Counselor: The report was that a 14-year-old boy was "freaking out" in a local supermarket. The counselor and salespeople needed help in handling him. We stayed with him for two hours. Through our local private psychiatrist we got an emergency tranquilizer and had him admitted to the hospital overnight . . . his home life was very disturbed. This kind of case is a strong reminder to me of how badly we need an emergency hostel in our community. I hope we can make it happen some day.

Conference with Volunteers: We organized the telephone coverage for our satellite clinic. I can't imagine what we would do without all the volunteer help we have.

Board of Directors Meeting: Main items on the agenda are budget cuts, our volunteer program, and fund raising. This agenda should give everyone a good idea of the problems and the future in running a human service program like this.

Besides the hard work of trying to keep our program afloat financially, sometimes the amount of human tragedy we see really gets to me. If I didn't have someone to talk to, I don't think I would manage very well. It helps to have a well trained team of crisis counselors, and it's a lucky thing that we get along well together. The only problem about our group is that there are never enough of us to do everything that needs to be done.

BARMAID

This is the dumpiest bar I've ever worked in but I really enjoy it . . . I like the people. When I quit my last job and came here, a lot of the old men followed me. There are all kinds of bars, but if it weren't for bars like this a lot of old people and "down and outers" wouldn't have anyplace to go. Our "regulars" don't have anything or anyone, and they admit it. I feel like a counselor a lot of times.

One of my customers, a pretty young woman, has had several children taken away. When her caseworker called me to ask if I thought she was ready to have her child back, I said *no;* and I told the woman too.

This bar is really the only social life that some people have. Take Montana. She's about seventy years old and used to be a popular dancer. Now she just goes from bar to bar and is taken care of . . . everybody loves her.

I think the people I feel closest to are the old men who are lonesome or widowed. I always talk to them when they come in. One old man does carving for a hobby, so he whittled out a little church and gave it to me.

One guy who shouldn't drink at all stayed on the wagon for quite a while, then went on a three week binge. His girlfriend told him that she didn't want him anymore if he didn't stop drinking. So he came in here and got sick after two drinks. He fell on the floor and hurt himself. I called the police and asked them to take him to the hospital. He threatened to kill me and screamed all the way to the hospital. I called the girlfriend, and she and I both convinced him to stay in the hospital for at least 30 days. When he got out, he came in and thanked me. This is really rewarding.

I work hard at helping people get on the right track, and I'm really tough on people who don't do anything with their lives, like these old guys. I know just how much they can drink. Take Ben, he can drink only three and I tell him, "O.K. . . . you can have them either all at once or you can stick around for a while." I was brought up to respect my elders, and I don't want to see these guys go out and fall on their faces. A lot of people working in bars might not agree with me, because I think they're more interested in making money. But I don't want any part of helping guys mess themselves up by too much drinking.

In a way, working here is really kind of sad . . . you know these old people come down here for company . . . some of them don't have anyone who cares about them except me.

This bar has changed a lot in the past few years. It used to be a rough and tough place. Then I got to know the University nursing students who come here. We became good friends. Now we don't have any of the fighting we had in the old days.

When the University had the Writers' Conference, one of the writers came in and I felt like refusing to serve him. He stood here giving advice to everyone. Finally I told him, "If you want to come in here and drink your drink, O.K., but don't tell my people what to do." He got it together after that. Ken Kesey came in and was really nice . . . He talked to Montana and mixed with the people . . . I remembered him from the picture on his book.

Then there's Casey . . . He's not very stable, I guess, but is really sweet. He's a patient at the State Mental Hospital. Every so often he sneaks out of the hospital and comes in here. They always come and get him. One time I told him to go home and shave and not to come back until he did. He shaved his whole head, but at least he looked neat and clean.

I have a good friend who's a priest. We argued for years about my work in the bar. He told me for a long time that I shouldn't work here. Finally he agreed that it wasn't a bad thing to do. Someone has to do it.

APPENDIX

Service Forms*

Specifications for Use of Forms[†]

Initial Contact Sheet

Comprehensive Mental Health Assessment
  Rating Scales
  Client Self-Assessment Worksheet
  Client Assessment by Other Worksheet

Continuation Record

Interim Assessment

Termination Summary

Follow-up

Service Contract

Authorization for Release of Confidential Information.

Child Screening Checklist

*Reproduced by permission of the Erie County Department of Mental Health; Mental Health Services, Erie County, Corporation IV, South East Corporation V, and Lake Shore Corporation VI.
These forms and specifications were developed by a Task Force of workers representing Corporation IV, South East Corporation V, Lakeshore Corporation VI, and the Erie County Department of Mental Health. Members: Marsha Aitken, Maureen Becker (Chairperson), Barbara Bernardis, George Deitz, Lee Ann Hoff, Elizabeth Keller.
† For samples of forms not included here and for complete specifications for use of these forms, the reader is referred to Erie County Department of Mental Health, 95 Franklin Street, Buffalo, New York 14202.
Note: All forms reproduced have been reduced to approximately 60% of actual size.

SPECIFICATIONS FOR USE OF FORMS

These service forms are designed for use within a human service delivery system which focuses on the client as a member of a social network. The underlying philosophy of the forms emphasizes that the stability of a person's social attachments strongly influences his or her ability to function within the community.

The forms are designed to assist in the achievement of several objectives:

1. To provide workers, clients, and collaborating agencies with information that is relevant and organized in such a way that the client's level of functioning, goals, and methods for attaining them can be sharply defined and used as a guide in the course of service.

2. To provide supervisory staff with information necessary to monitor service and assure quality care to clients on an ongoing basis.

3. To provide administrative staff the data base necessary to monitor and evaluate service program outcomes in relation to stated objectives.

INITIAL CONTACT SHEET*

This form is intended to provide basic demographic and problem information at the time the client requests service or is presented for service by another person or agency. This information should provide the worker with sufficient data to make several key decisions early in the helping process:

- How urgent is the situation?
- Who is to be assigned responsibility for proceeding with the next step?
- What type of response is indicated as "the next step"?

This form is used chiefly by the worker designated to handle all incoming calls and requests for service during a specified period of time.

CRISIS RATING: HOW URGENT IS YOUR NEED FOR HELP?:

Very Urgent: Service request requires an immediate response within minutes; e.g., crisis outreach; medical emer-

*Form reproduced on page 319.

gency—requiring an ambulance to be called (overdoses); severe drug reaction; police contacted if situation involves extreme danger or weapons.

Urgent: Response requires rapid but not necessarily immediate response, within a few hours. Example: low/moderate risk of suicide, mild drug reaction.

Somewhat Urgent: Response should be made within a day (approximately 24 hours). Example: planning conference in which key persons are not available until the following evening.

Slightly Urgent: A response is required within a few days. Example: client's funding runs out within a week and needs public assistance.

Not Urgent: When a situation has existed for a long time and does not warrant immediate intervention, a week or two is unlikely to cause any significant difference. Example: child with a learning disability, certain types of marital counseling.

COMPREHENSIVE MENTAL HEALTH ASSESSMENT FORMS*
Completion of these forms follows the "Initial Contact" and provides more detailed demographic and client information. It may take anywhere from one to several contacts with the client in order to complete all the relevant items on these forms.

Rating Scales
The rating scales are designed to provide a more objective picture of an individual's level of function or dysfunction by rating the person in ten Life Areas and six areas called Signals of Distress on a 5-point scale with standard definitions ascribed to each scale. Crises or mental health problems arise from broken life attachments in one of the ten life areas. Such broken attachments are also often manifested by signals of distress. The assessment rating scales enable workers to describe and evaluate individuals in a sufficiently comprehensive way so that specific service goals can be identified.

Since assessment is an *ongoing process* over time, these forms should assist the worker in recording changes in a client's level of functioning, which then has implications for revising the service contract.

*Form reproduced on pages 320–325.

Initial Assessment Phase: During the Initial Assessment Phase, the worker records a composite of several viewpoints or perspectives (Worker [W], Client [C], and Significant Other [O]) in relation to each life function or signal of distress. During or after the clinical interview(s), the worker should decide on a rating for the sixteen items. This decision is based on his/her observation and interviewing skills. Assessment can be further expanded by asking the client and/or significant others to rate the client's level of functioning. All the areas may not be assessed at any one time, but should be completed prior to completion of the service contract.

Working Phase: Reassessment may be done at any time during the service interval if the worker finds significant life changes or progress made on goals to *warrant* an interim assessment.

Termination Phase: At the completion of the service contract, when the client and counselor have worked toward termination, a final assessment is done to (a) suggest whether the level of functioning desired has been achieved, and (b) make a comparison between the initial and termination functional levels.

Follow-up: After termination of service, the person should be contacted periodically to ascertain whether any further service is needed or desired. The follow-up contact should be negotiated as part of the service contract and carried out unless the person states that he or she does not wish to be contacted after termination of service. Follow-up contacts are particularly important for the person who finds it very difficult to ask for and use help during early stages of a problem before a serious crisis develops.

ASSESSMENT RATING SCALE DESCRIPTIONS AND DEFINITIONS: Rating scale descriptions and definitions are intended to provide the worker with a more comprehensive understanding of the meaning of each assessment area. The examples cited in the definitions of each scale are just that, examples. The worker should recognize that there will be numerous other examples of real-life situations which will be analogous to those provided. Also, while no rating of a person can be *completely* objective, the scale definitions provide a framework for eliminating subjective assessment as much as possible.

A. LIFE FUNCTIONS
1. Physical Health
Description: This scale is intended to focus on a person's physical health needs as well as ability to identify, regulate, anticipate, and seek treatment for those needs. Physical illness refers to symptoms, whether real or imagined. Ratings should be made considering severity of illness and need for an immediate medical response. Considerations include: sleeping, eating, drinking, alcohol and drug use/abuse, weight, posture, motor mannerisms, physical complaints, general nutrition, personal hygiene, dental hygiene, activity level, medication, physical impairments/disabilities.

Ratings

#1 High: Person is involved in pursuit of physical health as a part of living. Is aware of and follows through on physical health problems when they occur. Enjoys good physical health with no present need for medical services.

#2 Moderate High: Person has health problems and can identify, regulate, and anticipate them.

#3 Moderate: Person has physical problems and can identify them; however, is inconsistent in seeking medical attention; e.g. sees physician for prescription, but self-medicates.

#4 Low/Moderate: Person has physical symptoms that indicate medical attention is needed. Has knowledge that a problem exists but is not making an effort to seek assistance. Person requires regulation by others and reminders that physical needs are important.

#5 Low Functioning: Person has physical symptoms that require immediate medical attention and are potentially life threatening (malnutrition, heart pain, dehydration, excessive obesity). The person is not concerned about the problem and is not making any efforts to seek medical treatment.

2. Self-Acceptance/Self-Esteem
Description: This scale is intended to assess an individual's feelings towards the self as a person—the degree to which he or she feels capable, adequate, and valuable as a person.

Ratings

#1 High Functioning: Individuals are enthusiastic about life and confident of their resources and capacities for personal adjustment. They employ a realistic standard of self-appraisal based upon awareness of both positive and negative traits. While not viewing themselves as perfect, they see themselves as capable and adequate. Their goals are realistically based upon their capacity for achievement and they choose appropriate means for goal solutions. They are capable of feeling guilt and anxiety when they have violated their own internalized standard of personal conduct. Their aspirations are consistent with their capacity and are organized within a systematic life style that permeates the past, present, and future. Failure can be accepted without damaging their basic sense of personal adequacy. They adjust relatively easily to frustrations of daily life and can change their goals consistent with personal and/or situational changes. Since they feel basically adequate, they are capable of total personality development and can creatively actualize the full range of their inner potential. Basic self-acceptance translates into basic acceptance of others and allows them to freely enjoy social interactions. It is important to distinguish those individuals with a genuine positive self-regard from those who practice denial of negative self-regard.

#2 High/Moderate: Individuals are usually productively involved in many areas of life. Their expectations are realistic and they usually set goals consistent with their ability. Since they realistically accept having some negative traits, they are relatively free from anxiety, guilt, and blame. They are committed to the development of their potential and usually view themselves as being in relative control of their life situation. They accept frustration as a fact of life and adjust their goals accordingly. Under extreme stress they may question their ability and self-worth and may experience a minor and temporary decline in functioning. They rarely have feelings of depression and they advance beyond personal responsibility to being able to assume responsibility in relationships with others.

#3 Moderate Functioning: These individuals characterize the majority of the population. Their sense of adequacy and competence is sufficiently strong to allow self-management and responsibility to others within the context of their daily lives. While there is awareness of both negative and positive traits, there may be some distortion of either. They may have some difficulty in accepting failures and may rely upon support from others in dealing with frustration. At times, they protect themselves through falsification of their own ability or the circumstances relating to failure of goal achievement. With sufficient stress they may temporarily underaspire or overaspire to goals and may engage in self-depreciation and/or blaming of others. Guilt and anxiety are determined by an appropriate internalized standard of personal conduct, but at times they may accept responsibility for events over which they lack control. Some negative traits may be denied and some positive traits exaggerated. While being reasonably self-confident, they may become defensive when their behavior or accomplishments are challenged. Their means-goals relationships are appropriate and usually consistent with their capacity, although they usually do not develop their full potential. At times they may experience mild depression and have fleeting fantasies of suicide which are not acted out in actual behavior. They usually have a few close friendships and are capable of interpersonal relationships based upon the acceptance of others.

#4 Low/Moderate: Individuals are inconsistent in their self-evaluations. While usually feeling inadequate in managing their problems, they have sporadic periods of renewed confidence in their coping ability. They basically feel inadequate, guilty and self-condemning with frequent fantasies of suicide and possible attempts. While they are cognitively aware of some positive traits, they generally feel negatively toward themselves and act accordingly. Periods of positive mood are reactions to situational determinants rather than to positive self-regard which may also represent attempts to overcome unwanted depression. They experience their daily life as stressful and feel unable to manage ordinary problems.

#5 Low Functioning: Individuals are preoccupied with a sense of personal failure and guilt. They generally feel inadequate and incompetent and characteristically focus upon their negative traits and are unaware of and deny having positive traits. The tendency to condemn themselves is overt and prominent to the extent of self-punishment, including frequent suicide ideation or actual attempts. There is obvious defenselessness and open admission of worthlessness. Frustration tolerance is weak with a lack of capacity for coping with stress resulting from personal and situational changes. There is a pronounced inability to plan objectives realistically. Individuals may underaspire or overaspire to goal achievements which lead to actual failure due to their unrealistic standard of self-expectation. There is a sense of hopelessness, pessimism, self-doubt, and acute depression. Unfavorable comparison with others often leads to social withdrawal. These people cannot accept responsibility for themselves or for others. Basic self-rejection usually results in a critical and condemning attitude toward others.

3. Vocational/Occupational

Description: This area focuses on the person's present employment/vocational role in terms of:

- Extent to which it meets his or her financial needs.

- Individual's degree of satisfaction with present employment or role, e.g. Are you working to your level of capacity—or above it? If unemployed, do you have any job skills or education that could be developed? If unemployed, ascertain the degree of activity around job search. e.g. What have you done to find a job? Are you working two jobs which interfere with family life?

Occupation refers to: student, homemaker, retired, as well as usual occupations.

Ratings

#1 High: Person is employed and working at full capacity. Person expresses satisfaction with job or retirement.

#2 Moderate/High: Person is employed. Satisfied with job, not actively seeking for better paid work, but says, "I wish I could make more." Or, person is retired and quite satisfied with self-support.

#3 Moderate: Person is employed but expresses dissatisfaction with present job in terms of (a) pay, (b) advancement,

(c) hours, and/or; (d) nature of work. Has fairly stable job history and can get and keep jobs. Is aware of skills, but does not show much activity around changing jobs for self-betterment. Person is only moderately happy with retirement role and lacks options for use of time.

#4 Low/Moderate: Person is unemployed at present, has worked in past, but work history is sporadic. Takes jobs when he or she can get them, but leaves, gets fired, or laid off. Has some skills but is not aware of them. Is retired and has few options for satisfying use of time.

#5 Low: Person is unemployed. Has no vocational goals. Cannot assess self in terms of future employment. No skills. Is retired and has no satisfying outlets.

4. Immediate Family

Description: This scale is intended to assess the ability of family members to provide support and problem-solving assistance during crisis as well as on a day-to-day basis.

Ratings

#1 High: Person is able to rely on the family as a unit during times of emotional crisis as well as on a day-to-day basis. Family is usually always able to meet the person's needs and can offer both positive as well as negative feedback in a constructive way.

#2 Moderate/High: Person relies on family members in times of crisis; however, family members are not always able to respond completely or in a consistently constructive way.

#3 Moderate: Person relies on at least two family members and can depend on them in times of need. Person has no real sense that these people would help for extensive periods of time.

#4 Low/Moderate: Person has one family member that he or she talks to; however, does not rely on them except in extreme cases. Feels family doesn't care about him or her.

#5 Low: Person feels like family is never around when needed—acts as if he or she were not a member of the family. Person depends on nonfamily members when in trouble. Person is isolated and does not have a regular support system.

5. Intimate Relationships

Description: Intimate relationship is defined as ''a close, familiar, and usually affectionate or loving relationship'' which is usually limited to one or a few people. This rating measures the extent to which a person can have such a relationship in which there is mutual sharing of positive/negative feelings. Such relationships are often characterized by a sense of openness, honesty, and feelings of support. Although sexual intimacy may also be an important part of this relationship, the scale is intended to emphasize social or psychological intimacy even where a sexual relationship may not exist, e.g. a close brother-sister relationship.

Ratings

#1 High: Peron has intimate contact with a few others and the intimacy is acknowledged by all. There is a strong sense of permanency and future interactions are seen as important to maintain. Relationships are relaxed, open, and mutual understanding exists through honest interaction. Time is spent together by choice and significant moments are treasured.

#2 Moderate/High: Person has intimate contact with (at least) a few others and the feeling of closeness is shared by both. The relationship has permanent qualities and though it may be closed in some areas, time is spent together by choice and for extended periods.

#3 Moderate: Person can identify a close relationship in which there is intimacy and an honest sharing of feelings. A sense of permanence has existed or does exist, at least potentially, and some time is spent together.

#4 Low/Moderate: Person has or had some marginal intimate relationships that were seen as somewhat supportive. These relationships may be strained, but feelings about the other can be discussed and there is a possibility for developing a relationship.

#5 Low: Person has no intimate contacts with others, real or fancied. Is closed, defensive, and resistant to talking about feelings for others at present or in the past.

6. Residential Situation

Description: This area refers to a person's basic shelter needs, how he or she meets those needs, and the degree of satisfaction the person expresses about his or her residence, e.g. How do you judge your housing situation?

Is the person concerned about poor housing or is there little awareness that housing is substandard. e.g. If living situation is poor, what are you doing to improve your living situation? Does your living situation contribute to other problems, or (if the situation is good), does it improve your functioning? Is there overcrowding, rent too high, safety hazards, adequate heat and plumbing, lead paint, etc.?

Ratings

#1 High: Living conditions are more than adequate. Owns home or lives in excellent surroundings. Person expresses satisfaction with present living situation and privacy is available at any time. Living situation is stable.

#2 Moderate/High: Living conditions are adequate in terms of size and state of repair, with some degree of privacy, but not entirely satisfactory to the person. Is actively searching for better housing that is affordable. May include a transitional living situation that is adequate but temporary.

#3 Moderate: Living conditions are adequate, but premises need repair or lack the degree of privacy that would be considered appropriate. Person expresses dissatisfaction, but is not actively looking for alternatives or is complaining about the state of disrepair of an unsafe neighborhood; does not do anything to correct the situation.

#4 Low/Moderate: Living conditions are below standard, with no activity around improvement; or person is being evicted, not actively searching for other placement. Eviction due to non-payment of rent or other problems is viewed as the landlord's fault. Feels there is not much that can be done about living conditions.

#5 Low: Currently has no place to live, is living in temporary housing, or is living in conditions which require a change due to health problems. There is a definite need to provide alternative housing immediately. Living conditions are unstable.

7. Financial

Description: This area includes:

• Extent to which a person's financial needs are met. e.g. Do you make enough money to comfortably support yourself?

• Source of income. If unemployed or retired: Are you on welfare? Social Security? Veteran's benefits?

• Ability of the person to budget the money which he or she does have.

Ratings

#1 High: Person has a sufficient source of income and moderate to extensive savings. Anyone would be willing to lend him or her $500 without concern. Has excellent credit rating. Has some potential for finding other sources of income if current job was terminated. Budgets income well and is capable of making good investments.

#2 Moderate/High: Person has a good source of income and perhaps some savings or investments to fall back on if income were suddenly discontinued. Has some friends/family or a good credit rating which could be drawn upon if necessary.

#3 Moderate: Person has a fixed source of income or a job which permits basic needs to be met, but requires some careful budgeting in order to purchase desired "extras." Has limited borrowing power from a few friends or other resources. Is generally able to budget funds but would be hard pressed if income were suddenly terminated.

#4 Low/Moderate: Person has income either through public assistance or from a job, but it meets only the most basic needs. Person may or may not be able to meet the stringent budgeting required for living on a fixed income.

#5 Low: Person has no source of income at present. May also owe money on some/several debts. There is no money to cover the coming week's expenses. His or her credit rating is nil and person has no one whom he or she could borrow from. Must have immediate assistance in order to cover basic living costs.

8. Decision Making Ability

Description: The purpose of this scale is to assess the strategy, process, and effectiveness of the person's decision making and problem solving performance relative to goals and actual outcomes. Emphasis should be focused upon the person's cognitive functioning with less attention paid to emotional factors that are involved in the decision making process.

Ratings

#1 High: Individual is very task oriented and sets realistic goals consistent with ability. He or she thinks before acting and shows evidence of logical thought process in goals-means-ends relationships. Individual feels basically secure and self-confident as decision maker. He or she approaches problem-oriented situations with necessary emotional detachment—appropriately scanning the field; collecting relevant information, while holding extraneous factors constant; reviewing alternative solutions to the problem; and considering consequences of each alternative before implementing actions. If the choice is incorrect, the person shifts to a more appropriate alternative rather than clinging compulsively to the original one, and he or she accepts responsibility for the decisions.

#2 High/Moderate: The individual enjoys a full emotional life but is quite capable of task orientation when making decisions. There is usually no apparent emotional interference with the continuity and logic of thought process, except when numerous problems occur simultaneously or when individual problems have severe consequences. The belief in oneself as decision maker is stable, and the person more often than not accepts the consequences of his or her decisions, even during those infrequent times of acting impulsively. The individual sometimes chooses a particular course prematurely; considers consequences of alternative solutions before acting, sometimes acting impulsively; usually shifts to a more appropriate alternative if actual experience shows original alternative to be incorrect; and usually accepts responsibility for decisions, although sometimes he or she will blame the situation or other people for mistakes. At times feelings may confuse thought processes and the person may either temporarily withdraw or rely upon others for help in problem situations.

#3 Moderate: Individual shows a blending of task- and self-orientation. At times, goal priorities may be in mutual conflict or goals-means relationships may be inconsistent. Nevertheless, the person is reasonably capable of making effective decisions most of the time. He or she collects relevant information, sometimes scanning either too narrowly or broadly; reviews alternative solutions, sometimes choosing a particular one prematurely; and considers consequences of alternative solutions before acting, sometimes acting impulsively. The person usually shifts to a more appropriate alternative if actual experience shows the original alternative to be incorrect; and usually accepts responsibility for his or her decisions, although sometimes either blaming the situation or other people for personal mistakes. At times feelings may confuse thought processes, and the person may either temporarily withdraw or rely upon others for help in problem situations.

#4 Low/Moderate: Individual is mainly self-preoccupied and is unable to concentrate for the necessary period of time to arrive at a problem solution. Thought processes are scattered and shifting; and impulsively arrived at solutions are implemented without considering alternatives. There is a noticeable degree of compulsive clinging to alternatives in spite of their ineffectiveness in actual experience. The person will quite desperately accept advice from others and will doubt his or her own capacity for decision making. Beliefs are often without foundation in reality and the person frequently thinks in a fatalistic way that he or she is incapable of altering surrounding situations.

#5 Low: Individual is quite disorganized and reveals an obvious emotional interference with thought processes. He or she is self-preoccupied, impulsive, inconsistent, and distracted. When faced with a problem situation, the person becomes frightened and withdrawn and may either seek support and advice from others, or avoid social contact altogether. Solutions to problems are impulsive and later regretted and disowned. Goals are inconsistent and unrealistic and means-goals relationships are inappropriate. Thought processes are scattered with considerable distractedness and shifting. Beliefs may take the form of compulsions and delusions and, at times, hallucinations may be present. Events taking place in the person's life appear to have no order or purpose and seem to be outside the individual's control.

9. Life Philosophy

Description: This area examines the extent to which a person has life goals and a system of values. One's values guide a person in determining the "rightness" or "wrongness" of an idea or action. It is essential to assess whether there exists a system of values upon which goals and actions follow; not whether a person's value system is consistent with and/or acceptable to society's view of life. Certain life styles have special ritual/taboos or "laws"/guidelines/norms which are consciously followed or ignored. A client's ability to "judge" a certain situation or to have a sense of a "good" or "bad" conscience are indicators of the existence of a value system. The person's value system forms the basis for various life goals and aspirations.

Children and those persons with certain mental handicaps (e.g., mental retardation or psychosis) will tend to utilize their parents' or significant other's value system to guide their behaviors and attitudes.

Ratings

#1 High: A system of values exists that reflects the origins of "right" and "wrong" judgments. This system can be described by the person and is used as a guide for goals and behaviors in ambiguous or ill defined situations of varying kinds. The person's behavior reflects actions that are consistent with this value system. The person has set meaningful goals and has achieved them to his or her satisfaction.

#2 Moderate/High: Person is in the process of defining his or her own value system and goals, and recognizes the need for same. Is usually satisfied with knowing "right" from "wrong." Experiences occasional confusion or ambivalence when facing complex situations involving "ethical" issues or decisions which are neither "black" nor "white" but in "gray" areas. May also be confused occasionally about what he or she wants out of life.

#3 Moderate: A hierarchy or degrees of "rightness"/ "wrongness" exists with some things being considered "forbidden." Behaviors are not entirely consistent with these judgments. Person can acknowledge the existence of a value system but it is "imposed" or "inherited" from others rather than truly integrated and acknowledged as one's own. Goals very often are those set for the sake of others or in response to pressure rather than for self. The value systems of most children would fall into this category.

#4 Low/Moderate: Person has a value system which allows individual actions to be labeled as "right" or "wrong." There is no underlying scheme, so behaviors may not always be consistent. Similar situations can produce unexpected or different reactions. Person has poorly defined life goals and is generally frustrated in his or her attempts to achieve goals.

#5 Low: Has no value scheme that expresses itself in a consistent pattern of behavior. Actions and decisions appear inconsistent and haphazard. Person appears at times to have "no conscience at all," and is generally directionless.

10. Leisure Time Use/Community Involvement
Description: This area refers to how a person uses leisure time and the degree of satisfaction that he or she obtains from it. Leisure time can be monitored by the extent the person uses available community resources appropriately and the extent to which these resources are sought out. Community involvement is determined by the extent the person participates in the community outside of his or her home. Leisure time is any time when the person is not at place of employment or not occupied with childrearing and/or other housekeeping activities. It would include going to the movies, the pool hall, playgrounds, etc. Is a person's leisure time so limited that there is no time for self, significant other, or family relationships to develop (as in the case of the person who works two jobs)? Does a person have too much leisure time (as in the case of being unemployed or retired)? e.g. Do you have ample leisure time which helps you function in other life areas? Is leisure time a burden? A lonely period? A real bore?

Ratings

#1 High: Feels comfortable with amount of leisure time. Realizes the necessity for leisure and uses this time for constructive projects, meetings, and recreational activities. Does not become over-involved. Regulates leisure time use very well. Is quite aware of community resources and actively involves self in several community activities. Has some sense of responsibility to his or her community.

#2 Moderate/High: Has definite ideas about how to use leisure time and is aware of the need for it. Expresses satisfaction, but sees room for improvement and actively pursues it. Has knowledge of his or her community and becomes involved in the community on occasion.

#3 Moderate: Recognizes the need for leisure time and has some available. Tends to become over-involved on occasion, but does not recognize this as a pattern. Has difficulty in regulating use of leisure time. Only occasionally will the person seek community activities or involvement due to some limited social skill or lack of transportation to community resources/activities.

#4 Low/Moderate: Uses leisure time inappropriately. Is interested in some activities, but is inconsistent in pursuing them. Wants to do something, but doesn't know what. Has a talent or interest but cannot bring self to pursue it. Participates in community activities if encouraged, but would not initiate such activities for him/herself. Depends almost totally on others for knowledge of community resources.

#5 Low: Never has any time to relax. Never knows what to do with leisure time. Sits and ruminates, feels like nobody cares. Not interested in anything outside of home. May engage largely in passive activities, e.g., watching television. Has never developed or engaged in outside interests, or did so only in the distant past. Person is almost totally unaware of potential community resources.

11. Feeling Management
Description: The intent of this rating is to measure the person's awareness of feelings and ability to appropriately use and manage feelings in various situations. This rating concerns the way in which a person's defense mechanisms protect him or her against problems in living; the person's ability to regulate impulsive behavior; the person's ability to control or work through painful feelings, e.g. How would you judge your ability to handle your feelings?; or your ability to accept and value positive feelings?

Ratings

#1 High: Person is aware of feelings, can express them at will, and can take appropriate action to discharge or regulate them. Person can effectively acknowledge and appreciate the value of both negative and positive feelings which can lead to the "actualizing" state of living.

#2 Moderate/High: Person can generally express and regulate feelings in all but a few situations. Can discriminate between positive and negative feelings most of the time.

#3 Moderate: Person has an awareness of feelings that can be expressed and behavior is usually appropriate to the feelings, but mechanisms for working out feelings are not generally available.

#4 Low/Moderate: Self-corrective and control capacities are limited to survival activities on a physical level. Person is a "victim" of feeling states. Cannot regulate actions in accordance with appropriateness of acts, but responds to feelings in a reactive way. Tends to be able to identify only strong negative feelings, for example, anger.

#5 Low: Has no self-corrective or control capacity and requires structure and control to be imposed upon him or her from others. Has no awareness of feelings that can be expressed. Feelings tend to "erupt" and tend to be quite destructive to the individual or to others. Behavior tends to be incongruent with feelings after inappropriate over-/under-reactions.

B. SIGNALS OF DISTRESS

12. Lethality Toward Self

Description: This scale is intended as a guide to assess the suicide potential of a particular individual at the time of assessment. Specific signs (based on the study of completed suicides) are applied to the individual in an effort to predict as accurately as possible whether or not a person is likely to commit suicide. The person should be assessed as to:

- Suicide Plan: a person with a well-thought-out plan including specific time, place, circumstances (e.g., excluding possible rescue) with a readily available high lethal method (gun, jumping, carbon monoxide poisoning, barbiturates, hanging, car crash) is a high risk for suicide; e.g. How are you planning to kill yourself? Do you have a gun? Do you have pills? What kind? How many?

- History of Suicide Attempts: a person who has made previous high lethal attempts or changes plan from low lethal to high lethal is a higher risk than a person with history of low lethal or no attempts.

- Resources and Communication with Significant Other: any person with poor coping ability and loss of interpersonal support system or inability to maintain communication with existing resources is a high risk; e.g. Is there anyone you feel you can turn to when you're really down? Does _____ know that you're feeling like killing yourself? What is _____'s response to your threat, plan, etc.? This last question is included because significant others may, in fact, encourage would-be attempters by not caring or, in fact, telling them to go ahead.

- Age, Sex, Race: suicide risk increases with age for white males. More white males than females commit suicide. Among racial minority persons, there are more suicides under the age of forty than among older persons.

- Marital Status: more divorced, separated, and single persons commit suicide than married persons.

- Physical Illness: presence of physical illness increases suicide risk.

- Drinking and drug abuse: drinking or other drug abuse, accompanying impulsiveness, and loss of control increase suicide risk, especially in the presence of available high lethal methods. In addition, use of either legal or illegal drugs such as barbiturates, sleeping medications, or LSD may also raise impulsiveness and cause loss of control.

- Recent Loss: personal loss or threat of loss such as of a spouse, parent, status, money, or job increases suicide risk. In some situations a job promotion may actually be perceived as a loss because the individual feels he or she no longer has the capabilities to handle the situation, or the supports to carry through.

- Unexplained Change in Behavior: e.g., sudden reckless driving and drinking by a previously careful, sober driver can be an indicator of suicide danger. Another unexplained behavioral change to look for is the giving away of valued possessions suddenly, making a will, or purchasing a large life insurance policy.

• Isolation: a person who is isolated both emotionally and physically is at greater risk than a nonisolated person. This may sometimes be a sudden and unexplained withdrawal or self-imposed isolation.

• Depression: signs include sleeplessness, early wakening, weight loss, anorexia, amenorrhea, sexual dysfunction, crying, agitation, hopelessness: e.g. How is your appetite? Do you sleep well? Have you lost weight lately? Depression is not *universally* present in all high lethal persons.

• Critical Life Event: a person experiencing the stress of a life crisis situation who lacks internal/external resources for satisfactory resolution of the crisis is a greater risk for suicide than others.

Explicit, direct questions must be asked of the person regarding all these signs if the information is not already available through other assessment data.

Ratings

#1 High Functioning: No predictable risk of suicide now. No suicidal ideation or history of attempts, has satisfactory social support system, and is in close contact with significant others.

#2 High/Moderate: Low risk of suicide now. Person has suicidal ideation with low lethal method, no history of attempts, or recent serious loss. Has satisfactory social support system.

#3 Moderate Functioning: Moderate risk of suicide now. Has suicidal ideation with high lethal method but no plan, or threats. Has plan with low lethal method, history of low lethal attempts; e.g., employed female, age 35, divorced, with tumultuous family history.

#4 Low/Moderate: High risk of suicide now. Has current high lethal plan, obtainable means, history of previous attempts, is unable to communicate with a significant other; e.g., female, age 50, living alone, with drinking history; or black male, age 29, unemployed, and has lost his lover.

#5 Low Functioning: Very high risk of suicide now. Has

current high lethal plan with available means, history of suicide attempts, is cut off from resources; e.g., white male, over 40, physically ill and depressed, wife threatening divorce, is unemployed.

13. Lethality Toward Other
Description: This scale is intended as a guide to assess the homocide potential or danger of assault by a particular individual at the time of assessment. The following signs are applied to the potentially homicidal individual:

• Homicide Plan: the person with a high lethal specific plan and available means for homicide is a high risk; e.g. Do you ever get so angry that you feel like killing? How do you plan to do it? Do you have a gun?

• History of Homicide, Impulsive Acting Out, or Homicide Attempts: e.g. Have you ever felt like hurting anyone before? Did you carry out your urge to kill someone? If so, what happened? Did someone stop you? Were you able to stop yourself? Do you ever feel like you are losing control of yourself? What do you usually do when you feel you are losing control?

• Resources and Communications with Significant Other(s): most homicides occur within family units or between/among individuals previously acquainted; e.g. How do you usually express your anger toward someone close to you? Is there someone you feel you want to get even with? Are you open to exploring other more constructive ways of expressing your anger?

• Drinking/Drug Use-Abuse: a person who drinks frequently and also has a history of impulsive acting out behavior is a higher risk for homicide or assault than a non-drinker. Drinking and accompanying impulsivity and loss of control through substance use and abuse may also raise homicidal lethality, especially in the presence of available high lethal methods.

• Other Criteria: the person who is suicidal as well as homicidal is an even higher risk because the consequential effects of homicide are not a possible deterrent. In the event that homicidal threats or references are made, however trivial these may seem, such references should be thoroughly checked out.

Ratings

#1 High Functioning: No predictable risk of assault or homicide now; e.g., no homicidal ideation, urges, or history of same; basically satisfactory support system, social drinker only.

#2 High/Moderate: Low risk of homicide now; e.g., has occasional assault or homicidal ideation with some urges to kill, no history of impulsive acting out or homicidal attempts, occasional drinking bouts, basically satisfactory social support system.

#3 Moderate Functioning: Moderate risk of homicide now; e.g., has frequent homicidal ideation and urges to kill, but no specific plan; history of impulsive acting out, but no homicide attempts; episodic drinking bouts; stormy relationships with significant other with periodic high tension arguments.

#4 Low/Moderate: High risk of homicide now; e.g., has homicidal plan; obtainable means; drinking history; history of impulsive acting out, but no homicide attempts; stormy relationships and much verbal plus occasional physical fighting with significant others.

#5 Low Functioning: Very high risk of homicide now; e.g., has current high lethal plan; available means; history of homicide attempts or impulsive acting out and feels a strong urge to "get even" with a significant other; history of drinking with possibly also high lethal suicide risk.

14. Substance Use
Description: This area refers to use and abuse of prescription or nonprescription drugs of all kinds (e.g. heroin, methadone, hallucinogens, amphetamines, barbiturates, tranquilizers, antidepressants, LSD) and alcohol.

The emphasis is on the person's ability to control consumption of drugs (social drinking and prescription diet pills can be examples of controlled consumption). When the controls break down, use changes to abuse. Abuse can be measured by how and to what degree it is self-destructive, the potential lethality (e.g., alcohol and barbiturates —high lethal combination), the degree to which use interferes with usual everyday functioning, or actually prevents the person from functioning.

This area also considers the person's awareness of drug use as a potential problem, current abuse as a problem, and the person's level of activity around alleviating or changing the self-destructive behavior.

Ratings

#1 High: Never a problem. All substance use is constructive and controlled.

#2 High/Moderate: Rarely a problem. Usually drinks or takes drugs within socially acceptable limits or on prescription, but feels a need every now and then to get drunk or high. However, this generally does not interfere with his or her social and family network or normal functioning.

#3 Moderate: Some problems. An occasional "drunk," or periodic consistent drug intake. Drug use sporadic and can be traced to a precipitating event, e.g. "I got depressed because . . ." Person realizes danger of becoming potential substance abuser and shows some activity around preventing this.

#4 Low/Moderate: Frequent problems. Usually drinks or takes drugs "to get/keep going." Frequently the pattern gets out of control; person goes on binges or has "weekend highs." Constantly promising to improve. Social and family network weak, but intact. Tends to be cyclical. Potential danger not perceived because person is always "starting over."

#5 Low: Constant problems. Currently abusing drugs/alcohol to the extent that it has caused a breakdown in social and family network; actual or threatened loss of employment due to absences; financial problems. Person denies problem with abuse, little activity around changing or alleviating situation, even though situation is perceived as stressful. There is an expression of "no hope."

15. Legal Problems
Description: This area focuses on the *degree* to which the person's current legal involvement is a problem which interferes with everyday functioning, and the *nature* of the legal involvement.

On the "degree of involvement" continuum, how do his or her legal problems interfere with:

- Job possibilities
- Mental health
- Physical health

Under "kind of involvement," assaultive behavior toward others is included, as well as differentiation between crimes against persons vs. crimes against property, or both.

If the arrests and charges concern driving while intoxicated, or include other drug involvement, the degree of substance use needs to be better assessed.

The person's concern or lack of concern about the consequences of his or her actions should be taken into consideration and should be related to a homicide/suicide lethality assessment.

Also, a clear picture should be obtained of what charges are pending against the person, and the severity of those charges, i.e., violations, misdemeanors, or felonies.

Divorce action generally does not include a legal problem.

Ratings

#1 High: Has never been arrested, convicted, or charged with any misdemeanor or felony, or has never been to family court. Is able to retain an attorney if he or she needs one, or knows how to obtain one through Legal Aid or the Public Defender's Office.

#2 High/Moderate: Has been arrested or fined or charged with a family (civil) and/or criminal offense once, but has had no subsequent arrests or problems with the law. The person has or knows of an attorney to handle legal problems.

#3 Moderate: Person has been arrested or fined or charged with a family offense or a criminal offense but did not serve time. May be on probation, but accepts responsibility of probation.

#4 Low/Moderate: Person has a history of offenses, has served time, and when on probation/parole goes to probation/parole officer only when he or she feels like it.

#5 Low: Has presently pending charges and is awaiting court hearing or trial. Is currently on probation, parole, or both, and may have to serve time if convicted of present charge.

16. Agency Use

Description: This area refers to the person's ability to negotiate with helping systems in the community in order to obtain his or her goals for service. Assessment should consider:

- Individual's degree of knowledge about existing services; e.g. Do you know where to get the help you need?
- Ability to contact agency.
- Ability to follow through with contacts.
- Ability to insure that he or she gets the service from the agency or goes to a more appropriate agency; e.g. When you don't get the help you need, what do you usually do?

Agencies are defined as service clusters that exist in the community or within reachable distance, e.g., lawyers, doctors, and welfare system.

Ratings

#1 High: Always successful. Has knowledge of agencies and is able to contact the appropriate agency to fill need. Follows through on contacts. Is able to find out about new agencies and use them appropriately. Expresses satisfaction with agencies. Can relate to the agency as a whole.

#2 High/Moderate: Usually successful. Has good knowledge of agencies. Is able to contact agencies and follow through. Usually contacts agencies appropriate to needs. Has had favorable experience with some agencies, but not with others. Does not understand that requests for services may be inappropriate to a particular agency. Feels it depends on the person you contact whether or not you get services.

#3 Moderate: Sometimes successful. Has fair knowledge of resources and contacts agencies for help. Follows through only if agency follows up or contacts person after "dropping out." Feels like he or she doesn't "want to bother anyone" with problems.

#4 Low/Moderate: Seldom successful. Has limited knowledge of resources. Has understanding of needs, but cannot select appropriate agency. Contacts agencies but does not follow through: "agency shopper." Feels "nobody really understands" his or her problem.

#5 Low: Never successful. Has no knowledge of existing services. Does not understand own needs or how an agency can meet them. Feels no one can help, no one can do anything about his or her problems.

TERMINATION AND FOLLOW-UP

A Continuation Record, an Interim Assessment, a Termination Summary, and a Follow-up form are all based on the sixteen items rated and described on the Comprehensive Mental Health Assessment.

OTHER FORMS USED BY THE WORKER

Service Contract form gives client and worker a format to deal with specific problems in the areas evaluated in the Comprehensive Mental Health Assessment (see page 326 for form).

Authorization to Release Confidential Information protects the client's right to privacy when he/she authorizes the release of information by another agency to the worker's agency. The form assures the client that the worker's agency will *not* release the acquired information without client's permission.

Consultation form is used by a consulting professional.

Child Screening Checklist records concisely the child's social and developmental history (see page 327 for form).

INITIAL CONTACT SHEET

Today's Date _____   Walk-in _____   ID # _____
Time _____ AM   Phone _____   SS # _____
PM   Outreach _____   Welfare/
          Written _____   Medicaid # _____

SERVICE REQUESTED FOR
Client's NAME _____
          First   Middle   Last

          Permanent _____
Address _____   Temporary _____
          Street   City/Town   Zip   County   Catchment Area _____
Phone # _____ Means of Transportation _____
Directions to home _____
          (if outreach)
Sex ___ Male _____   Date of Birth _____ Age _____
          Female _____

SERVICE REQUESTED BY
☐ AGENCY   Name _____   Phone # _____
☐ OTHER   Address _____   Time(s) seen by
☐ SELF   If Agency- Contact Person _____   the agency _____

PRESENTING SITUATION/PROBLEM - What made you decide to seek help today?
          (use other side if needed)

Have you talked with anyone about this?   Yes _____ Who? _____
Address _____   No _____   Phone # _____
          Date of last contact- _____
Are you taking ANY medication now?   Yes _____   What? 1. _____
          (If more than 3 begin list on MH-2) No _____
          2. _____
CRISIS RATING How urgent is your need for help?
☐ Immediate (within minutes)   3. _____
☐ Within a few hours
☐ Within 24 hours
☐ Within a few days
☐ Within a week or two   Comments

DISPOSITION (Check all that apply)
☐ Crisis
☐ Medical Emergency
☐ Assessment (specify)- _____
☐ Discharge Planning
☐ Expediting/Advocacy
☐ Other (explain)- _____
☐ Referral made to- _____   Confirmed—Yes ___ No ___ Date _____
Date of Next Cont act _____ Assigned to _____
Date of Assignment _____ Request taken by _____

MH-1

Form 1: The INITIAL CONTACT SHEET provides basic demographic and problem information at the time client requests service (see pages 294–295).

COMPREHENSIVE MENTAL HEALTH ASSESSMENT

ID # _____

Name _____

First   Middle   Last

Assessment Date _____ Time _____   AM   Place of Assessment _____

                                                                         PM

RATING SCALE

1	2	3	4	5
High Functioning	High/Moderate Functioning	Moderate Functioning	Low/Moderate Functioning	Low Functioning

(W = Worker; C = Client; O = Other)

A. LIFE FUNCTIONS
   1. Physical Health   -Medical Information (Include relevant items; eg. illnesses, surgery,
       physical impairment, allergies, pregnancy, birth defects)

Current medical care   Yes ___ No ___
Family Physician or Medical Clinic(s) NAME _____
Address _____ Last time seen _____
Phone _____
Medication Use   Name   Dosage   Duration   Physician/Clinic ____
   1. _____
   2. _____
   3. _____
   4. _____
   5. _____
Comments:

                                                                         W   C   O

                                                                         __   __   __

   2. Self-Acceptance/Self-Esteem

       Comments:

                                                                         W   C   O

                                                                         __   __   __

   3. Vocational/Occupational ___ Employed ___ Homemaker ___ Student ___ Other ___
       Employer/School
       Name _____ Job Title (Functional) _____
       Address _____ How long? _____
       Phone # _____ Unemployed _____ How long? _____
       (Optional) Education/Training _____

       Comments:

                                                                         W   C   O

                                                                         __   __   __

                                                                         MH-2

Form 2: The COMPREHENSIVE MENTAL HEALTH ASSESSMENT records a
composite of several viewpoints: worker, client, and significant other. Each person
rates the sixteen items on the form (see pages 295–319). The worker form is shown
here, pages 320–324.

4. Immediate Family   Parental Status-

　　　　Children?   Yes____No____How many? _____

　　Comments:

　　　　　　　　　　　　　　　　　　　　　　　　　　　　　　W　　C　　O

　　　　　　　　　　　　　　　　　　　　　　　　　　　　　　__　__　__

　　(Refer to Child Screening Checklist if appropriate)

5. Intimate Relationships   Martial Status-

　　Never　　　　　　　　　　　　　　　　　Living　　　How
　　Married_____ Married_____ Widowed____ Divorced_____ Separated____Together_____ Long ____

　　　Comments:

　　　　　　　　　　　　　　　　　　　　　　　　　　　　　　W　　C　　O

　　　　　　　　　　　　　　　　　　　　　　　　　　　　　　__　__　__

6. Residential   Living situation-

　　Lives alone ____Lives with family____Other ____(specify)_____

　　Comments:

　　　　　　　　　　　　　　　　　　　　　　　　　　　　　　W　　C　　O

　　　　　　　　　　　　　　　　　　　　　　　　　　　　　　__　__　__

SIGNIFICANT OTHER INFORMATION

Name	Nature of Relationship	Age	Grade *	Within Household	Outside Household	
					Address	Phone

*Special Class Placement　　　　　　　　　　　　　　　　　　　　　　　　MH-2A

Form 2 for worker continued.

COMPREHENSIVE MENTAL HEALTH ASSESSMENT (con't.)

Name _____   ID# _____

7. Financial   Source of income _____
       Comments:

                                                              W   C   O
                                                              __   __   __

8. Decision Making/Cognitive Functions
       Comments:

                                                              W   C   O
                                                              __   __   __

9. Life Philosophy/Goals
       What are your life goals?   1. _____
                                           2. _____
       Comments: 3. _____
                                                              W   C   O
                                                              __   __   __

10. Leisure Time/Community Involvement
       Comments:

                                                              W   C   O
                                                              __   __   __

11. Feeling Management

       Comments:

                                                              W   C   O
                                                              __   __   __

Form 2 for worker continued.

RATING SCALE

1	2	3	4	5
High Functioning	High/Moderate Functioning	Moderate Functioning	Low/Moderate Functioning	Low Functioning

B. SIGNALS OF DISTRESS

12. Lethality-Self   History of Self-Injury-

Date _____ Method _____   Outcome_____

_____ within last month   _____ Medical Treatment Only
_____ within last 6 months   _____ Hosp. Intensive Care
_____ within last year   _____ Hosp. Psychiatric
_____ over 1 year ago   _____ Out-pt. Follow-up
                                                                   _____ No Treatment

Total number of suicide attempts _____ Date of last attempt _____

Comments: (include ideation and threats)

	W	C	O
	—	—	—

13. Lethality-Other

History of Injury to Other   Client   Outcome   Other

Date(s)_____ Method-   ____ Medical Treatment Only   ____
____ within last month   ____ Hosp. Intensive Care   ____
____ within last 6 months   ____ Hosp. Psychiatric   ____
____ within last year   ____ Out-pt. Follow-Up   ____
____ over 1 year   ____ No Treatment   ____

Total number of assaults_____ Date of last assault _____

Comments: (include ideation and threats)

	W	C	O
	—	—	—

14. Substance Use-Drug and/or Alcohol

Other Drug Use (include alcohol use)

	Type	Present Use	Past Use	Duration
1.				
2.				
3.				
4.				
5.				
6.				

Comments:

	W	C	O
	—	—	—

15. Legal

a. Pending Court Action   Yes____   No ____   When _____

b. On Probation   Yes____   No ____   Probation Officer _____

c. On Parole   Yes____   No ____   Parole Officer _____

d. Conditional Discharge   Yes____   No____

Comments:

Form 2 for worker continued.

COMPREHENSIVE MENTAL HEALTH ASSESSMENT (cont.)

Name _____ ID# _____

16. <u>Agency Use</u>
Previous Mental Health Service Contacts

Outcare: Name of Agency_____ Phone # _____
Contact Person_____ Date of last Contact _____
Address_____

Incare: Name of Agency _____ Phone # _____
Contact Person_____
Address_____ Date of last Hosp._____
Reason for Admission _____
How often_____How long_____ Avg. length of stay _____

Comments:

W   C   O
— — —

<u>Optional Information</u>
Religious Concerns____ Yes____No____ What_____
Ethnic Cultural Background Problems Yes ____No____ .What _____

<u>Narrative Summary of Assessment</u>:

Form 2 for worker continued.

COMPREHENSIVE MENTAL HEALTH ASSESSMENT

Client Self-Assessment Worksheet

Date_____ Name _____

1. Physical Health

    Circle one for each question.

    How is your health?

    Comments: _____

    _____   Excellent
    _____   Good
    _____   Fair
    _____   Poor
                                                            Very Poor

2. Self-Acceptance/Self-Esteem

    How do you fell about yourself as a person?

    Comments: _____   Excellent
    _____   Good
    _____   Fair
    _____   Poor
                                                            Very Poor

3. Vocational/Occupational

    (Includes student & homemaker)
    How would you judge your work/school situation?   Excellent
                                                            Good
    Comments: _____   Fair
    _____   Poor
                                                            Very Poor

4. Immediate Family

    How are your relationships with your family and/or
    spouse?   Excellent
                                                            Good
    Comments: _____   Fair
    _____   Poor
    _____   Very Poor

14. Substance Use (Drug and/or Alcohol)

    Does use of drugs/alcohol interfere with performing your responsiblities?   Never Interferes
                                                                                Rarely Interferes
    Comments: _____   Sometimes Interferes
    _____   Frequently Intereferes
    _____   Constantly Interferes

15. Legal

    What is your tendency to get in trouble with the law?   No Tendency
                                                            Slight Tendency
    Comments: _____   Moderate Tendency
    _____   Great Tendency
    _____   Very Great Tendency

16. Agency Use

                                                            Always Successful
    How successful are you with at getting help from agencies (or doctors)   Usually Successful
    when you need it?   Moderately Successful
    Comments: _____   Seldom Successful
    _____   Never Successful

    Any additional comments?

MH-6A

Form 2: The COMPREHENSIVE MENTAL HEALTH ASSESSMENT for use by
client and significant other is structured differently from the worker's form. Portions of
side one and side two of the client form are shown above.

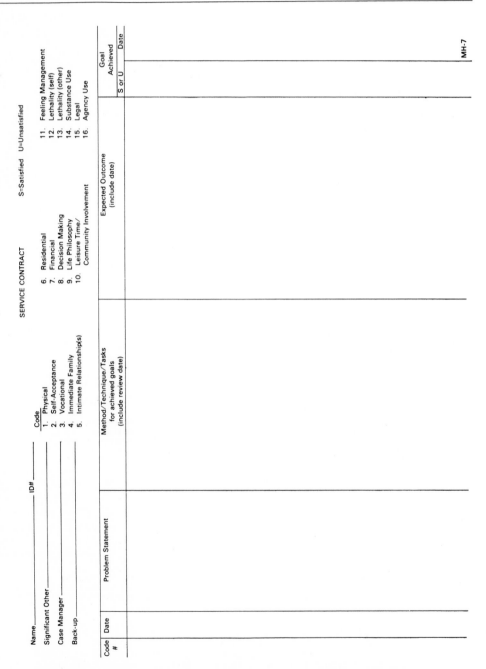

Form 3: The SERVICE CONTRACT is filled out by client and worker together. Problems are stated, solutions suggested, and specific dates assigned for an expected resolution.

Child Screening Checklist

Child's Full Name _____ Sex _____ Birthdate _____

ID# _____

School Problems
a) poor grades ___
b) does not get along with students ___
c) does not get along with teachers ___
d) suspended ___
e) poor attendance ___

Family Relationship Problems

does not get along with: father___ mother___ brothers___ sisters___; refuses to participate in family activities___; refuses to accept and perform family responsibilities___

Peer Relationship Problems

prefers to be alone___; prefers to be with adults___; does not associate with age mates___; not accepted by others___

Dyssocial Behavior

excessive lying___ hurts others___ hurts self___ destructive___ runaway___ substance use___ court involvement___ other___

Personal Adjustment Problems

temper tantrums___ easily upset___ speech problems___ sleep disturbances___ nervous mannerisms___ eating problems___ fearful___ lacks self-confidence___ clinging and dependent___ wetting, soiling, retention___ other___

Medical and Developmental Problems

chronic illness___ allergies___ physical handicaps___ accident prone___ seizures___ physical complaints___ lengthy or frequent hospitalizations___ medication___ surgery___ MR___ other___

Development Milestones (Administer to all pre-schoolers. Check behaviors present, up to and including present age.)

Age		Activity	Age		Activity
1	___	imitates speech sounds	2½	___	climbs stairs, alternating feet
1	___	feeds self with fingers			
1	___	pulls self to feet	3	___	forms sentences
1½	___	uses single words	3	___	dresses self - no fasteners
1½	___	walks alone	4	___	recognizes three colors
2	___	understands simple directions	4	___	throws ball overhand
2	___	scribbles with pencil or crayon	5	___	speaks clearly
2½	___	combines words into phrases	5	___	buttons clothing

In years or months, at what age do you think your child is functioning ____

Strengths and assets -

Comments -

Screened by _____ Date _____

Form 4: CHILD SCREENING CHECKLIST

INDEX